John Elving

THE PSYCHOLOGY
OF
CONFESSION

STUDIES

IN THE HISTORY OF RELIGIONS

(SUPPLEMENTS TO *NUMEN*)

XXIX

ERIK BERGGREN

THE PSYCHOLOGY
OF
CONFESSION

LEIDEN
E. J. BRILL
1975

THE PSYCHOLOGY
OF
CONFESSION

BY

ERIK BERGGREN

D.D., University of Uppsala

LEIDEN
E. J. BRILL
1975

ISBN 90 04 04212 1

CONTENTS

INTRODUCTION

The study that follows here is an attempt to make a psychological analysis of Christian confession. The subject is thus confession made to another person, earnestly felt and carried out, of the kind met with in Christian churches and movements.

The material has been drawn from Roman Catholic and Protestant sources : from the practice and observations of Catholic confessors and, too, from what individuals have experienced by making confession. On the Protestant side, evidence has been derived from such quarters as the old Oxford Movement and the newer Oxford Group (now "MRA"), also from particular spiritual advisers who have introduced private confession.

After a "phenomenology of confession" has been presented, there comes a survey of what psychiatry and psychology can teach us about what really takes place in the penitent's mind during the act of confession.

The third section gives closer scrutiny to the way in which psychiatric knowledge may be applied to the psychology of confession.

Parallelling such knowledge with experiences of confession has its definite limits, however. We have a religious factor to deal with in Christian confession, and this as a rule does not manifest itself during psychiatric treatment. An attempt is made in the last section here at elucidating the importance of the religious element in confession, at showing how it finds expression and what consequences it has in unifying a disintegrated personality.

I would like to place particular stress on the fact that the aim of this examination is purely of a scientific nature : my intention is nothing more nor less than to explain what happens in the act of confession. Accordingly, "practical" points of view have not been taken into consideration—which, of course, in no way implies that basic research of the kind involved here could not yield practical results. But readers are left to draw conclusions of that kind for themselves.

PART ONE

A PHENOMENOLOGY OF CHRISTIAN CONFESSION

CHAPTER ONE

THE NEED FOR CONFESSION AND ABSOLUTION

It is common human knowledge that talking about painful and disturbing memories or experiences which have lain on our minds unburdens us of them and affords a sense of relief. This means that such recollections or experiences may be felt as a weight. They induce a psychic pressure which can create worry and depression. The pressure, as if by its own force, impels a release; the process may take the form of a powerful need to make disclosures, to speak openly about oppressive secrets. This need finds expression in two ways : either in personal confidences to a trusted friend or as a written description. In the latter case, the memories involved have perhaps left the writer no peace until he "got them out of his system". The cathartic element involved is of importance in explaining the genesis of all literary confessions since Saint Augustine's *Confessions*.[1]

An authority on the romantic movement in German literature, Ricarda Huch, supplied good examples both of confessions which poets of that school imparted orally to friends and those they wrote down.[2] She related that the poet Nikolaus Lenau often made disclosures to his friend and fellow-writer Justinus Kerner, a man who evidently possessed the qualifications required for hearing confessions. Once, after an intimate conversation with Kerner, Lenau remarked of his need to communicate : "Confessing that was necessary to me. Now you are supporting it along with me". And literary expression of the same need is exemplified by the correspondence of Clemens Brentano and of his sister Bettine. Their letters to friends were nothing else than written confessions.

This need to reveal embarrassing and disturbing secrets might be expected to exist in direct proportion to the importance that the experience in question has for the speaker's or writer's personality as a whole. Accordingly, the need should be felt with special intensity

---

[1] A survey of religious confessions in literature was given by Anna Robeson Burr in her work *Religious Confessions and Confessants* (Boston, 1914).

[2] R. Huch, *Die Romantik*, II (Leipzig, 1920), in the chapter "*Romantischer Katholizismus*"; p. 230 ff.

when the values that he or she places highest are involved, those
with an essential bearing on that individual's entire way of life.
If we accept this to be so, we must find it obvious that the recollection of having broken an ethical principle related to religion—in
other words, of having committed a sin—will often be very hard to
endure, assuming naturally that both the religion and the moral
assessments founded on it are vital factors in a person's life. Because
of the guilt feelings there attached, the sin may engender a psychic
pressure that makes the need to find release through confession a
powerful force.

Abundant documentary evidence of the need, observed in the general
history of religion, was provided in Raffaele Pettazzoni's work *La
Confessione dei peccati*.[3] However, that study did not cover the sphere
of Christian religion. The need for confession asserted itself very
early in the history of the Christian church. Confession was there
connected with penitence, and later it became an integral part of
the penance sacrament in the Roman Catholic Church. In that way
the original need to confess was prepared for and developed; it received
a place in a religious exercise that would become a central element in
the fostering and training work of the Catholic Church. For Luther,
too, confession had the importance of a sacrament; he commended
it warmly, though he forbade compulsory practice of it. In the course
of time confession would, for various reasons, fall more and more
into disuse where the Reformed churches were concerned.[4] However,
there have been attempts to give it life in those churches. We shall
soon see here how the need to confess has emerged in the Protestant
as well as in the Catholic domain.

While Roman Catholic doctrine assigns confession a central place
in the penance sacrament, it is to be preceded by a meticulous examination of the penitent's conscience : he must look for all his serious
sins—those that violate God's Ten Commandments or break the Five
Commandments of the Church. Here the so-called "confession mirrors",

---

[3] Published in three parts (Bologna, 1929-36). Examples of confession to another
person are given in III, Index, p. 235 F. ("*morfologia*").

[4] For a history of Christian confession, see O. D. Watkins, *A History of Penance*,
I-II (London, 1920), and H. C. Lea, *A History of Auricular Confession and Indulgences*,
I-III (London, 1896). Among the works to which readers may be referred for Luther's
view of confession is N. N. Rathke, "*Die lutherische Auffassung von der Privatbeichte
und ihre Bedeutung für das kirchliche Leben der Gegenwart*", in *Monatschrift für Pastoraltheologie*, vol. for 1917; p. 29 ff.

drawn up as questionnaires, are used to aid the penitent. The self-examination is accompanied by remorse for sins committed. If the confession and absolution are to be valid, repentance must really be *contritio cordis*, contrition of the heart. The confession itself, *confessio oris*, follows this inward scrutiny : here the penitent must conscientiously enumerate his sins to the priest. If a serious sin should be deliberately omitted, the entire confession is not only nullified but becomes in itself a grave sin added to the burden on the penitent's conscience. When the priest finds that the penitent has duly fulfilled the requirements, he provides a certain means of atoning for the sins committed. This penalty, *Satisfactio operis*. is meant to replace—to redeem—the earthly or temporal punishment which ought really to fall on the penitent. There remains the eternal punishment, and this is remitted in the solemn pronouncement that constitutes the keystone and the crown of the whole penance sacrament. With his utterance of this phrase—*Ego te absolvo a peccatis tuis, in nomine Patris, et Filii et Spiritus Sancti*—the priest's divine function as custodian of the acrament is clearly revealed. By virtue of his office he deputizes for God as the forgiver of sins. Meanwhile, in the sacrament God has to do directly with the penitent whatever that person's psychological state may be and uninfluenced by the fact that the priest who administrates the sacrament may be an unworthy custodian of it. The sacrament has effect in accordance with the classic definition *ex opere operato*. It follows that, through absolution, the person becomes essentially pure, relieved of all sin.[5]

In view of the Church's doctrine on penance and absolution, it might be expected that devout Catholics would avail themselves often of confession as an established practice in order to achieve the purity from sin that they can gain thereby. And such is indeed the case. But great obstacles and difficulties lie on the way to absolution. Primarily it is examination of the penitent's conscience that proves awkward, but the degree of compunction required may give rise to anxiety. People who are genuinely pious often ask themselves : Have I really included everything in my self-examination ? Have I come to

---

[5] See F. Heiler, *Der Katholizismus* (Munich, 1923); p. 227 : "*Sobald von des Priesters Lippen die Worte ertönen* : *ego te absolvo a peccatis tuis in nomine etc.—erstrahlt die sündige Seele im Glanz der heiligmachende Gnade*". Works to which one may also be referred for accounts of Roman Catholic doctrine on the penance sacrament are Otto Schöllig, *Die Verwaltung der heiligen Sakramente* (Freiburg-in-Breisgau, 1936), and F.-D. Joret, *Aux Sources de l'eau vive* (Lille, Paris, Bruges, 1928).

true repentance ? And after absolution has been received, they may suffer dreadful pangs because they have forgotten to confess a certain sin or because they doubt that their contrition was sincere. If they are conscious of having infringed against instructions of the Church, their confession can produce an effect opposite to what was intended. With all this in mind, we are unlikely to find any exaggeration in Friedrich Heiler's remark that the danger of scrupulosity hangs constantly over the Catholic penance sacrament.[6] Yet it is of interest that, in spite of the demands placed on the devout by penance and of the risks they run when undergoing it, they usually are willing to submit; and this is evidently because of an often powerful need to make confession and because of a longing to find release through absolution.

Every Catholic is enjoined by the Church to confess at least once a year. Annual confession usually takes place at Easter-time, as a preparation for taking Communion. But ecclesiastical authorities recommend more assiduous—preferably weekly—confession. And as a rule good Catholics are frequent penitents. Among great figures and leaders of the Church, confession has been and remains the great and universal means employed in their aspiration to attain moral perfection.

One famous confessor, the mystic and ascetic Jesuit Louis Lallement, went so far as to recommend daily confession for people filled with "a special desire for perfection".[7] The chief principle he followed here was one prevalent in Catholic mysticism : that moral perfection is achieved only by purity of heart. And such purity is attainable only through confession and absolution.

The Dominican leader Henri Lacordaire was among the eminent Catholics who have held a similar view. It is claimed that, to an astonishing degree, confession gave him a sense that his sins were forgiven. And he confessed extremely often—so often that it is impossible to state "even approximately" the number of his general confessions.[8]

---

[6] F. Heiler says (*op. cit.*; p. 261) : "*Gerade im Beichtwesen wird jene in der Gesetzesreligion wurzelnde Seelenkrankheit der Skrupulosität, an der so viele fromme Katholiken leiden, akut. Die Beichte ist nicht nur eine Stätte des Trostes, der Hilfe und Gesundung, sondern auch ein Ort der Seelenangst und Seelenqual*". It is clear that "*unsäglich viel Skrupulosität und eingebildete oder eingeredete Gewissensqual in katholischen Beichtstühlen ein- und ausströmt*" (p. 263, quotation by Heiler from statements of Catholic writers).

[7] F.-D. Joret, *op. cit.*; p. 221.

[8] F.-D. Joret, *ibid.*; p. 217 (note).

Obviously, the need to make frequent confession goes together with a sensitive conscience and with personal piety. However, in certain cases when people keep returning to the confessional at the briefest intervals, their scrupulousness assumes an unhealthy tinge : what their confessors have to deal with is really scrupulosity. These people are left no peace by their perpetual feelings of guilt. And the absolution accorded in the penance sacrament does not assuage them. Rather, confession has the effect of increasing their burden of guilt; for they reproach themselves with having failed to fill the require- ments of penance and having omitted from the enumeration of their sins what they regard as important transgressions. In general they regard the most insignificant omissions as the gravest of offenses, and they accuse themselves of sins which they may not in fact have committed. These hapless people, dominated by their compulsive notions, give confessors much trouble with their constant insistence on confessing.[9]

Quite aside from cases of pronounced scrupulosity, too frequent confession appears to involve a risk that the act may lose its seriousness and true meaning, thus becoming a formality observed by perturbed people with a view to obtaining momentary peace of mind. However, the danger of superficiality exists for confession as a whole, even when penitents confess at long intervals. No doubt to some extent the risk derives from its compulsory character, from the fact that it is imposed by the Church and must be practised if people are to share in the divine grace of absolution. It follows that confessing can easily become no more that the outward observance of a ritual, merely a required convention.[10] Ecclesiastical authorities have not failed to issue warnings against such an attitude; and of course the demand for earnest and profound repentance remains a safeguard against it. As for very frequent confession, François de Clugny, a well-known confessor of the seventeenth century, was among those who have regarded it with healthy scepticism. He feared that, with penitents

---

[9] Concerning scrupulosity and handling in the confessional of those afflicted with it, see for instance O. Schöllig, *op. cit.*; p. 335 ff.

[10] A former Catholic priest, Josef Leute, wrote in his book *Der katholische Priester* (Göttingen, 1914; p. 87 f.) about how, in some cases, "penitents" who felt under severe constraint to make confession failed deliberately to follow the requirements. They confessed insignificant lapses but kept serious sins to themselves. Though they did not want to avow these, they nevertheless submitted to confession because they were ordered to do so and refusal would have got them into difficulties.

who came often to the confessional, the desire to confess was not, as it ought to be, dictated by abhorrence of sin, but sprang rather from too great a wish simply to acquire an easy conscience.[11] Similar doubts in the matter were put forth in the eighteenth century by another Catholic authority, Jacques-Joseph Duguet. He cautioned his penitents against hastening to the confessional as soon as some sin troubled them. They should first reflect on their deed and consider their moral situation—not run precipitately and confess the sin merely to be free of it and forget it.[12]

The tendency to frequent confession is, it seems, connected not only with a conscientious desire to ensure that one's sins are forgiven or that one is advancing on the road to moral perfection, but also with a need, inherent in the psyche, to communicate. An observation about how this need expresses itself with different people may throw light on the need for confession in general. While people of a fairly extravert nature sometimes find it very easy to speak about their innermost secrets and thus unburden themselves of what weighs on their minds, those of a more introvert disposition are inclined to be reticent and have difficulty in confiding to another person. Here we might recall how Ernst Kretschmer and C. G. Jung classified types of temperament. Jung's division placed the inward-turning or "introvert" type on one hand and the "extrovert" or outward-turning type on the other.[13] And the same general characteristics are found in Kretschmer's two types : the cyclothymic and the schizothymic.

Clearly, the need for confession manifests itself more strongly where people of a more extravert nature are concerned. Clemens Brentano may be cited as an example of the type. We have recently seen here something of his willingness to communicate. This appears also in the attitude he took towards Catholic confession. During his turbulent youth the Roman Catholic faith long remained alien to him, and doubtless his craving for confession played an essential part in his return to it. When he complained to Luise Hensel, the young

---

[11] Henri Bremond, *Histoire littéraire du sentiment religieux en France*; vol. VII, p. 293. The entire work comprises first eleven volumes of text (Paris, 1921-33) and then a twelfth volume with index of the others (1936).

[12] H. Bremond, *ibid.*; vol. VIII, p. 417.

[13] C. G. Jung, *Psychologische Typen* (1st ed. 1921 ; that used here—10th thousand— Zurich and Leipzig, 1942). For the general division of types as employed here, see the introduction to that work, pp. 7-13. Cfr. pp. 624, 641 and 686 f. (*Extraversion, Introversion* and *Typus*).

daughter of a Protestant pastor, about the difficulties and loneliness of his life, with a sound instinctive comprehension of what he required she directed his footsteps toward the Catholic confessional. He took her advice, and it was largely through her influence that he became a devoted son of the Church.[14] But long before his return to the Church came into question, he had remarked to his friend Georg von Arnim about his need to confess and confide to others : "When I was still a small boy and pious, and went to confession, I always felt a deep, pleasurable fear before entering the confessional. Though the passing of time was to deprive me of my faith, it could never take from me my need to confess".[15] He said that the love and attachment he felt for his friends had been able to compensate for the solace once received from the sacrament; his wish to communicate, his yearning for sympathy, support, and guidance, were more or less satisfied by their company. But he came at last to a state where the help he received from them no longer sufficed.

When we encounter people who find it very easy to confess—whether they do so in accordance with Catholic practice or otherwise—we may often assume that they are of Brentano's communicative type. And, equally, when we regard the numerous cases of Catholics who must force themselves to go to confession, we may suppose that their reluctance is explained to some extent by their being naturally of a reserved and introvert temperament. One reason frequently given for an unwillingness to confess—that confession must be made to another person—indicates precisely an absence of Brentano's communicative quality. The shame felt by a self-enforced penitent in the presence of the priest who will hear his confession is sometimes very intense.[16]

As well as this natural obstacle to confession which arises in certain cases only, there are hindrances that assert themselves for all Catholics, even for those whose temperament allows them to speak and make confidences with more ease. The requirements described earlier here—that a penitent's self-examination must be conscientious, his repentance genuine and his confession complete—form such impedi-

---

[14] Concerning Brentano and Luise Hensel, see L. Bopp, *Moderne Psychanalyse, katholische Beichte und Pädagogik* (Kempten, 1923), p. 61 f., and Frank Spiecker, *Luise Hensel als Dichterin* (Evanston, 1936) especially pp. 48-53.

[15] R. Huch, *op. cit.;* p. 239.

[16] This emerges from examples of confession to appear in what follows here. Readers are referred particularly to the case of the French writer Joris-Karl Huysmans (more closely examined in Chapter 8).

ments. Added to them is the dread with which numbers of Catholics approach the taking of a holy sacrament. The fact that all difficulties are overcome, that faithful Catholics rather often make confession, seems to bear witness not only to the self-discipline they exercise in following instructions of the Church but also to the fact that confession and absolution (here in their Catholic form) fulfil a primal need of people in general to speak about what afflicts them and thus find relief.

We can study how difficulties appear before confession and also the need to confess in the results of an investigation carried out by Georg Wunderle, a Catholic psychologist with religion as his field.[17] The main aim of his analytical survey was to discover what the feelings of people were before they went to confession. He used the questionnaire method and received answers from thirty devout Catholics. These "subjects" of his received numbers. Nos. 1 to 13 were men : 1 and 2 being laymen, 3 to 9 students of divinity or priests ("*Weltgeistliche*") and 10 to 13 munks. Nos. 14 to 30 were women : 14 to 19 being of secular occupation and 20 to 30 nuns. Wunderle knew them all to be serious people, with a reflective attitude towards their spiritual lives. To the question of whether any particular feelings were experienced at the immediate prospect of confession, No. 16 stated what hers were : "Shame in my own eyes, before God and the confessor, also anxiety and even a thorough disgust. The mere thought that I am to receive a sacrament upsets me, or, rather, alarms me; then, too, there are my worries about whether I have been searching enough on certain points (in the examination of conscience)".

But, in the midst of all the disinclination and anxiety felt by most of the subjects, their longing for absolution came as a surmounting force that drove all before it. To give one instance, No. 29 said : "For that reward, gaining God's love once more, I do in fact submit to a penitent's obligations, which I always dread". And, similarly, No. 5 declared : "The thought of confessing arouses a certain aversion in me, but also a kind of yearning (*Verlangen*)". Such aversion seems to depend largely on the system of examining a penitent's conscience in detail before and during confession. In this process trifling matters must often be dealt with, "pardonable sins" which according to doctrine need not be confessed. It is scarcely surprising if in cases where the penitent has no serious sin on his conscience the examination

---

[17] G. Wunderle, *Zur Psychologie der Reue* (Tübingen, 1921).

can prove laborious and distasteful. But there is evidence that the thought of confession brings a presentiment of liberation; it does so more especially when the person knows that he has committed a grievous sin. No. 13 was probably noting a typical experience when he said : "The thought of confessing is disagreeable and embarrassing to me if I have committed only pardonable sins, but when I have had more serious things to avow the thought of confessing them was a comfort to me". When a sin is oppressive of course the need to be rid of it is heavy, too. Then, the longing for a final release through absolution vanquishes inhibitions.[18]

In consequence of all this, faithful Catholics must often approach the the confessional with very complex emotions. While such deterrent forces as an anguished conscience, a sense of shame and dread hold penitents back, the need and longing to speak of what truly afflicts them, to be delivered from this by absolution, impels them forward.[19] That the strongly retarding elements are usually conquered appears to be a good measure of the power behind the need for confession and absolution.

Need for these has given rise to the practice of confession in the Protestant, as well as in the Catholic, domain; or it has created conditions that encouraged confession and ensured a response when certain spiritual guides have offered such care for troubled minds. We may observe that the introduction of confession by individual churchmen or religious revivalists has led as if spontaneously to its frequent practice. With psychological intuition, the innovating Protestant preachers have grasped that people have an innate need to

---

[18] The Catholic faith has been able to express the psychological situation in which the need and longing for absolution overcome the obstacles to confession. See, for instance, *Tridentinum* in H. Denzinger's and C. Brannwart's edition of *Enchiridion symbolorum* (Freiburg-in-Breisgau, 1928), 900, p. 297, and 896, p. 294.

[19] Further examples of mingled feelings before the making of confession might be given from Ricarda Huch's work on the German Romantics. She supplies comments on the subject not only by Clemens Brentano but also his brother Christian and Wilhelm von Schütz; and she remarks that Christian Brentano's account of his first confession shows the state of mind in which he found himself, how he on his way to the confessional *"von Angst und Sehnsucht wechselweise gemartert und zum Himmel gehoben wurde, als ginge es zur Begegnung mit einer Heissgeliebten"*. (R. Huch, *op. cit.*; p. 239 f.) She adds that when reading such descriptions we receive the impression of a compelling necessity in the mind to cast off its burden. This impression is confirmed by testimony from converts of the German romantic movement in general about the effect confession had on them. (*Ibid.*; p. 238.)

escape from the sins they have committed; the soundness of this insight is proved by the fact that, repeatedly, a renaissance of individual "cure of souls" has followed when the initiative has been taken to provide it. That result is confirmed by studying the influence of—to give some instances—the nineteenth-century Oxford Movement, the Norwegian theologian Knud Krogh-Tonning, the German revivalists Johan Christoph Blumhardt and Wilhelm Löhe, the Swedish "Laestadian" movement and the twentieth-century Oxford Group.

In the Oxford Movement, which grew forth from High Anglicanism, E. B. Pusey was the chief propagandist of confession along Roman Catholic lines. In 1846, he preached a university sermon at Oxford on "The Keys of the Kingdom and the Complete Absolution of Sinners"; thereupon he had to receive confessants in increasing numbers from all over England. Wherever he went, he was called on by people who wanted to make confession to him and receive absolution from him.[20] One writer indicates the frequency with which this happened when he says that confessing to Dr. Pusey became something of "a fashion".[21] In some cases this view of the attraction was not perhaps unjustified. But it would surely be shallow and misleading to stamp the use of confession offered by Dr. Pusey as a mere convention of the time. On the whole, the spontaneous way people flocked to him and to other "Oxford" men, particularly John Keble, showed that the opportunity given them to confess answered a natural need they felt to be free of their sins and thus take a new turn in life.[22]

As for Knud Krog-Tonning, the Protestant theologian mentioned, his ecclesiastical and theological opinions closely resembled those held by members of the Oxford Movement, from which he received an incentive.[23] He keenly advocated re-introduction of confession and absolution by the Church of Norway, and in 1881 he published an appeal on the subject. The following year he took up duties as chaplain not only at a hospital in Oslo but also of both a workhouse

---

[20] P. Thureau-Dangin, *La Renaissance catholique en Angleterre*, II (Paris. 1903), p. 98 f.; cf. p. 54 ff.

[21] G. Faber, *Oxford Apostles* (London, 1933), p, 402,

[22] E. S. Purcell in his *Life of Cardinal Manning* (London, 1896; vol. I, p. 497) said about the frequency of confession following upon the Oxonians' initiative : "Penitents, wherever the Tracts for the Times and sermons of Pusey and Keble reached, were springing up like blades of grass in the early spring".

[23] The account of his development given in his memoirs, *En Konvertits Erindringer* (A Convert's Recollections; Copenhagen, 1906), is followed here.

(really a workshop-prison) and a poorhouse. Especially in the prison, this function gave him ample opportunity to study the benefits conferred in practice by the private confession he had called for in print. As result of his new observations he regretted deeply that Protestantism had abandoned private shriving. He said that in the case of many an inmate he had been able to witness "what a blessing it brings just to be given the chance of speaking frankly and honestly to his pastor about the most intimate concerns of his life". But he believed that even more salutory effects would have been achieved if he had possessed the means and authority to end confessions with a proper absolution. As a clergyman, he felt that he was empowered to take measures in this regard; so he created a pronouncement of absolution himself (none being included in the church service-book). In the same way as the English ritualists, he was led to make a new "adherence to Catholic practice". Use of this in his chaplaincy work gave him great satisfaction. "I remember eyes that radiantly met mine through tears of joy, and hands stretched out to me in fervent thanks for such an act, this particularly with people who felt that they could breathe freely for the first time after years of bearing the heavy yoke laid on them by awareness of grave sins committed, misdeeds which they had never before dared avow to anyone".

One of the Germans mentioned, Johann Christoph Blumhardt, started his revival in Möttlingen, a parish of Württemberg, during the 1840's. Confession sprang up of itself in his parish and became an important factor in bringing many people to religious faith. How he received the idea for his practice of confession emerges from his own account of events. The first person who came to him seeking release from a painful conscience was a man disliked by the local populace. He asked if the pastor believed there could be any salvation for him. Blumhardt wished to test the man's sincerity, and told him that he must confess what his sins were. But at this the man grew wary and went away. He soon came back, however; and on his third visit he gave up all resistance and made a confession. In spite of this, he remained extremely grieved, and no consoling words could assuage him. "He thought", said Blumhardt, "that if he was to be set completely at peace I must give him pardon by virtue of my office".[24]

---

[24] F. Zündel, *Johann Christoph Blumhardt* (Giessen, 1926), p. 157. Cf. Blumhardt's words in the following (p. 157 f.) : "*Den Eindruck aber, den die Absolution auf mich und den Mann machte kann ich nicht vergessen. Eine unaussprechliche Freude leuchtete*

Blumhardt comforted him by saying that all would be put right next time. And the man was back next morning, reiterating his wish to be given real absolution. So, while the man knelt, the pastor laid hands upon him and pronounced an absolution. This is how Blumhardt describes the impression it made : "When he rose from his knees, his entire face was transfigured, it shone with happiness and gratitude."

As word spread of the sinner's confession and the change that had taken place in him, Blumhardt was soon overwhelmed with people who wanted to confess and receive absolution. The procedure evolved with that first confession served as pattern for his general way of hearing confessions. Again in Blumhardt's case, the great stream of people who came for private spiritual healing showed that his practice of it met a powerful need. So many would-be confessants called on him that he scarcely had the strength to receive them all.[25]

In a similar way, confession and absolution entered the Laestadian movement. This religious revival had originated towards the middle of the last century and spread through the northernmost part of the Scandinavian peninsula. Here, too, a preacher wished to relieve people who were afflicted by their consciences and needed to be told, in plain and clearly understandable terms, that they were accorded divine foregiveness. The preacher who instigated the practice of absolution was Johan Raattamaa. In 1848 he went to teach at the missionary school in Lainio, a village in the Lapland parish of Vittangi. People of that village gathered in the evenings at meetings in the school, and Raattamaa read aloud sermons published by Lars Levi Laestadius, founder of the movement to which they all belonged. After some time these meetings began to result in a mood of repentance seizing the listeners. Because the sermons of Laestadius adhered strictly to the commandments, calling down judgement and punishment on transgressors, Raattamaa's hearers fell into awful dread; they were so terrified of the torments to be suffered in hell that Raattamaa did not know how he could comfort the poor souls. "They threw themselves on the floor, like Luther in his cell, and there twisted like worms in their abysmal anguish".[26] It so happened that

---

aus dem Angesichte des Mannes, und mir war's, als ob ich in eine ganz neue, mir völlig unbekannte Sphäre hineingezogen wurde, in welcher heilige Geisteskräfte rege würden".

[25] See Zündel, op. cit.; p. 160 ff.

[26] C. Edquist, Ropande röster i ödemarken (Voices Calling in the Wilderness; Stockholm, 1916), p. 26.

Raattamaa then became acquainted with Luther's views on absolution. He is thought to have read a sermon by Luther for the first Sunday after Easter.[27] This takes as text *John* 20 : 19-31, and Luther there maintains that all Christians, though particularly those holding clerical office, possess the power to mediate divine grace. According to the Gospel, they have been charged by Christ with the duty of aiding and consoling fellow-Christians who are in distress over their sins and of releasing them from those sins in plain words. From the practice of absolution later in the Laestadian movement, it would appear that Luther's statement on how forgiveness should be formulated made a deep impression on Raattamaa. Luther held that if the pronouncement was to possess any validity it ought to run as follows : "I set thee free of they sins, not in mine own name nor in that of any saint, nor for the sake of any human merit, but in the name of Christ and empowered by His commandment".[28] Here Raattamaa encountered the basic concept of the Lutheran reformation : God bestows unmerited grace on sinners; this is revealed in the summons to seek unqualified absolution in the spirit of Christ and at Christ's behest. Answering that call, Raattamaa conveyed to the people of Lainio unconditional pardon for the sins which caused their despair. Instantly, their anguish was transformed into jubilant happiness. "In the exuberance of their joy, they began to skip about, to dance and embrace one another".[29]

Later, Laestadius himself gave approval to the procedure developed by Raattamaa, with its special emphasis on the unconditional nature of absolution.[30] And so it became established practice among Laestadians for sinners to confess either before the entire congregation or privately to a single member of the church, usually the preacher.

---

[27] In *Dr Martin Luthers, Sämmtliche Werke* (Erlangen, 1827); vol. XI, 321 ff., and in the Weimar edition of Luther's writings : vol. XXI, p. 289 ff. and vol. XLIX, p. 143 ff.

[28] Luther, *ibid.* (Weimar edition); vol. XXI, p. 296.

[29] C. Hasselberg, *Under Polstjärnan* (Under the North Star; Uppsala, 1935); p. 247. This is one of the works giving descriptions of the Laestadian movement.

[30] Laestadius spoke with a certain disdain about the conditional pronouncement generally used by priests. In the Laestadian community the wording could be : "Your sins are pardoned through the blood of Jesus," or "I announce to you the forgiveness of your sins through the blood of Christ." See G. A. Fleege, *Den laestadianska rörelsen i Kyrkslätt församling* (The Laestadian Movement in Kyrkslätt Parish; Borgå, 1910), p. 17. The writer adds , "If this formulation is not used forgiveness is uncertain".

The preacher then pronounced absolution.[31] Though this power to mediate the redemption of sins really belonged to the congregation as a whole, he exercised it on their behalf. (In a subsequent chapter here, we shall have occasion to lay special emphasis on a preacher's position in his congregation.) Absolution was to exert, in the future history of the Laestadian movement, the same effect as when Raattamaa first imparted it in Lainio. The sense of liberation and the joyous emotion it produced would often—in accord with the ecstatic spirit of the movement—find tumultous expression.

In more recent times, confession has gained new topicality in Protestantism, partly because of the energetic way it was taken up by the Oxford Group. The method of confession practiced by that movement differs, however, from the forms previously dealt with here, for the person who wishes to be relieved of his sins is not the only one who confesses : the person who listens to him does so also. But the latter's confession would probably be more exactly termed "testimony". He tells the real confessant—a still unconverted sinner— how in his experience divine grace can deliver people from sin. The confessant thus receives encouragement to go on confessing until a definite outcome is reached and he is "changed". In principle, the two participants are placed on the same footing by their exchange of confidences. The "confessor" cannot, therefore, convey any form of absolution by virtue of his office or position. But it might be said that absolution is replaced by the comfort and guidance which the recipient, with his greater experience in spiritual matters, can offer by sharing what he has come to know of liberation through divine grace. Confession becomes a stage in a personal transformation. As the person confessing confronts his past, the wish grows in him to be cleansed of its sins and thus enabled to live in a state of grace. Here, as in so many other aspects, the movement was marked by its founder, Frank Buchman; he emphasized how, after his spiritual conversion, it had become clear to him that for a person "to keep his sense of the divine his heart must be empty of all sin, of every vestige of his discordant past".[32]

---

[31] Public confession was not compulsory, though as a rule it was required for sins that had given general offence. Private confession otherwise sufficed. (See C. Hasselberg, *op. cit.*; p. 251.)

[32] Cited by Harold Begbie in *Life Changers* (London, 1923); p. 40.

The Oxford Group made—as MRA it still makes—a distinction between "sharing" with a single person and public confession. But here the terminology is misleading, for "sharing" appears to be the real confession. Judging from descriptions of the public "confessions", they are usually more in the nature of testimonials. Rather than actually confess sins for the first time, people "bear witness", along lines well known in Anglo-Saxon religious revivals, as to how they have overcome sin. They generally speak about God's power to vanquish this and to conquer weakness in human nature. Here is the description of a Group meeting where probably testimony was presented in a fairly typical form : "With surprise I heard the confessions of people taking part, often young students who—with shining eyes and happy hearts, showing natural eloquence and humour— recounted how they had escaped from their inhibitions by placing themselves whole-heartedly at the service of Christ".[33] Testimony given in this manner before the congregation is evidently preceded as a rule by private confession and release from sins. The giving of such public testimony signifies official adherence to the movement and entrance into the religious community; at the same time, it strengthens the convert in his endeavour to keep on a new course in life. Lastly but of no slight importance, it is a kind of lay preaching which serves as propaganda for the movement.

In at least some quarters of the Oxford Group "sharing" has been advocated with a certain doctrinaire insistance. "As long as a person's sin has not been made known to others", it is said, "just so long that person has not come seriously to grips with his sin".[34] Opposition made to the demand for confession is readily interpreted as evidence of pride, evidence that the old self, unchanged and with its egotism intact, remains in command. An informant of Harold Begbie when he wrote on the Group (obviously an eminent representative of it, whom he called "Persona Grata") went so far in his claims on the necessity of confession as to declare : "I don't think it is too much to say that until a man confesses his sin to another man he can never really be spiritually vital. One knows scores of men who carry guilty consciences, and who think they square accounts by confessing their sins in secret to God, and genuinely trying not to commit those sins again. Such

---

[33] J. F. Laun, *Unter Gottes Führung* (Gotha, 1931).

[34] Sverre Norborg, *En märklig världsväckelse* (A Remarkable World Religious Revival; Stockholm, 1935); p. 31.

men can never help one another; such men haven't the ghost of an idea what redemption means. They pretend. Their religion is a form. Their life is a dead letter".[35] Of course, the bias and exaggeration in that statement are striking. But the fact that representatives of the movement do make such comments indicates how significant a part "sharing" has played in the way their lives have changed. If their remarks on confession as the only saving grace are to be understood they should be placed against the background of the speakers' personal experience. Abundant testimony has been provided by the movement on the decisive importance of confession, and later here we shall have occasion to study more of it. It clearly reveals that, by requiring confession and using the method we have described, the Oxford Group has answered a need in people to speak frankly about their sins and thus be freed from them. Doubtless, a great deal of the attention and support drawn by the movement may be attributed to the fact that, by making confession so vital an element in its way of changing lives, it satisfies the need to confess.[36]

We have of course presented these examples of Christian confession mainly with a view to ascertaining the extent to which the need for confession and absolution has there asserted itself. And we have been able to verify that the need appears forcefully within the framework established for its expression by the Catholic Church, also that it seems to spring up spontaneously when the opportunity for its fulfilment is provided on the initiative of certain churchmen and religious revivalists. To illustrate the need still further we might, finally, call attention to the sense of release—an emotion very often vouched for—that comes after confession has been made. Later, we shall discuss in detail that reaction on the part of confessants. Meanwhile, it can be noted here as a sign that confession involves the release of a heavy psychic pressure, the existence of which in many cases explains why people are driven to confess in spite of inward opposition. Their mental situation may demand some expression, and the need to confess is then likely to assert itself with elemental force.

---

[35] H. Begbie, op. cit.; p. 116.

[36] H. W. Clark, who has devoted special study to the movement, speaks about the proselytizing importance of its practice of confession : "It is noteworthy that Moral Rearmament has owed the success of its program in part to the use of confession". (The Psychology of Religion : New York, 1958; p. 117.)

CHAPTER TWO

THE NEED FOR AUTHORITY

A confessant needs to make his confession to a person with authority : this seems clear from an analysis of his mental state both before
he confesses and when he is confessing. It may be emphasized to
begin with that, quite obviously, somebody bent on confessing does
not turn to anyone available but goes to a person in whom he places
trust. Where confession exists as a sanctioned usage of the Church
and ends in absolution, or in cases where the demand for absolution
may arise spontaneously, it is self-evident that the confessant will
approach the person who by virtue of his position can impart absolution. The authority of this figure is needed as a guarantee that
confession will have the intended effect : deliverance from sin. Even in
cases where no absolution is required, it is natural that would-be confessants should approach someone who inspires confidence, though here
this is not founded primarily on the confessor's position but on his
purely personal qualities. Thus, we see the confessant's need for
authority emerging merely from the fact that he reveals his most
intimate secrets when confessing, and that he has a deep need or
instinct to be relieved of oppressive guilt and expects help from the
confessor in getting free of it.

The need to encounter authority becomes still plainer when we
consider that the confessant seeks not only to be liberated from
his sins at the time but also help and guidance for the conduct of his
future life. He who sincerely repents his sins and confesses them
ought in so doing to turn his back on them, resolving not to repeat
them and to lead a better life. Catholic confession makes altogether
sure of this decision by requiring the penitent to state it explicitly
in what is called the "special resolution". But such a resolve, however
firmly and clearly expressed, by no means always suffices for a penitent to mend his ways. He often finds himself in a state of some crisis.
By making confession, he has usually become more lucid about
himself and his nature, and he needs aid and counsel from the confessor
if he is to carry out his resolve and live differently in the future.
Doubtless, in many cases he gains insight into the weaknesses which
make certain temptations particularly difficult for him to withstand,

and this leads him to confess to a spiritual guide who has his confidence, for he expects from that confessor the wise and perceptive advice which can carry him through temptation. It may be that a penitent has had the crushing experience of again and again committing misdeeds which he opposes with all his conscious being, which he has tried to resist as unworthy of him, because incompatible with the ethical standards he has set up for himself. In such cases, a frequent reason for making confession is probably the need for authoritative guidance. The great desire for this explains the esteem and renown enjoyed by certain confessors who are able to provide it.

As with the need to communicate and to confess, the need for authority varies from person to person. It is commonly advanced that an important reason for the attraction which the Catholic Church exerts on some Protestants and people without religion is that authoritative attitudes there on life and faith cannot be called into question. Certainly the need to be given firm personal direction is often a vital motive behind conversion to Catholicism. Meanwhile, the need for confession seems to run parallel with that for leadership and authority. The convert obtains satisfaction of both needs from a confessor who not only receives his confession but also gives him instructions on his way of life.[1]

In the previous chapter, we took the case of the poet Clemens Brentano as an example of a powerful need to communicate. He fits in again here as an illustration of a pronounced need for authority. Brentano knew his own nature, and before his return to the Church he declared that only complete submission to a spiritual leader accorded with his temperament.[2]

It is tempting here to hazard a connection between the need to communicate and the need for authority. Undeniably, people who are extrovert and communicative—"sociable", as Kretschmer characterizes the type—appear to have a specially strong need for authority. The very ease with which they speak about all that lies on their minds seems to indicate a need to gain acceptance and approval; or, inversely, that they need to be censured, but in such case they

---

[1] This has been emphasized by, among others, the Danish church leader H. Fuglsang-Damgaard, who remarked : "...And long, extremely long, is the line of converts who have been drawn to Rome because confession is lacking in their own church". ("*Privat-skriftemaalet*"—Private Confession—in *Svensk Teologisk Kvartalskrift*, 1939.)

[2] R. Huch, *op. cit.*; p. 238.

want to be guided and assisted out of reprehensible circumstances which they find intolerable. Introverts, on the other hand, have more difficulty, because of their natural reserve, in attaching themselves to an authority and submitting to its rules. Even so, in all likelihood the need for authoritative guidance is generally present in the confessant's situation.

The great French psychiatrist Pierre Janet spoke of the need for authority ("*le besoin de direction*") as a very common phenomenon among *les psychasthéniques*—his term for people psychically of too little strength to face and cope with the problems of life alone.[3] He gave many examples of such weakness : where, for instance, parents stood as authorities for their children, husbands assumed an authoritative position for their wives, or the other way about. The relationship became altogether clear only when the authority was lost. Then the dependent person might react neurotically and be forced to seek treatment. Janet remarked that the same pattern could be seen in cases of people who left monastic life and attempted to live out in the world again : after a time they longed to return, for they felt incapable of going on without the carefully appointed, disciplinary schedule and daily routine of their monastery or convent. Similar cases could be found of neurotics who were incapable of getting along in the undirected freedom of civil life, where too much depended on their own initiative, but to whom a period of military service brought almost complete mental health. Janet observed that confessors were often able to check the outbreak of a neurosis by imposing definite precepts on a penitent.[4]

All this shows a need for direction on the part of neurotics; but of course the need revealed by the outbreak of their mental aliments is simply a magnification, or a displacement, of that which exists in normal people. The need for authority becomes altogether dominant in the emotional lives of some unbalanced people and they yield to

---

[3] Pierre Janet, *Les Médications psychologiques* (Paris 1919); vol. III, p. 379 ff.

[4] "*Le fait doit être fréquent, car les psychasthéniques doivent être nombreux dans les confessionaux*". (*Ibid.*; p. 384.) In his work *Les obsessions et la psychasthénie* (Paris, 1903; p. 707), Janet said that by taking many examples from the letters of Bossuet and Fénelon he had been able to establish that those confessors had instructed neurotic penitents. He spoke, too, of having had the co-operation of confessors for the guidance of a number of his patients. "I ought to say also that some priests to whom I have sent mentally ill people with a number of recommendations have fully understood the rôle I wanted them to play".

it unrestrainedly. Yet the same need is part of a normal emotional life and lies deep in the psyche. Its place there has, incidentally, been given particular prominence by William McDougall, who assumed the instinct for submission to be a basic propensity of the psyche; and this instinct is nothing else than a tendency to place ourselves under the domination of an authority.[5]

If we want a typical example of the need for authority where confession is concerned, we can take that of E. B. Pusey in his relationship with his confessor. Such need was markedly plain in the emphasis he placed on the confessor's being above all banal and everyday things. The confessor had to be a sacred person.

Pusey's insistence on this fitted together with the general concept of the church in the Oxford Movement : its affirmation of institutionalism, the way it upheld the loftiness of clerical office and the sublimity of the sacraments.[6] Pusey's example shows that among representatives of the movement it was a religious necessity to truly experience, to deeply know, the spiritual meaning of that concept. Thus, Pusey felt the clergyman's authority in his rôle as confessor and spitirual leader to be of indispensable value.

Pusey was of a scrupulous disposition. He suffered from an extremely heavy burden of guilt; but, even when he had long been receiving confessions, it took much time before he could make up his mind to confess himself. He regarded his sins as being too grave. Finally, however, he decided that he would confess to John Keble, a friend who was also prominent in the movement. He had written to Keble earlier describing how he felt about his sins. Then he had said that, in the midst of all the mercy and guidance he received from God, he was filled with shame : "I am scarred all over and seamed with sin, so that I am a monster to myself". He went on : "I loathe myself. I can feel of myself only like one covered with leprosy from head to foot; guarded as I have been, there is no one with whom I do not compare myself, and find myself worse than they; and yet thus wounded and full of sores, I am so shocked at myself that I dare not lay my wounds bare to anyone".[7] And all this in spite of his having

---

[5] William McDougall, *The Energies of Men* (3rd ed., London, 1935); p. 98. Cf. his *Introduction to Social Psychology* (10th ed., 1916); Chap. III, p. 45 ff.

[6] Y. Brilioth, *The Anglican Revival* (London, 1925); see not least A. C. Headlam's preface.

[7] H. P. Liddon *et al.*, *Life of Edward Bouverie Pusey* (London, 1894); vol. III, p. 96.

so often seen the benefit that confession and absolution conferred on those who came to him and made confession.

When nearly two years had passed after his writing of that letter, Pusey happened to fall ill, and he then felt much inclined to settle with what lay on his conscience. So he wrote again to Keble, this time asking to have precepts for the penance he wished to undergo. He explained that he had a great need to place himself under a personal authority; the life he led being without this, he regarded himself as in an unnatural state.

Finally, half a year later, Pusey made his request : Would Keble receive his confession ? Keble replied accepting to do so, and he urged his friend not to go too far in self-torment. But for an entire month Pusey prepared himself with awful intensity. He observed the strictest asceticism, wore a hair shirt next the skin and fasted so much that his doctor warned him there was risk for his life. In his letters to Keble at this period his deep need for authority was clearly apparent. He adressed his friend as "Father" and in closing was "grateful" and "unworthy". He was anxious to stress the distance between himself as penitent and Keble as confessor-authority. He did not wish to go to Keble's rectory as a guest. And their meeting before his confession was not to be marred by any commonplace actions or exchange of phrases. He wrote : "Come to me please when it suits you; but when you come, come as God's priest. If I might ask do not shake hands or—anything of this world".[8]

And so Pusey made his confession to Keble. Some days afterwards he wrote—the letter beginning characteristically "My dearest Father" —and said he could not doubt that through Keble's direction and power of mediation he had received God's grace as never before. Everything now appeared different to him. However poor he thought his prayers to be, he felt in possession of a love and a hope that had never existed in him before. It seemed to him that he was entirely transformed : as if his old, sinful ego had been entirely obliterated by confession.

When making his confession, Pusey had with him detailed precepts as to how he should conduct his life, and these he submitted to Keble's authority. Earlier, for his period of penance, he had urgently requested Keble to supply him with such disciplinary rules. But Keble had not wished to provide any definite instructions; instead, as was his wont

---

[8] Liddon, *op. cit.*; p. 100.

with other penitents, he got Pusey to find for himself the ways of behaviour and the spiritual exercises that suited his own temperament. At the time of confession, Keble subjected Pusey's precepts to careful scrutiny. Though he dissuaded or cautioned on a number of points, he considered other rules worth following. He wanted to try many of them himself. This we may take as a sign that he wished to defend himself against having the authority in his person placed too high. The same wish emerges from his reply to the letter mentioned earlier, where Pusey describes his experiences during confession. As if in echo to Pusey, a powerful note of self-reproach enters Keble's answer. Nevertheless, Keble's authoritative rôle in Pusey's life was now established; and it would be maintained through the years. Pusey made a habit of confessing to him at least three times annually. And Keble had to accept his position, not only for Pusey's sake but because it belonged to the concept which he held himself of the church and the clergyman's office.

From our analysis of the penitent's situation and from evident examples, it is thus clear that a confessant has a deep need to encounter authority in the person of his confessor. What gives the confessor his authoritative position from the penitents' point of view is his ability to satisfy their wish to be released from sin through absolution; or perhaps the ability to create in some other way a certainty that God's grace affects their sinful state. When a penitent chooses a a confessor whom he believes can provide what he needs, he has, as it were, obtained beforehand a guarantee that his confession will have the effect intended. Another thing that gives a confessor authority for confessants is the ability to instruct and advise with which they credit him. The essential reason why a confessor inspires their confidence appears to be the assurance that he can satisfy those needs, mentioned here, which are clearly evident in the confessant's situation.

We shall next see how the church or religious community and certain spiritual leaders have answered the confessant's need for authority : we shall, in other words, observe how they have built up an authoritative position for those receiving confession.

CHAPTER THREE

THE CONFESSOR'S AUTHORITY

The Catholic Church meets people's need for authority and absolution with its doctrine on the penance sacrament and its teaching
that the priest possesses divine qualities to administer the sacrament
and exercise moral authority. During the ceremony of ordination,
God Himself has made a priest the instrument of His power in this
world. Thus, the priest is endowed with a *character indelebilis* which
distinguishes him from all secular persons and qualifies him to carry
out his mission as intercessor between God and Man, indeed even
to deputize for God among mortals.

A Catholic writer has said that the priest shows his extraordinary
qualities as director of souls by his "apostolic zeal, knowledge of God's
ways and supernatural wisdom".[1] But those gifts are not enough
for a priest when he officiates in the penance sacrament. They could
have their effect also outside that sacrament. As administrator of
the sacrament he possesses a special and divine instinct : this shows
him the way when he instructs penitents on remedies for their sins
and gives them guidance on their future conduct.[2]

Such an image of the priest's high office is inculcated in Catholics
by their creed itself. A good Catholic accepts a priest's authority;
consequently he is prepared in advance to follow confessional advice
and to comply in all matters with directions as to his way of life.[3]

This maintenance of clerical authority has an integral place in the
structure of Roman Catholic doctrine. It is connected there both
with the concept of the Church as a whole and with teaching on the
sacraments. While in the Protestant domain the clergyman's authority
does not receive the same support from a dogmatic outlook, when
confession comes into question it is affirmed by other means. True,

---

[1] F. D. Joret, *op. cit.*; p. 227.

[2] *Ibid.*; p. 229.

[3] Officials of the Church require that each and every adherent shall place himself
under a priest's direction. A teacher of the Church, Vincent Ferrier, went so far as to
claim that God does not accord His grace to those who have the opportunity of putting
themselves under priestly guidance—thus to advance on the road to sanctity—but
fail to do so. (Joret, *op. cit.*; p. 224.)

in some areas of Protestantism an approach is made towards Catholic institutionalism; but in others we may observe how a preacher's authority stems from the position accorded to him as the leader of a revival or as a religious personage. There is often no very clear distinction between the esteem which a churchman enjoys through being a man of the church and that deriving from his qualities as a person. In a subsequent chapter we shall see that even in the Catholic Church, where institutionalism is fundamental, the confessor's personal attributes may be of crucial importance in the effect exerted by confession and the consequence of this for the penitent's spiritual renewal.

It was in line with the High Church and institutional character of the Oxford Movement that members there should have stressed as we have seen they did the clergyman's authority as confessor and spiritual guide. In 1873 the leading "Oxonians" issued a declaration on confession and absolution : they summarized their views about the clergyman's powers where those matters were concerned.[4] Here they made reference to ordination in the Anglican Church, during which the words of Jesus to His disciples (*John* 20 : 22-23) are enounced to each of those consecrated : "Receive ye the Holy Ghost : Whose soever sins ye remit, they are remitted unto them; *and* whose soever *sins* ye retain, they are retained". In this connection the authors of that declaration were not thinking of the general absolution during divine service : what they had in mind was individual absolution as this is authorized by the *Book of Common Prayer* for use when a clergyman makes a sick-call on a person who is afflicted by his sins and who should therefore be encouraged to confess them. According to the prevailing dispensation, such a person was to be absolved with a distinct and unconditional pronouncement of absolution.[5] The Oxford Movement extended this dispensation so that it applied not only to the sick but to all other people afflicted by their sins. They too should be urged to confess, and when they had done so should be absolved with the pronouncement approved by the church. Members of the movement had no wish to make confession compulsory. They simply wanted to encourage practice of it, and thus open the way for a

---

⁴ Liddon, *op. cit.*; p. 266 ff.

⁵ "Our Lord Jesus Christ, Who hath left power to His Church to absolve all sinners who truly repent and believe in Him, of His great mercy forgive thee thine offences : And by His authority committed to me, I absolve thee from all they sins, in the Name of the Father, and of the Son, and of the Holy Ghost. Amen". (*Ibid.*; p. 267 f.)

return to that means of spiritual liberation and purification, forgotten by their church.

In drawing special attention to the Keys of the Kingdom as a privilege of the clergy, of course the movement showed an inclination towards Catholic teaching on the sacral nature of the priesthood. It had, indeed, to defend itself against charges of "popery", some of them directed precisely at confession and absolution. E. B. Pusey thought it of consequence to stress how the movement differed from Rome. He stated the most essential differences in a letter of 1836. Confession in the Anglican church is not, as in the Roman church, a sacrament. While for Roman Catholics it serves as a second baptism that completely eradicates sin, for Anglicans it is "a token of God's future mercy" without entirely obliterating sin. In the Catholic penance sacrament the priest performs as a judge and examines the penitent in order to ascertain both the nature of his sins and the immediate circumstances involved. Not so with us, Pusey said in effect; here in the movement a clergyman is only a clergyman, God's instrument, assigned by Him the task of transmitting His forgiveness to sinners by pronouncing absolution.

On at least the first of these points, Pusey's distinction would seem difficult to maintain. Absolution should of course be unconditional. If it is, then to be of purpose it must be an eradication of sin or what is enounced by the words : "I absolve thee from all thy sins". And as to the second point— a distinction between the Anglican clergyman's purely "ministerial" capacity and that empowering a Catholic priest to stand judgement—this would probably not prove very great in practice; for it behoves also the Anglican confessor to interrogate his penitents on their sins and the motives behind them, so that he can give advice suited to each individual case. Indeed, it was characteristic of Pusey himself that he made an exceedingly close analysis of his penitents, one so careful that it occasioned some unflattering comments from his critics.[6]

In whatever way these matters are construed, the Oxford Movement did seize such opportunities as were offered by the Anglican church system to bring out the clergyman's competence and authority as confessor. We have seen, for example, how very keen Pusey was to impress on Keble the necessity of conducting himself with authority.

---

[6] Faber, *op. cit.*; p. 402. His scrupulousness here was maliciously inferred to be morbid exaggeration of an innate inquisitiveness !

We interpreted this as an attitude dictated by Pusey's need for firm direction. Naturally, it can also be said to coincide with his course of elevating the clergyman's authority as confessor. In his own case, he insisted on respect for the clerical mission which God had entrusted to him. One evidence of this was that his penitents addressed him as "Father"[7]; he obviously thought well of the practice, for he followed it himself when he came under Keble's spiritual direction.

With H. E. Manning—who, before he went over to Rome, could be counted a member of the Oxford Movement[8]—the demand for authority found rather original expression. The external arrangements he made for a confession to begin with, and his ceremonious behaviour during it, were calculated to induce great respect in the penitent. He received penitents in the church, and there usually seated himself in a large and dignified chair with arms, before the altar. A penitent was expected to sink on to his knees before him and make confession in that position.[9]

One of his penitents has related how Manning met him in an empty church and proceeded towards the altar, wearing his gown, with a folio-sized prayer book in his hands.[10] Manning bade him kneel and then read a deeply earnest prayer from the book : "Renew in him, most loving Father, whatsoever has been decayed by the fiend and malice of the devil, or by his own carnal will and frailty !" The narrator continues : "I have never forgotten the deep seriousness of those moments". After the prayer, he made his confession with much gravity, firmly resolved to combat sinfulness. No questions were put to him about his sins. The rite concluded with absolution.

The various testimonies about Manning's confessional practice were summed up by Purcell : "His manner was solemn, impressive in the extreme, and 'almost awful', as one of his penitents described it. He spoke with absolute assurance and authority, as one holding the keys. He never allowed any one for an instant to forget his position as a penitent on his knees before him, mentally as well as physically".[11]

---

[7] Thureau-Dangin, *op. cit.*; vol. II, p. 98.

[8] Though Manning certainly took his own course in many matters, he publicly professed himself to be a Tractarian, and in that circle he maintained animated relations particularly with Newman. (See Thureau-Dangin, *ibid.*; p. 82 ff.) He was co-author of Tract 78 in the Puseyite volume. (Liddon, *op. cit.*; vol. III, p. 479.)

[9] That Manning, like other "Oxonians", received confessions in the church nave definitely accorded with the movement's general endeavour to stress the holiness of the church nave and its central place in the religious life of the congregation.

[10] E. S. Purcell, *Life of Cardinal Manning*; vol. I, p. 493 (note).

[11] *Ibid.*; p. 494.

Manning's insistence on the confessor's authority and the arrangements he made to impress it on his penitents did not deter people
from confessing to him. On the contrary, they felt drawn to a spiritual
director who, while noted for his personal piety and sagacity, was
also so imposing.[12]

A similar case of great emphasis being laid on the church as an
institution and on the clergyman's station is that of the German
preacher Wilhelm Löhe.[13] In 1837, when he became pastor of Neuen-
dettelsau, in Bayern, he found that a religious revival was under
way among his parishioners. He believed later that this would have
passed without trace if private confession had not provided him with
the means of sustaining the new spirit. He advocated such confession
in his sermons. And his appeal met with such response that soon the
great majority of his parishioners made it their rule to confess to him
before taking Holy Communion. Löhe set great store by the institutional character of confession and, accordingly, also by the clergyman's authoritative position.[14] One evidence of this was the procedure
followed when people notified that they wished to take Communion.
They did so in church after the weekly Friday service before a Sunday
when Communion would take place. Löhe stood, a commanding presence, at a table in the middle of the choir, and those so inclined went
forward to him, one by one. He noted who they were "with a fleeting
but penetrating glance". People guilty of serious demeanours remained
until the end; Löhe then gave them a severe lecture and urged them
to repent. Only after remorse and penitence had come to them were
they granted pardon and given permission to attend Communion.

The eminence of the clergyman and of the established church was
enhanced by the arrangements made for private confession. Löhe
always received penitents in the church vestry. When he began with
confession, he listened to them while standing; for, as he regretfully

---

[12] However, some statements conveyed by Purcell show that Manning's behaviour
could at times make too dominating and "awful" an impression. Many people who
went to him were so overwhelmed by his severity and the steadfast faith that emanated
from him that they did not dare place their doubts and difficulties before him. (*Ibid.*;
p. 497.)

[13] J. Deinzer, *Wilhelm Löhes Leben*, I-III (Nürnberg and Gütersloh, 1874-92). See
particularly the chapter *"Löhe als Beichtvater"*; vol. II, pp. 157-169.

[14] See G. Wehrung, *"Wilhelm Löhe und seine Lehre von der Kirche"* in *Theologische
Literaturzeitung* (1941); col. 177 ff. : Löhe *"liess durch die Ordination den Amsträger
gerade über den Stand des allgemeinen Priestertums erhoben werden"* (col. 180).

said, one of his predecessors had "ordered the confessional to be hewn to pieces". But later he would use a confessional, at least in the deaconesses' institution where he was spiritual adviser. Löhe developed—according to his admiring biographer—the qualities of a great director of conscience as he pursued his course. What characterized him specially was a "solemn dignity in all his dealings with the penitent". Confession ended with absolution, which Löhe pronounced standing. The stringent self-examination was thus succeeded by benediction, dread and despair by a sense of liberation : and release must have been experienced with an intensity rendered all the greater by the confessor's previous severity.[15]

While in the cases we have examined hitherto priestly authority was doubtless upheld primarily by emphasizing the church as institution and the loftiness of clerical office, we shall see in what follows that a confessor's authoritative standing may derive from other factors as well : from his position as a revivalist and, above all, his personal qualities.

This was the situation with, for instance, Johan Christoph Blumhardt. The revival in his parish, Möttlingen, got truly under way only when he began to receive confessions.

That revival was preluded by some striking cases of faith cures. Three members of a family in the parish suffered from what were evidently serious hysterical disorders : they assumed that they were possessed by devils, which was also Blumhardt's view.[16] After long and arduous efforts, he finally succeeded in restoring them to well-being through prayer and laying-on of hands. We can easily imagine what a great impression this must have made in the parish. Blumhardt noted later, with concern, that many people preferred to talk about his cures than about the subsequent revival and showed a greater wish to learn more on that subject. Certainly, the healings had a great deal to do with the fact that his appeals for an intensified

---

[15] Deinzer expressed this eloquently, if also a trife bombastically, when he said of absolution from Löhe's lips : *"Wie tröstlich klangen dann diese hohen Gottesworte und wie giengen sie den Seelen ein, lindernder als Oel und Balsam, erfrischender als Thau, süsser als Honig und Honigseim"*. (*Loc. cit.*)

[16] In 1850 Blumhardt published an account of his most sensational faith cure : that of Gottliebin Dittus, who recovered so completely from her illness that she was later able to carry out duties as teacher in the infant school established by Blumhardt. His account of the cure was republished in 1934. (See the review of it by Emil Ott in *Theologische Rundschau* for 1937; p. 369.)

spiritual life in the parish gained a response from his listeners. And it is likely that they helped to bring him into demand as healer for the inner dissociation which his parishioners became fully aware existed within themselves when they heard his sermons exhorting repentance.

We find in Blumhardt's case none of those exterior arrangements, of that ritualistic behaviour, designed to impress penitents and underline the dignity of church and clergy. But he had a very effective way of stressing the seriousness of confession itself. He made penitents come at least three times before he granted absolution. He did not permit them to go through confesssion casually, but insisted on getting thoroughly to the root of a sin : on making an analysis sufficient for a spiritual guide to give advice which could bring the penitent real liberation in future. Only when he was satisfied with the analysis did he bestow absolution.[17] The gravity of confession was given due prominence by this procedure. At the same time, Blumhardt had strengthened his authority as confessor—an authority that was ultimately founded on his personal qualities as a director of conscience.

We see how this authority was built up : by the esteem that derived from his faith cures and by the spiritual power he evinced as a preacher, also by the emphasis he placed on the seriousness of confession, and by the experience his penitents acquired of his ability as mental healer.

A genuine revivalist preacher can win a dominant influence over his faithful flock by his sermons. On a listener shaken by his words, he can play as on a sensitive instrument. Such is especially the case in movements, like the Laestadian one, where religious ecstasy makes its appearance. An as illustration of what takes place, we can take this eyewitness description of a Laestadian meeting.[18]

The preacher begins with a penitential sermon in which he depicts the misery of sinners and the horrors that hell holds in store for them during the life to come. "The preacher's words reverberate round the cot. Men and women groan with dread. The women fall into a swoon. Sobs of terrified children can be heard among the cries of anguish. But, finally, when the place is filled with the lamentations of horror-

---

[17] However, Blumhardt could make exceptions to his rule that penitents must come three times before receiving absolution. He might give it on the first visit in a distressing case when the greatly perturbed penitent was in utter despair over his sins. (See Zündel : *op. cit.*; p. 159.) Here we are reminded of Raattamaa and the Laestadian movement.

[18] Märta Edquist, *Lars Levi Laestadius* (Stockholm, 1922) : p. 136 f.

stricken people, the preacher allows a new note to ring out. A ray of light suddenly penetrates the gloom. Salvation is to be found. Now complete and entire confession is on its way. A commotion arises in the multitude. One after another, and soon several together, those present gain the strength to confess what has, perhaps for many years, been entwining and tormenting their consciences. Very sombre words may be spoken about sin and vice, but bringing all this forth into the light involves a boundless liberation". Then : "When sin is confessed some people know such relief in their hearts that they feel they no longer belong to the earth. At the same time, it is as if something must fill the space left empty when sin was driven out. With the preacher's picture of heavenly glory, such blessedness pours in that it seems their hearts will burst. People lift hands to throats which are about to choke. Then the tension breaks. It is dissolved in a shout of joy". *Liikutuksian*—group ecstasy along the same lines as in the early Pentecostal Movement—begins.

At the revivalist meeting depicted here, many taking part were not yet "awakened". The description shows that their confession signifies entry into the religious community and their adoption by the faithful. Meanwhile, confession is practised by "awakened" members of the congregation as an oft-repeated purgatory for serious sins. It may, as we have seen, be made either before the congregation or privately to the preacher, and the preacher generally confers absolution on behalf of the congregation. It is precisely his power to do this which elevates him to a position of extreme authority, above what he would occupy only as a revivalist preacher.

A writer with special knowledge of the subject has remarked on this : "In the Laestadian movement it seems as if the great majority would not recognize any other God than the preachers".

If we wish to have a more modern instance of a confessor whose authority was founded solely on his position as a revivalist (in so much as it did not stem from his personal attributes), we might well take that of Frank Buchman.

As leader of the Oxford Group revival, he was *a priori* in a situation that induced feelings of confidence and respect in those who approached him. He was an example of the famous revivalist who travels from country to country, from town to town, awaited with eager anticipation wherever he goes. Word of his ability to influence people has reached all ears. The success of his revival is in itself a sign of such power. Perhaps preparations for his arrival are made by representatives sent out for the purpose; some local residents may have taken part previously in meetings and given their impressions of them. People have read about the movement in books and newspaper articles; and now they have received invitation cards to the big assembly. When the leader and his assistants—his "team"—draw near, an atmosphere of expectation has been developed. The leader makes his appearance at "the psychological moment". People attend the meeting for different reasons : some perhaps out of simple curiosity, others from a deep spiritual need. All this held true in Buchman's case. His assistants gave testimony about how they had been "changed", and some local people joined in. The audience was struck by so much candour. Many present found in it an indictment of the way they themselves lived. They wanted to hear more about the path to a new life. And they very much wished to meet the leader of the movement. He must surely be a true spiritual guide and transformer of lives to have achieved such results![19]

When a personal meeting of the kind takes place with a revivalist leader, his authority is accepted without reserve by uncritical people. They are prepared to follow at once his advice and directions. Frank Buchman was evidently well aware of his position in this respect, and he knew the value of an authoritative manner when he had a still wavering and reluctant person before him. If someone hesitated to make a confession, he was capable of issuing a plain order to do so. Or a person who found it difficult to make up his mind would be summoned to accompany "the team" on an evangelizing tour.[20] A somewhat censorious adherent of Buchman's was once shocked by his imperious way of proceeding.[21] And, from the fact that the spiritual experiences of his disciples were so much in line with his prescripts, a number of his critics have inferred that he exercised a dictatorial influence on his followers. But rather, of course, we see a natural consequence of Buchman having created the movement with its special methods and requirements.

---

[19] See, for instance, the experience of "Princeton" described by Begbie, *op. cit.*; p. 143 f. Cf., incidentally, J. B. Pratt's description of how the psychological background for a revivalist's public appearance can be created in such a way. (*The Religious Consciousness* : New York, 1921; pp. 165-194.)

[20] For example. see the summonses to "Persona Grata" and to "Greats" recorded by Begbie : *op. cit.*; p. 115 and p. 82 for the respective cases.

[21] "Greats". See Begbie : *idem*; p. 85.

Frank Buchman's position and his self-confidence were important elements behind his success as a confessor. They induced respect in people who were disposed to confess and inspired an advance attitude of trust in them; so the great revivalist, who had been able to effect a startling change of heart in so many others, was approached by such people with high expectations, and a fairly certain prospect of receiving help. It is easily perceived that this gave Buchman a very favourable situation to start from, both in the matter of getting a confession and of exerting influence on the confessant. But it is also evident that, in the long run, his success as spiritual guide did not depend only on his position and prestige as a revivalist leader, but on his wholly personal attributes—without which, for that matter, he would not have become the religious leader he was. Briefly, those qualities of special importance to Buchman as director of souls were his ability and his willingness to project himself into each individual who came to him for help, to discover the special difficulties of every one by interesting himself in exactly that person's problems, to find the most suitable remedy for them through his experience and knowledge of human nature. Buchman was, to quote two estimations of him from writings on the Group movement, a "soul surgeon" (Begbie's epithet) and an unsurpassed "psycho-analyst" (Hambro's).

Our survey of the confessor's authoritative position has shown how it is upheld by institutionalism in the church and maintained also by the confessor himself. Assertion of such authority may appear in doctrinal views, as with the Catholic Church. We have come across a similar conception in certain Protestant quarters. But especially where Protestantism is concerned, the authority of a spiritual guide seems to be founded ultimately on his possession of certain entirely personal qualities. This clearly means that in Christian confession we must take two kinds of confessor into account : with one type importance rests on outward authority derived from priestly office; with the other it belongs rather to an ability, determined by the confessor's own faculties, to enter into spiritual fellowship with confessants. In the first case, the main thing about a confessor's behaviour seems to be the authoritative way he issues orders and requires obedience. (Meanwhile, the penitent responds with docile submission). In the second case, principal stress lies not on a dominant position granted *a priori* but on the confessor's power to interest himself personally in the confessant : here the relationship between the two who take part in the act of confession is not characterized by any remoteness but rather by mutual sharing and a sense of communion. In a phenomenological study of Christian confession, it can be convenient to separate the two types of confessor and also the relations of each with confessants. But that must not lead us into so isolating one type from the other that we misconstrue the complex reality involved. An examination of the trustful relationship in confession may reveal a portion of the real situation.

The trust of a penitent both in confession as a divine institution and in his confessor seems to be required if his confession is truly to have the desired effect on him. Of course it is plain that the need to confess contains in itself both an urge to confide and to give confidence to another person; we do not confide to anyone at all but to somebody in whom we can feel confidence. It is clear, too, that a would-be confessant turns to a person who, in some way, can help him get rid of the sin that weighs on his conscience, and who can also give him advice for the future. All these needs on his part mean that his confessor must possess authority. Definite importance is attached here to the confessor's external position as priest or clergyman and as director of souls. But the confessant often wants more than this of his confessor : he hopes to meet with comprehension, interest and sympathy. The trust given a confessor in an earnest and profound confession, also the wholehearted surrender to him and belief in him, then appear to be inspired to a determining degree by his altogether personal qualities; and this is so even when confession is of a strongly institutional character, as in the Catholic Church. On the other hand, if we look at religious communities where emphasis is not laid on the outward authority of the confessor but rather on his personality and the reciprocal element in his relations with confessants, it seems that even there a confessant cannot help regarding his confessor as in some sense an authority. The authority then resides principally in the comparatively greater religious experience of the person who receives confession. In what follows, we shall see that this holds true even with so pure a form of confession to a layman as that practised in the movement created by Frank Buchman.

CHAPTER FOUR

RELATIONSHIP OF TRUST
BETWEEN CONFESSOR AND CONFESSANT

From what we have now observed, the confessant's trust in his confessor—obviously an essential element in any serious confession—may be said to depend on an authority which the confessor possesses in some exterior way, also on his entirely personal attributes and individual conduct. Having dealt in the last chapter more particularly with the part played by external authority, we ought now to examine specially the nature and importance of the confessor's personal qualities. First, we may note that the confessor should acquire what could be called an inner authority through his own involvement, through his willingness to comprehend and enter into the confessant's troubles : such authority of the confessor is rooted in the confessant's mental situation, and thus he can exercise a profound influence on it. In what follows, we shall study the evidence of a confessant's trustful attitude founded on authority of the kind.

Let us, to begin with, turn to confession in the Catholic Church and see what significance is attached to the personal element there. The confession we meet with might of course seem to be of a purely institutional kind : in principle it should function *ex opere operato* and thus have its effect whatever the confessor's personal attributes and manner of proceeding; so the personal factors ought really to be of no consequence. But closer investigation shows this to be a rather superficial view, applicable only when Catholic confession is practised in a routine fashion. The actual situation is that, even if the penance sacrament is objective in principle, the personal element seems to have asserted itself and broken through the institutional framework. We shall take first some examples which illustrate indirectly the importance of the confessor's individual faculties : these will reveal how a number of penitents reacted when they had confessors who did not suit them. Instances will then follow where the confessor's personality expressed itself directly : confessors who have been able to enter into genuine communion with their confessants will here come under view.

When the German psychiatrist A. Muthmann wished to gain information about the psychological factors which are in operation during confession, he questioned carefully devout Catholics whose confidence he enjoyed.[1] From answers received, it was clear that not all priests could achieve the right results when their penitents confessed. As a case in point, one priest was too tactless and insensitive about the penitent's emotional reaction to a particularly burdensome sin. Another priest reprimanded so sharply[2] that the act of confession became too painful for the penitent; he could no longer submit to it, however much he wished to recieve absolution. Muthmann did find in his survey that absolution always brought a sense of "release of tension", notwithstanding that the priest might have been a bad confessor. But it is worth noting that, even if the penitent was convinced of having received full absolution for his sins, his emotional state after confession varied in accordance with the confessor's personal behaviour.[3]

Henri Bremond depicted the response of a French mystic, Marie de l'Incarnation, to a mechanical sort of confessor. She went one day to Notre-Dame in Paris, and while there felt a powerful impulse to confess. Put in the mystic's language : "I perceived so clearly from an inward illumination the significance of making a good confession; and I acquired so strong a conviction that I ought to make one, I could not doubt that I should".[4] Consequently, she entered a confessional. But the priest who took her confession proceeded in a very routine manner, without establishing what was of importance to her in it. She afterwards related that her heart closed and she could no longer confess as she had planned to do, in accordance with the promptings that had newly come to her.

Sensitive people are put off by a customary and unadapted method of confessing. Bremond added some reflections of his own to his account of the case given. Often, he said, when he passed a confessional and pictured all the fine-souled penitents who had perhaps found only dense and common-minded ("*épais, vulgaires*") priests behind the grill there, he thought of the severe blows that must have been dealt

---

[1] A. Muthmann, "*Psychiatrisch-theologische Grenzfragen*", in *Zeitschrift für Religions-psychologie*, I (Halle an der Saale, 1908); pp. 49-75.

[2] "*Der andere Geistliche schilt so sehr*". (*Ibid.*; p. 65.)

[3] "*Der Gefühlston aber sei auch bei der beruhigenden Überzeugung völliger Absolution je nach der Art des Geistlichen ein verschiedener*". (*Ibid.*; p. 65.)

[4] Bremond, *op. cit.*; vol. VI, p. 17 (note).

to them. And he went on : "Who among us can pride himself on never having 'resealed' a single soul ?"[5]

François de Sales provided a good illustration of what can happen when a person wants to confess in the Catholic Church. The would-be penitent arrives at a church, thinks of nothing else than making his confession, waits for an opportunity of talking to a confessor... But perhaps the confessor has numerous other penitents. When the person's turn comes, to get matters over quickly the priest deals summarily with his confession and with instructions to him. And as soon as this penitent leaves the confessional a mass begins. He is looking for the peace that can give composure to his soul and make room there for reverence and attachment to God...[6]

A routine confession of that kind does not suffice. It is not enough that penitents should simply be referred to what is established by the Church. For a confession to be wholly adequate, the confesssor must obviously be able to inspire the penitent's confidence in a personal way. For the act of confession itself to exert full effect, this is to all appearances a necessity. And it is of most particular importance if the penitent is really to heed his confessor's directions and advice in the future. Without the existence of a personal relationship between confessor and penitent, the priest's function as spiritual guide is probably illusory.

In fact, ecclesiastical teachers of the Catholic Church attach considerable weight to personal qualities when they draw up the requirements for a confessor. We may see an early illustration of this in the writings of Origen. In his second homily on Psalm 37, he gives advice to someone bent on confessing to a leader of the Church : "Look about with care for the person to whom you will confess your sins. Accept first as the physician to whom you will lay bare the source of your affliction one who knows how to be weak with the weak, how to weep with him who weeps, one who has the ability to share in sorrow and

---

[5] *Loc. cit.* Cf. P. Janet, who said that many confessors have understood how to handle people suffering from compulsive neuroses. But he declared that there are also priests who show a quite incredible ignorance and obtuseness when they have to do with over-scrupulous people and those suffering from compulsive neuroses; such priests are "*assez sots pour raconter des niaiseries sur le diable à des pauvres esprits tourmentés par des obsessions sacrilèges*". ("...Stupid enough to relate naive nonsense about the devil to simple souls tormented by sacrilegious obsessions". P. Janet, *Les Obsessions et la psychasthénie*; p. 708.)

[6] Bremond, *op. cit.*; vol. IX, p. 115.

suffering : do this so if he who first shows himself to be a wise and compassionate physician has said something to you, if he has given you counsel, you will act accordingly and follow it".[7]

Here, briefly described, we have the essential personal requirement for a confessor. He must possess an aptitude for sympathy in the true meaning of that word : for sharing the feelings of others. Along with this, he needs to have wisdom in order to give fitting confessional advice. It may perhaps seem less remarkable that Origen paid such consideration to the confessor's altogether personal qualities when we remember that in his day penance and confession had not yet acquired the stability they would later have as institutions of the Church.

But even in our time Catholic pastoral theology which establishes norms makes similar requirements as to the confessor's personality and behaviour. In a much-praised handbook on the priest's administration of the sacraments, Otto Schöllig, a professor who taught at a seminary for priests in Freiburg, places chief emphasis on the following temperamental qualities of a confessor.[8] He must be endowed with "pastoral wisdom", which means that he should possess a feeling for the personality and situation of each individual, thus being able to deal with penitents and give them directions as suits the nature of each; in that way he best serves the aim of the penance sacrament, which is to overcome sin and increase the penitent's sanctification. The confessor should feel great eagerness to help souls in distress. He must be supplied with much patience, gentleness, paternal kindness, and a never-ceasing readiness to help. The highest requirement placed on him personally was expressed in Saint Ambrose's words on the priests as a *"vicarius amoris Christi"*. In relations with penitents, the confessor must shun everything that could be construed as springing from an absence of affection and sympathy. Through awareness of his own weakness, he ought to be humble. He is not the master of his penitent, but the penitent's loving and sympathetic father. Here, Schöllig quotes from the *Tridentinum* : "Good will towards the person who should be reformed often works better than authority, encouragement better than threats, love better than power".[9]

---

[7] Quoted from O. D. Watkins, *A History of Penance*; vol. I, p. 139.

[8] O. Schöllig, *Die Verwaltung der heiligen Sakramente*; p. 218 ff. See the review of this work in *Zeitschrift für katholische Theologie*, 1937; p. 154 f.

[9] *"Saepe plus erga corrigendos agit benevolentia quam auctoritas, plus exhortatio quam comminatio, plus caritas quam potestas"*. (Schöllig, *op. cit.*; p. 221.)

The confessor's personal attributes ought to mark his conduct in his various functions during the act of confession. It is commonly said that he is then to be father, physician, teacher and judge.[10] The fatherliness should evince itself in particular as benevolence and sympathy for penitents. The priest is warned against an unresponsive attitude and a severity that will render confession more difficult for the penitent; it should be remembered that the penitent approaches the holy sacrament with dread and has perhaps had trouble in overcoming a natural reluctance to lay his sins before a priest. The heavier a penitent's sins lie upon him, the easier his confessor should, through kind encouragement, make it for him to confess. Not only is paternal affection often regarded as necessary to get the penitent started with his confession, it is required no less during the course of confession. The priest must then restrain himself from showing signs of impatience, surprise or disapproval : in other words, from any response that could make the penitent feel alarmed or humiliated, thus causing him to break off his confession in fear or rhame. True, the way a confessional is constructed, with a grill separating the two people there, serves to screen the confessor's visible reactions from his penitent.

The confessor's personal attributes are again of much consequence when we come to his function as physician of the soul. This involves his tracing the causes of a sin, prescribing a remedy for it and preventing its recurrence. For the success of his efforts here, certain qualities are bound to be decisive : discretion, his ability to grasp the mental state and individual character of his penitent, also the faculty of projecting himself into the penitent's mind. Particularly where this last is concerned, attention is called to the importance of taking proper time with a penitent. Warning is issued against routine confessional procedure; every penitent must receive careful treatment. François Xavier's words apply as a *sententia aurea* : "It is of more value to hear a few well-made confessions than many that are made in haste and will be without effect".[11]

A confessor's personal sensibility, tact and discernment are perhaps most necessary of all when he appears in his function as judge. One thing he must then do is determine the gravity of various sins, distinguishing between serious or mortal sins, on the one hand, and those

---

[10] See the article on *"Confession"* in *Dictionnaire de théologie catholique*; col. 942-960. Cf. Schöllig, *op. cit.*; pp. 223-245.

[11] Article on *"Confession"* in *Dictionnaire de théologie catholique*; col. 944.

which are pardonable or venial, on the other. To do so, he must investigate the circumstances in which a sin was committed.[12] Here, especially, the confessor is cautioned against proceeding too rigorously. He must not torture his penitents with questions, as certain confessors are capable of doing. That can engender a dread of confession and an aversion to the whole system of penance. Another danger is frequently pointed out : if the confessor lacks understanding of his penitent, he can indicate new possibilities of sinning through his questions.

These are the general demands we read of with regard to the purely personal qualifications a confessor needs for his task. We shall now see how two exemplary Catholic confessors maintained the principles concerned and put them into practice. We shall also see how, in doing so, they gained the confidence and complete devotion of their penitents, thus creating a relationship of fellowship which is advantageous to the effect of confession".

François de Sales' opinions on the confessor are regarded as highly authoritative; and he is himself considered to have been a model confessor. Indeed, he is held up as the classic director of conscience and given a kingly position among those of the Catholic Church.[13]

Saint François made clear that it is not enough for the confessor to possess the knowledge needed for his vocation. He must not only understand how to question and examine penitents about their sins but must also be their friend and confident. Nor does it suffice that he is revered as one endowed with special grace to administer the sacrament : he must also be loved as a person. According to Saint François, the would-be penitent ought to choose his confessor with great care and make his choice among a thousand—no, ten thousand. The confessor should at once hold the authority that derives from his knowledge and virtue, and in the eyes of penitents be invested with a prestige beyond compare. He must be something more than an ordinary person : a divine being, "an angel". But the divine element is not to

---

[12] In *Katolsk katekes för det apostoliska vikariatet i Sverige* (Catholic Catechism for the Apostolic Deputyship in Sweden; Stockholm, 1937) this is stated in the following manner : "Important circumstances are ones that greatly increase the sin. Those belonging here are, primarily : l. circumstances by which a sin is rendered a mortal sin (for example, *larger* theft, *considerable* injury); circumstances which substantially alter the character of a sin, as another Commandment is also broken (for example, theft of *church* property, maltreatment of *parents*)".

[13] *Bremond*; vol. IV, p. 136. Cf. F. Vincent, *Saint François de Sales. Directeur d'âmes* (Paris, 1923); p. 550.

be so magnified that real human trust can find no room beside the penitent's awe for his confessor's holiness. Saint François even spoke of friendship (*amitié*) as being the proper relationship between the two. Theirs is to be a genuinely personal attachment and basically a reciprocal one. Presupposing an actively personal attitude on the confessor's side, Saint François made an urgent request to the penitent : "Place extreme confidence in him, so mingled with holy reverence that the veneration in no way diminishes your trust and the trust does not impede your reverence. Commit yourself to him with the respect that a daughter has for her father, and honour him with the sense of reliance that a son has for his mother". The friendship should be firm and gentle, dedicated and divine.[14]

And François de Sales himself fulfilled the requirements he placed on a spiritual leader : this is shown by the statements in which his penitents expressed their faith in him. One of his spiritual sons, Jean-Pierre Camus, wrote to him that he believed a secret spiritual power flowed into his words from on high. "You may do what you like with me. Your judgement has such power over me and your will so completely governs mine that I ponder on your words as on an oracle's reply".[15]

Another of Saint François' penitents, the mystic Jeanne de Chantal, had been dissatisfied when she confessed to a previous confessor, But after her very first confession to Saint François she felt so calmed and so restored that she believed an angel from heaven had talked with her : "I listened to the holy prior as if a voice from heaven were speaking to me ; he seemed to be in a state of trance from the way he collected and searched after his words, one after another, as if it were difficult for him to speak".[16] And she experienced the most sweeping sense of transformation : "Oh God, what a day of joy for me ! It seemed to me that my soul put on another face and left the inner prison where the directions of my first confessor had kept me until then". Of course, this case illustrates with particular clarity the importance of the confessor's personality in the Catholic Church ; for Jeanne de Chantal was able to obtain from one Catholic confessor the understanding that she had missed when the penitent of another.

---

[14] In François de Sales' *Introduction à la vie dévote*, quoted from F. Vincent, *op. cit.*; p. 407.

[15] Bremond; vol. I, p. 169 f.

[16] Bremond; vol. II, p. 548.

Similar testimony may be found concerning many other famous Catholic confessors : how, by their strength of personality, their feeling for the penitent's individual character, their wise course of procedure, they won their penitents over completely—for themselves and thereby for their aim of leading on towards holiness. We might take from Henri Bremond's work another description of how an ideal Catholic confessor performed his task and appeared in the eyes of his faithful following. Charles de Condren is the confessor this time.[17] It is said of him that when someone came under his direction he devoted himself to that single person's spiritual development as if he had nothing else in the world to do. He possessed a "universal ardour in his soul" : though he had as much love for each one as if none other existed for him, he wanted to reach so many people. His goodness, to begin with, but also his wisdom as a spiritual guide inspired the complete confidence of his penitents and their great devotion. M. Olier, who was both a penitent and the leading disciple of Condren, expressed his own experience and that of Condren's confessants generally when he said : "One found oneself at such complete repose under his direction that there has never been any child of his who did not count it among his greatest bounties that he had got to know so good a father".[18]

Linus Bopp, on the subject of how important the confessor's personality is in Catholic confession and the power it usually exerts there, gave as his opinion that only people whose character is stamped by self-forgetful love possess the ability to understand others and lead them aright. He cited various confessors of such exemplary character in the Catholic Church.[19]

As for confessors in the Protestant sphere, it doubtless emerged from what was put forward in the last chapter how the confessor's per-

---

[17] Bremond; vol. III, p. 407.

[18] *Loc. cit.*

[19] *"Gleichwohl kommt auf die Persönlichkeit des Beichtführers sehr viel an. Die grossen Seelenführer wie Franz von Sales, Vinzenz von Paul, Fénelon, Vianney von Ars, Overberg, Klemens Maria Hoffbauer, Sailer u. a. waren alle Männer selbstlosester Liebe. Nur solche sind imstande den Mitmenschen zu durchschauen und zu verstehen".* (Bopp, *op. cit.*; p. 88.) Cf. J. Leute, who from his experience as a Catholic confessor emphasized very strongly the importance of the confessor's personal qualities. They are, he said, of particular significance when advice and solace to the penitent are involved : *"Je persönlicher und je mehr aus der eigenen Seele geschöpft dieser Zuspruch erschien, desto mehr ging er zu Herzen. Mit einer reinen Schablone ist nichts zu machen".* (*Op. cit.*; p. 95.)

sonal attributes usually assert themselves there; also that those qualities appear ultimately to be decisive for his position as a spiritual adviser. We have already seen evidence of the confidence felt by confessants in Protestant confessors. But here we might give two further examples which throw into particular relief the intimate relationship and harmony of mind between confessor and confessant.

A friend of John Keble found the explanation of Keble's ability to create a spirit of communion with his penitents in his extraordinary benevolence : "It was like loving goodness itself. You felt that what was good in him was applying itself directly and bringing into life all that was best in you. His ready, lively, transparent affection seemed as if it was the very spirit of love opening out upon you and calling for a return such as you could give".[20]

Relations between Keble and his penitents were strongly emotional in character; the penitents effaced themselves and depended entirely on their confessor's authority. The friend just quoted gave token of their self-abnegation in the following way : "What I think is remarkable is not how many people loved him, or how much they loved him, but that each and every one of them seemed to love him with the very best kind of love of which they were capable".[21]

We might turn with advantage to the writings on Frank Buchman and his work in order to study further how the personal qualities of a confessor make themselves felt, and how in consequence he gains his confessant's devotion. In the gallery of Oxford Group figures supplied by numerous books on the movement, one of the most interesting personalities is the figure whom Harold Begbie calls "Greats". He is of special note because he tested the Group's message with a critical sense; also, in spite of having been vitally affected by the movement, he preserved a critical attitude towards it. Particular importance should without doubt be attached to his testimony for that reason, During his first meeting with Frank Buchman they both behaved characteristically : "Greats" showing his natural scepticism, Buchman using his ability to overcome a doubting attitude and to establish a spirit of community under the most unfavourable auspicies.

"Great's" sole preoccupation during that first conversation was, at first, how most conveniently to get rid of the unpleasant American. But soon a change set in. He forgot what it was he found so disagreeable

---

[20] W. Lock, *John Keble* (London, 1895); p. 207.
[21] *Loc. cit.*

about the man. The conversation continued, and then Buchman got up to go. "Greats" said afterwards : "Something overwhelming had come over me. It was an insult to play with this man".[22] And then he confided his troubles to Buchman. "For the first time in my life I had deliberately and gladly made a fool of myself before a perfect stranger. I had told him things I had never breathed to another". He added : "I put it all down to some uncanny personal quality of the man, some quasi-hypnotic influence". And later, when he had thought over his experience in Buchman's company, his sardonic attitude vanished and he switched over to self-reproach about the way he had responded to Buchman's "simple goodness".

At later meetings with Buchman, "Greats" saw the Oxford Group leader as an eminent representative of God. No one before had given him such a sense of God's nearness. "It was a particular individual experience which I have had but a few times in my life, and perhaps never with the same intensity" : this was the experience of "standing before God". "Greats" concluded : "Whatever I may subsequently think of F. B. [Buchman] cannot alter my conviction on this subject".

Begbie received similar testimony about Buchman's personality and the trust he inspired from a student called "Rugger Blue" in Begbie's book.[23] Buchman made a profound impression on "Rugger Blue" the first time they met. They did not discuss ethics or religious problems. (Often, it may be noted, Buchman did not want to bring on any religious crisis by "talking religion" as soon as an opportunity was offered for a private talk.) "Rugger Blue" related : "F. B. never pusued me. But I couldn't shake the thought of him out of my mind. I got no line from him, never heard a word about him, never met him. Yet, from that moment of out first meeting he was hardly ever out of my thoughts. I've talked to other fellows since about their first impressions of F. B., and I find that he took many of them as he took me. It was a strange strong feeling that he really knew about one, and could help one..." A crucial conversation soon followed that first one. The two met again later when the student had decided to make a confession; there came to him again, prompting him in his resolve, the feeling that Buchman could help him : "I knew then, absolutely and with a regular blaze of certainty, that he could clean me out. I told him the whole trouble, everything".

---

[22] Begbie, *op. cit.*; p. 70 ff.
[23] *Ibid.*; p. 96 ff.

Harold Begbie also gives an account of how "Persona Grata"—later a prominent Oxford Group figure—was won over by Buchman. While "Persona Grata" was attending a school of divinity in Hartford, Connecticut, and undergoing a period of great temptations and severe disharmony, Buchman came to lecture there. "P. G." received "the immediate feeling" that "he could speak with complete frankness and confidence to this stranger—stranger no longer, for the touch of his hand had conveyed an instant feeling of friendliness".[24]

Numerous other examples could be given of Buchman's faculty for arousing trust : getting people to abandon their reserve and make frank confidences. But those presented will suffice to confirm this statement of Begbie's about the devotion of those came under his spiritual guidance : all, said Begbie, "regard him with an affection which is one of the many proofs I possess that his goodness has the true character of divinity—it is lovable".[25]

About the importance of the confessor's personal virtues in confession, we can make this general observation : the more in evidence they are and the greater the store which is set by them, the less the confessor's external authority comes into view; significance is attached instead to exchange and communion between confessor and confessant. François de Sales spoke of reciprocity between the two; and his entire method of confession and spiritual leadership (which we shall examine more closely in the next chapter) was aimed at creating a sense of unity between them. He emphasized that the confessor must show love for the penitent, and he must endeavour to be loved in return. If he succeeds in this his spiritual guidance will have gained an ally within the penitent. Ultimately, his leadership does not depend on his outward authority but on his personality. It is the confessor's personality which inspires the penitent to disclose himself wholly and to strive for the moral perfection that he sees reflected in his confessor. This applies to François de Sales' own case; it holds good also with the other eminent confessors whom we have encountered here : such men as John Keble, Johann Christoph Blumhardt and Frank Buchman. On the whole, it may be assumed that the key to their success as directors of conscience lay in their exerting their influence primarily through how they themselves were : through their strength of personality, their willingness and ability to give

---

[24] *Ibid.*; p. 112.
[25] *Ibid.*; p. 52.

of themselves and take an interest in each individual who came to them seeking release from spiritual troubles. Naturally, official authority has its importance : it gives the would-be confessant an indication of where to direct himself, and it raises in advance his expectation of finding satisfaction for his need to confess, to be freed from his sins, to receive advice and guidance. Such authority thus supplies the prompting which brings confession about. But after the act of confession has begun personal factors come into play, and these are of decisive importance for the entire effect of confession.

The mutual element and fellowship between confessor and confessant may in some cases be of such a nature that the person who, to start with, acted as confessor becomes the one who confesses or who receives spiritual direction. The two exchange their roles. Cases of this kind occur both in the Catholic and the Protestant spheres.

Henri Bremond described what could happen when certain Catholic mystics made confession : mystical women might begin to receive uncanny experiences and not understand themselves how to interpret these.[26] But a knowledgeable confessor would finally come to the aid of such a woman. Having observed her closely, he would urge her to banish all uncertainty about the provenance of the spirit that possessed her and surrender herself to divine grace. "During the first half of his intervention the priest is only a priest, by which I wish to say only an authority : he alone controls; one thinks of nothing else than obeying him".

Soon, however, a change takes place within the confessor, and his whole attitude is imperceptibly altered. He does not really want to be anything more for the mystic than the representative of God and his Church. But he cannot forget himself so completely. He sees the mystic as a being whose spirit opens to God's wisdom and all-embracing power. And when he has received her confidences, how can he withstand an inclination to give her, sooner or later, his own ? How could he be able to restrain himself from refreshing and strengthening himself at the spring welling up beside him ? So Bremond asks. And when the confessor has ceased to speak in the name of divine authority, the mystic sees him only as a soul to be restored and uplifted from the earth. She wants to share with him the gifts bestowed in abundance upon her. She makes no pretence of leading him ; she does not speak in an authoritative tone. But his manner of proceeding is no longer a

---

[26] Bremond; vol. II, p. 38 ff.

master's; instead he behaves as an apprentice, as the pupil. And she guides him by telling him about her experiences.[27]

Here, the confessor's authority, ecclesiastical and personal, and the method he employs both gradually prove superfluous; the liberating, creative ferment comes from the person who was to be directed. In a most obvious way, the personal element has broken down the prescribed plan of procedure. Naturally, this type of Catholic confession is exceptional. It is of interest, nevertheless, because it illuminates the part played by the personal factor in confession. Of course, in general the confessor's authority is meanwhile at least formally asserted. That authority is, to be sure, intimately connected with the character he assumes as administrator of the sacrament.

In the Protestant domain, we may expect to find the particular conditions for such reciprocal confession where the recipient has no accepted authority : in lay confession. The best-known examples of lay confession in our time have been provided by the Oxford Group movement. There, the method of confession used, "sharing", was designed to produce a sense of unity. Members of the Group have made the following statements about the practice. One said : "I shared everything that lay on my mind with a friend; I revealed my weakest sides to him, and he did the same to me".[28] And V. C. Kitchen told of how he and his wife exchanged confessions : "We told each other fully and freely the kind of people that we really were".[29] Here, it is evident that the form of confession may be compared with secret confidences made between friends. However, what characterizes "sharing" in Buchmanism is its religious coloration : confidences are felt to be something more than those in a relationship between two people. The participants sense that a higher power above them ultimately receives the confessions of them both. Emil Brunner considered it specially meritorious of Buchman to have understood that the absence of a "you up there" and "you down there" is an essential condition for the cure of souls : to have perceived that for the proper

---

[27] *"Elle stimule, elle insinue, elle rayonne, suave dominatrice qui règne à genoux".* (She stimulates, she suggests, she radiates, gracious dominator who reigns on her knees. Bremond; vol. II, p. 40.)

[28] *Ermatinger Tagebuch. Gruppenbewegung im Deutschland u. in der Schweiz 1932* (Gotha, 1932).

[29] V. C. Kitchen, *I Was a Heathen* (London, 1934); p. 100.

relationship of confidence to be engendered distance between confessor and confessant must be abolished.[30]

We have, to be sure, observed how important it is that the receiver of confession should be able to enter into personal communion with the confessant; but from the account given earlier here of the part played by authority in confession, it has probably emerged as plainly that a relationship of trust and mutual sharing can be achieved even though the confessor maintains a certain remoteness in dealings with his penitent.

And, in fact, strong as the emphasis is on reciprocity in "sharing" of the Oxford Group movement, the recipient's authority often seems to play a certain role there. His authority is apparently founded on his possession of somewhat greater religious experience than that of the person approaching a first confession. This person is encouraged to confess by hearing the other tell what he has gone through in a religious way, also about the faults and sins from which he was rescued by his conversion. The impulse to confess is quickened. The frankness and honesty of these revelations obviously calls for a response in the same spirit; and, when the new confessant makes his confidences, he evidently does so in the hope that the recipient—who has previously succeeded in gaining spiritual liberation—will help him find a way out of his troubles. This interpretation of what "sharing" implies is confirmed by the examples and statements which we will have occasion to cite in the discussion of confessional method that follows. Incidentally, we shall there see a good many instances of a trustful relationship between confessor and confessant.

---

[30] E. Brunner, "*Mitt möte med oxfordbevegelsen*" (My Meeting with the Oxford Group Movement) in *Kirke og Kultur*, 1933; p. 279 ff.

CHAPTER FIVE

CONFESSIONAL METHOD

The confessor's ability to inspire confidence is evidently connected with the method he uses for confession and spiritual guidance. It is clear, too, that a confessor endowed with special personal qualifications will create a confessional method worth following. He does so *sua sponte*, without reflecting closely on his course of action. Later, however, he may derive a system with clearly framed rules from his experience. We might study the methods of some prominent confessors, basing our examination either on clear and systematic statements, when such exist, or on what may be deduced from how those confessors practised : this should supply us with more information than can be gleaned by merely directing our attention at the confessor's personal virtues or "intuitive capacity".

One of the great figures in the Catholic cure of souls is—as we have already stressed—François de Sales. We ought to find that such an exemplary confessor had an ideal method for confession in its Catholic form. His ideas about spiritual healing are still valid and have a normalizing importance in the Catholic Church.[1] By examining his method we should consequently make a somewhat closer approach to how he could get his penitents to rely so completely on his direction —in, for example, such cases as those of Jean-Pierre Camus and Madame de Chantal.

The basic principle of Saint François' spiritual leadership is, we perceive, that the confessor should not force orders and regulations on the penitent. François de Sales assumes that his penitent has a strong desire to attain moral perfection, a desire which should be supported by the confessor's instructions. But he is quite aware of the psychological law that people resist commands and statutes

---

[1] Concerning the model set by François de Sales, Vincent said (*op. cit.*; p. 550) that one should always go to him for instruction. "Not one of his ideas as director of souls, not one of his lines of procedure, has gone out-of-date". Cf. Georges Goyau, *Orientations catholiques* (Paris, 1925), p. 68 ff., about the value of Saint François' principles in spiritual leadership : "...*Cette direction, qui est peut-être pour l'Eglise le plus subtil et plus efficace moyen d'ascendant*". (...This direction which is perhaps for the Church the most subtile and the most effective means of ascendancy.)

which are imposed from without and have no hold on their convictions. We find the basis of the old observation about the attraction of forbidden fruit in his words : "Just as there exist people who are unwilling to take a medicine, however good it tastes, simply because it is called a medicine, there are souls who are frightened of actions that are enjoined upon them simply because they are decreed. It is said that there was a man who had lived for eighty years quite contentedly in the city of Paris without ever venturing outside; but when, by royal edict, he was ordered to remain there for the rest of his life, he went out to look at the fields which all his life he had never cared to see".[2] One must not give strict orders and prohibitions to the person one wants to direct. That is to impede the work one wishes to perform or see bear fruit. Saint François wrote to an abbess who desired to carry out a reform in her nunnery that she ought not to make any stir about what she had in mind. "That would only mean", said he, "that all *sensitive souls* will have prepared themselves against you and become obdurate". He added : "They must *reform themselves* under your guidance".[3]

Saint François practised his own precept. Ordinarily, he issued no commands. He only advised his penitents, and that with a respectful diffidence (*"timidité respectueuse"*). For instance, after providing Jeanne de Chantal with instructions for her spiritual life, he wrote : "These are good and appropriate counsels for you, not at all commands"[4]

He wanted to allow great freedom to his penitents. He considered spiritual liberty to be a sacred thing, a view related to his basic concept of the human soul : for him the soul is the place of divine inspiration. There the creation of God goes on, and this must not be disturbed by petty interference from without. Francis Vincent, the biographer already quoted, says that François de Sales placed his guidance under God's : this meant that before giving his advice he carefully investigated the forces present in his penitent's soul. He perceived from these how God imparts to each person an unquenchable desire for a faultless life. The confessor's function is to distinguish between the divine and the human, then to sustain and promote the divine. The confessor can never lay claim to having instigated the new spiri-

[2] Vincent, *op. cit.;* p. 412.
[3] *Ibid.*; p. 413.
[4] *Ibid.*; p. 414.

tual life of a penitent. It is God who has created this, and the confessor has merely cleared away obstacles for the *creatio continua*.

Accordingly, Saint François' rules for the spiritual life were intended to support God's own creation. They should be applied in a general way. People ought not to rivet their gaze on details. It is as if we heard an echo of Luther's voice when we read words like these to Madame de Chantal : "I have often told you that one should certainly not go too much into detail with the exercise of virtue; rather, one ought to proceed quickly, candidly, childishly, or, to speak good French, with *liberté*, in good faith, *grosso modo*".[5]

His method was unusual; he was ahead of his time with his liberal principles, and his own penitents could occasionally wish for more definite directions. But in spite of the freedom he allowed them about particulars in the conduct of their lives, he wanted them to follow his general principles. As far as those were concerned, he took a firm line. If a penitent was not pleased, he had to choose another confessor. Saint François required that his penitents should have only one confessor; also that his authority should be preferred to the penitent's own will in all matters. Thus, both compulsion and freedom were involved. But constraints, commands and instructions should not be felt by the penitent as coercion. Saint François called them *"advis"* and *"conseils"*. The very word *"commandemens"* was detestable. And advice had to be given in a way that made it acceptable. François de Sales was masterly at so depicting the impeccable life and the path by which it could be reached that his penitent was seized by longing for it and eagerness to take the course indicated.

Instead of the authoritarian and imperative method, Saint François followed a more indirect procedure. He talked to himself as much as to his penitent. He might allow a third person to take part in the conversation aimed at spiritual healing, and speak to that person or let him speak. He gave praise for virtues that he wished to see in a penitent. He recommended good books. He wanted above all to set his spiritual children in motion, to so activate them that they participated themselves in penetrating secrets of the sacred life; and they would then become convinced that the right means for attaining moral perfection had been assigned to them. He was anxious that a person should retain his self-esteem and sense of dignity as a free human

---

[5] Vincent, *op. cit.*; p. 415.

being, instead of feeling completely subordinated, enslaved and self-abnegated beneath a strict authority.

It was characteristic, too, of the way François de Sales handled his penitents that he paid heed to the individual character of each and to the personal basis underlying it. Here he differed from the many spiritual leaders who have treated their confessants in summary fashion, not bothering to make any spiritual analysis and leading them all through an invariable, established procedure. Analysis of that underlying basis played a great part in Saint François' system. Just as he placed high value on making a thorough investigation to distinguish between the human and divine in a penitent's soul, he attached much importance to discovering at the same time what lay in the penitent's personal nature. He inquired into heredity, and scrutinized inherited leanings towards certain sins and virtues; he investigated moral strength and character generally. The directions he gave afterwards conformed with the results of this analysis. His instructions were intended only to aid the soul in moulding itself according to its own pattern, thus to reach the degree and form of perfection that corresponded to the person's specific disposition. Saint François did not ask of anyone more than was within that person's power. He took a soul as it was and did not try to achieve anything against its nature.[6] And in this—his course of not laying down the same morally improving rules for all—he was evidently rather exceptional among Catholic directors of conscience.[7]

We see that one of the secrets behind Saint François' success as a spiritual guide resides in his method of appealing first of all to the emotions. As we noted, he believes that nature has sown in each person a seed of love for God. This must be made to grow, to develop until God wholly fills the person's soul and completely determines his conduct. Knowledge and logical reasoning are factors entirely subordinate to feeling. It is by appeals to this that the heart is moved and the will set into operation. Ideas lead to results only if they enter the soul wholly enveloped by emotion. Strengthening the will is, essentially,

---

[6] He wrote to one of his spiritual daughters : "*Ne desirés point de n'estre pas ce que vous estes, mais desirés d'estre fort bien ce que vous estes*". (Do not wish at all to be what you are not, but desire to be very good as what you are. Vincent, *op. cit.*; p. 451.)

[7] Vincent, *ibid.*; p. 450 : "*Bien rares sont les directeurs qui ne tendent pas à réaliser dans autrui un type de perfection uniforme*". (There are very few directors of souls who do not tend to produce in others a uniform type of perfection.)

a matter of cultivating feeling. And Saint François is a master at using an affective educational method. Few others have understood so well how to speak about God and the suffering Christ so that the penitent is filled with love for them and reaches out to them. He understands also how to employ a more indirect method. He realizes that the best way for a confessor to perform his task is by making himself dear to his penitent. When he has succeeded in this, the penitent will be very receptive to his instructions.

One writer has said about Saint François' affective method : "François de Sales does not argue; he makes himself felt, he embraces, he caresses. He causes religion to be loved by making himself beloved".[8] And Saint François himself believed that he was endowed by nature to enfold others in the tenderest and purest love. With a certain self-complacency, he said that he thought no one else possessed to a higher degree the exceptional emotional gift involved.[9]

In his social intercourse with his spiritual children, Saint François addressed them in affectionate terms and a tender tone. This accorded with the mode of his time : there the period suited him admirably. Vincent points out that such epithets as *"ma fille"*, *"bien-aymée"*, *"ma tres chere fille"*, *"mon ame"*, *"unique"*, flowed from his pen. And he could vary these endlessly, adapting them to each person's individual character. He wanted to give every one of his penitents the impression that a special communion existed between them, a spiritual communion founded on love. To a nun who had recently placed herself under his guidance, he wrote : "The signs I have found in your soul of an earnest confidence in me and a fervent sentiment towards piety fill my heart with fatherly love for your heart. So rest assured, my good daughter, that we shall—you will see—achieve much". The union thus was sealed between confessor and penitent. She gave him trust; he gave paternal love. Confident of success, they could direct their gaze at the great task of attaining moral perfection.

To another penitent, a woman of the world this time, Saint François wrote : "*Mademoiselle*, my brother, who is coming to you, will perhaps tell you that I love and respect you very much; but you may believe

---

[8] Quoted by Vincent : p. 498.

[9] "*Il n'y a point d'ame au monde, comme je pense, qui cherissent plus cordialement, tendrement et, pour le dire à la bonne foy, plus amoureusement que moy; car il a pleu a Dieu de faire mon coeur ainsy*". (There is no soul in the world, I think, who cherishes more heartily, tenderly and, to express it honestly, more lovingly than I; for it has pleased God to make me so. Vincent : p. 499.)

that he does me this service from affection, so I want you to know that my heart truly cherishes this feeling. That is why I write thus with my hand and from my heart".[10]

On occasion, Saint François could identify himself with his penitent. A case in point : he wrote to one, Madame de Charmoisy (the "Philotée" of his work *Introduction à la vie dévote*) about "our soul", "our heart", "our love", "our progress". Thus, the interests of confessor and confessant were the same. Complete solidarity existed between them.[11] We have already witnessed here manifest examples confirming that penitents also experienced a sense of communion, and that they willingly, with complete trust, surrendered themselves to their beloved confessor.

François de Sales' method of spiritual direction has since been practised by many others in the Catholic Church. Its use by his younger contemporary and disciple, the Jesuit priest Jean-Joseph Surin, was a typical case.[12] Surin's special penitent was a woman mystic, Jeanne des Anges. She appeared to suffer from possession by the devil, but, between periods when so obsessed, she had experiences of divine inspiration. Before she became his penitent, Surin had himself been cured of similar attacks; thus, he was particularly able to understand her. He said of his principles as her spiritual leader that his main desire was to imbue her with a wish to attain inner perfection; and here he proceeded with great care. He never issued any express orders, but instead allowed her much freedom. He trusted that God would lead her where He desired; meanwhile, he observed closely the workings of the Holy Ghost in her soul. Evidently, he did exercise great influence on her. But when he wanted her to follow his intentions, he gave his instructions in such fashion that she was unaware of being directed by him. He said that he endeavoured to give her a love for God : this love would mean that she could place her own will under her leader's. And it did not take Jeanne des Anges long to declare that she had committed herself entirely to his leadership.

The most essential elements in François de Sales' method make their appearance here : attentive observation of the penitent's natural

---

[10] Vincent, *op. cit.*; p. 501.

[11] *Ibid.*; p. 503 : "*C'est plus que la collaboration : c'est une parfaite et douce communion*". (It is more than collaboration : it is a perfect and sweet communion.)

[12] Bremond; vol. V, p. 226. Surin carried on an extensive cure of souls. Fénelon was among his confessants. (See Bremond; vol. V, p. 268, note.)

inspiration, which is regarded as divine; careful directing of the penitent; the affective method, involving in part that the confessor should
make himself loved, thus to obtain the penitent's willing acceptance of
the ideas he represents.

It is obvious that the cautious and completely indirect method of
François de Sales is not appropriate in all cases. Whether the confessor
is Catholic or Protestant, with an irresolute and doubtful penitent
the occasion may often call for peremptory and distinct commands.
Certainly, such orders were given under the spiritual leadership of
Saint François de Sales. And Surin, whom we see as a typical exponent
of Saint François' method, was well aware of this. By his own statement, he had experienced how unendurable it is to find oneself under
spiritual direction where no definite response is made to the penitent's
anxious questioning. He said that he had come to know the truth in
the holy Teresa's words that there scarcely exists any greater and more
unbearable affliction than to fall into the hands of a timid, too cautious
confessor.[13] And Surin's penitent, Jeanne des Anges, did in fact
understand the limitations of his method. While admitting its great
value, she said : "I believe that it would not be of use for all kinds
of people".[14]

In spite of appearances to the contrary, we have already noted
that there lay a certain "hardness" in the method of François de Sales.
He was extremely firm where the main principles of his spiritual
care were concerned. It was only about the ways in which these
should be applied that he recommended discretion and mildness :
by exercising such qualities he wished to prevent penitents from
summoning up natural opposition to orders and prohibitions.

Examples could be given from both Catholic and Protestant quarters
of a severe and resolute attitude on the part of confessors. We observed earlier cases where confessors showed harshness because of
injudicious zeal or because they did not sufficiently understand the
penitent's particular nature and pressing troubles. But of course
there are also cases where the confessor takes a determined line as
consequence of the penitent's disposition and conduct. In general,
the natural course is for a confessor to decide his approach from the
confessant's own attitude and then adapt his method accordingly.
Certainly, it is no accident that the method of François de Sales is

---

13 Bremond; vol. V, p. 256.
14 *Ibid.*; p. 226.

best exemplified by cases where we see him as the spiritual leader of mystics or pious Catholics. His gentle direction can be put into practice with these and lead to success. It seems to be the ideal procedure in Catholic cure of souls. But when visitors to the confessional are not very devout—are perhaps people who take an altogether superficial view of penance and seek absolution merely to clear their consciences for a time—then a stricter and more resolute method does not seem to come amiss. As we have remarked, the instructions given to a priest charge him with conducting a rigorous inquiry if he has reason to suspect that the penitent's confession and repentance have not been profound enough. If he finds that they have not, the penitent can be refused absolution—though for the most part such a measure is postponed in the expectation that he will feel contrition, make the effort of will necessary to overcome sin, and reform. Absolution can be differed, too, until the penitent has banished certain undesirable elements from his life or made amends for transgressions against his fellows.

At times, the acts of atonement imposed in penance may evidently be rather severe. There are great differences between the penalties required by various Catholic confessors. Saint-Cyran, for instance, was very stern and liked to inflict stringent punishments.[15] Peter Rosegger has related from his youth that when confessing to a priest of his home parish he received what he thought was too heavy a penance. He protested, and was then refused absolution. As he wanted to take Communion, he decided to confess to another priest of the parish whom he knew to be more lenient. This time he heard nothing about a heavy penance, and the desired absolution was bestowed upon him.[16] When there is strictness in the confessional (and strictness is well justified from the viewpoint of Catholic pastoral theology), it usually seems to be directed either at inducing contrition and a change of heart in the penitent or at obtaining tangible proof that a change of heart really has taken place.

Other cases do occur—for example, when the penitent shows too much hesitancy about beginning his confession—where determined action by the confessor may lead to result. It did so with Charles de

---

[15] Bremond; vol. IV, p. 130 ff. Bremond cites similar procedure in the confessional practice of Saint-Cyran's contemporary Charles de Condren : vol. III, p. 325 (note).

[16] Peter Rosegger, *Waldheimat*, in *Ausgewählte Werke* (Vienna, no date); vol. I, p. 288 ff.

Foucault, to give an illustration. When that French poet was a young man, true religious faith came to him in the confessional. During a period when he was seeking his way towards faith, he got to know Abbé Huvelin, a famous confessor at the Church of Saint Augustine in Paris. He visited that church one day. Abbé Huvelin was sitting in a confessional but had no penitent for the moment. Foucauld entered there to consult the abbé about certain difficulties in matters of doctrine. As he talked to the priest, he stood and leaned against the grill, instead of kneeling in the usual way. He ended what he was saying with : "I am not a believer". The priest answered : "Kneel and begin your confession". "I have no faith", countered Foucauld. But the reply came : "Yes, you have! Confess!" And Foucauld capitulated : he made a confession with tears running down his cheeks. The ground was prepared for this result not only by his religious struggle but by his personal relations with the priest and his admiration for him.[17]

Even if such a procedure might occasionally be practised in Catholic confession because of the penitent's character and behaviour, the ideal confessional method there still seems to be either that of Saint François de Sales himself or one approaching his. This is clear from the great appreciation accorded by the Church to Saint François and his method. It is evident, too, from the great importance we have noticed that normative pastoral theology of the Catholic Church places on the confessor's personal qualities, particularly on his ability to enter into a spirit of communion with his penitents : an ability founded where he is concerned on paternal love. It fellows that, as a certain measure of personal fellowship is thought desirable in established Catholic confession and thus aimed at, confessional method there ought to pursue a similar course to that of François de Sales.

We may note the same tendency in confessional method and spiritual direction practised in the Protestant sphere : this is natural, for communion between confessor and confessant is usually a sought-after ideal there. We can find celebrated Protestant confessors whose methods bear close resemblances to those of François de Sales.

---

[17] Charles de Foucauld, *Ecrits spirituels* (Paris, 1930) ; p. 80 ff. The following words are enlightening about how the confession came about (p. 82) : "*Je demandais des leçons de religion : il [Huvelin] me fit mettre à genoux et me fit confesser*". (I asked for some lessons in religion : he made me kneel and confess.)

John Keble did not wish to command his penitents. He did not feel himself to be their master, but rather that he was an unworthy instrument in God's hand, one that could be used to aid people in distress. He was anxious that his penitents' attention should be drawn to the fact that he could not release them from their personal responsibility by absolution. They themselves would have to place their trespasses before God and seek pardon for them. Through his guidance, they might perhaps be helped from succumbing again to sin. But usually he was not willing to dictate to them how they should behave. "He suggests again and again to his penitents that they should make their own rules and even choose their own penances for themselves".[18]

It is likely, nevertheless, that Keble led his penitents according to his will. True, as far as possible he let them find their own paths, but probably the rules they set for themselves complied with his counsel. His personality and his judicious way of proceeding caused people to accept what he had to say. He possessed, as we have remared, an ability to bring out the best in others and to make himself loved by his penitents. And this—that penitents entertain affectionate feelings for their confessor—is, of course, the best prior condition for his getting them to conform with his opinions and advice.

Here, we may recall François de Sales' method of never commanding and of leaving as much as possible to the penitent's own efforts. We are reminded, too, of the emotional relationship he sought for and attained; his success in the matter probably being due in the main to what he himself was, though also to the deliberate means he used. In Keble's case there was no such conscious attempt to win affection. He gained it automatically through the force and benevolence of his personality; and by the way this manifested itself in profound understanding and sympathy for his penitents. Other noted Protestant confessors have also obtained an emotionally-charged position in the minds of their penitents by that same process—as was pointed out earlier.

A study of Frank Buchman's confessional method reveals many correspondences with the ideal one of François de Sales. It was characteristic of Buchman's approach to people that he avoided as far as possible taking an initiative when he noticed that something new was amove in their minds. He exerted his influence more through his personality than by directly sermonizing or exhorting people.

---

[18] W. Lock, *op. cit.*; p. 209.

It was the sinner who should work to bring about a change in himself. This person found himself removed, as it were, from a secure position when in Buchman's company, even if their talk was confined to neutral topics. It would become clear to him that he ought to speak about his troubles with the celebrated spiritual healer. A solution to them could be expected from Buchman. And Buchman's companion would often discover with surprise that he had come out with a confession. We have seen illustrations of how Buchman's personality worked in that way.

Buchman liked to keep very quiet during a conversation, only putting in a word or two now and then to guide the speaker in the right direction. On occasion, he would diagnose the person's spiritual state with a brief phrase that startled : its accuracy would either spur the talker on or cause him to resume the conversation later— to continue until, finally, he confessed his sins and placed the problems of his life before Buchman.[19]

Another similarity with the method of François de Sales : Buchman also perceived that the person himself should indicate his own way of achieving spiritual health and solving his difficulties. To bring this about, Buchman recommended a moment's silence during which the Holy Ghost would supply guidance. An example of this appears in his account of how he handled a certain business man.[20] When the man had come to the decisive point in a conversation with Buchman, he said : "Well, what do you intend to do with such a great sinner as me ?"Buchman on what followed : "I now looked at him as if I was expecting him to give the answer himself, and finally he said : 'I suppose that for a fellow like me there's nothing else to do than fall on my knees... But,' he added', 'I don't know what we'd be doing together on our knees'. 'I don't either', I said. 'Let's wait for the Holy Ghost to give us instructions. Can't we be quiet for a while before God ?' "[21] And during that brief silence the business man was inspired with faith.

We saw how François de Sales sought to attain communion with his penitents. The ideal relationship with them was one of trust and

---

[19] See as cases in point the descriptions of Buchman's conversation with the man Begbie calls "Beau Ideal" (*op. cit.*; p. 126 ff.) and with "A Young Soldier" (p. 153 f.).

[20] J. F. Laun, *op. cit.*

[21] A similar example is given by A. J. Russell in *For Sinners Only* (London, 1934); p. 116.

friendship. The same spirit of fellowship was Buchman's aim. Of course, it constituted one of the elements on which he based his confessional method of mutual sharing. Spokesmen of the Oxford Group movement have testified that it was precisely "sharing" that wrenched them from their personal isolation. They were filled with a powerful new feeling, with a warmth and enthusiasm that caused them to talk readily about everything that weighed on their minds until they no longer held any secrets from one another. They cast their old sinful lives behind them, resolving that they would surrender themselves to God and follow His commandments in accordance with the absolute requirements stated by the movement.

An illustration of Buchman's method is given by "Persona Grata" in Begbie's book. After meeting Buchman and a first conversation with him, "P. G." talked about his troubles and temptations. He relates : "I turned to him and said, 'My mind is filled with a cloud of evil thoughts; why do I have these evil thoughts?' To my astonishment he said at once, 'Why, P. G., I have those evil thoughts'." The account goes on : "Directly he had said that I had the feeling he knew what to do with them. There was a deep sense of relief in my mind. He said nothing more to help me. All he added was that I must come to see him later that day. But I felt extraordinarily happy, exactly as if the fight was over".[22] That sense of relief can be ascribed mainly to the feeling of community that "P. G." experienced when he heard Buchman's confidential words about having troubles of the same kind himself.

Begbie's "Greats", who also appeared earlier here, describes the impression made on him when he had a similar sense of communion with Buchman : "He was no longer a second focus of consciousness, but was somehow sharing in mine".[23]

Emil Brunner said of Buchman that he fully realized what it means to people to have a spiritual guide who feels altogether united with his confessant.[24] The latter must be given to understand that his religious adviser is speaking as from one sinner to another. By talking frankly of his own weaknesses and mistakes, he will get the confessant to be candid in return. Brunner claimed that, if the confessor acts in this way, dread of making confession will disappear.

---

[22] Begbie, *op. cit.*; p. 113.

[23] *Ibid.*; p. 70.

[24] E. Brunner in *Kirke og Kultur*, 1933; p. 279 ff.

This is how "sharing", as established by Buchman, is generally carried on in the movement : the person who has "made himself over" gives evidence, publicly or privately, to someone who needs to know how another was tormented by sin and has overcome it. What the speaker desires is that a fellow-being should open his eyes to his own sinfulness, gaining a real knowledge of its existence and nature. A characteristic element in Buchman's method derives from his wish to imbue people by every means with abhorrence of sin, with longing to be released from this, with love for the good.[25] Personal sermons in the form of "sharing" ought to serve that end.

The destruction and poisoning of human life are depicted in "sharing". And so is the path by which liberation can be reached. As well as feelings of guilt in listeners, and of disgust with their sinfulness, the personality of the testimony-giver plays a great part in arousing their yearning to follow that path. Of course, eloquent object lessons demonstrate that the commended way to spiritual health leads also to success. The "teams" of people in the movement provide (if one may express the matter so) good advertising for it. Happy people are involved, with bright and smiling faces. They raise a desire to attain a new spiritual life by reflecting the opportunities that such a life offers. Meanwhile, the ultimate aim of "sharing" is to draw a response : the listener should answer the confidences received by confessing his own troubles. "Sharing", according to Laun, "immediately inspires trust and creates an atmosphere of frankness." [26]

It is interesting that we find so much that is identical in the method of the foremost spiritual director of the Catholic Church, François de Sales, and the best-known spiritual healer of recent times in Protestantism, Frank Buchman. Resemblances are significant of the fact that the two each perceived intuitively what psychological factors come into play in the confessant and the sort of relationship which should exist between him and the confessant. Let us summarize the common elements in the views of Saint François and Buchman on confession. Initiative is allowed to come from the confessant. (The two did not force themselves on confessants, and did not readily issue orders or decrees.) If possible, the confessant is himself to find a way out of his troubles. The divine inspiration in a penitent, which François de Sales said should not be disturbed, corresponds to the "quiet

---

[25] Russell, *op. cit.*; p. 64.
[26] Laun, *op. cit.*

time" recommended by Frank Buchman, when the Holy Spirit will give guidance. Both appealed to the imagination and the emotions in order to engender detestation of sin and an earnest desire for good. The principal aim of both was to enter into close communion with their confessants. Saint François achieved this by giving as much as he could of his dedicated personality : he used his affective method. Buchman also attained that end by giving of his innermost self : in the form of "sharing".

PART TWO

TEACHINGS OF PSYCHIATRY

CHAPTER SIX

PSYCHIATRIC OBSERVATIONS AND THEORIES
RELEVANT TO THE PSYCHOLOGY OF CONFESSION

The preceding investigation here aimed at establishing some vital requirements for the act of confession. We found one of these on the confessant's side to be a great need brought on by remorse for sins committed and a sincere desire to escape from sin. We discovered, too, that the confessant feels the need for an authority, one which may on occasion be regarded as a guarantee that the redemption of sins really will take place; also, the possessor of authority should be able to supply such guidance as the confessant requires for his future life. We noted further that the needs mentioned are both answered and supported by the authoritative position which the confessor occupies : a position maintained in part by the endorsement he gains from the church as an institution and partly by his altogether personal virtues. For an ideal confession, we have observed that a relationship of confidence between the two people involved is of crucial importance; and in achieving such a relationship the confessional method employed plays a great part.

When these prior conditions are met, a confession generally results in the confessant experiencing a more or less powerful sense of relief and liberation. We have seen how such feelings appear, and how they can be given the most tumultous expression—in the Laestadian movement, for example. In what follows, we shall give closer examination to that sense of release and study various significant statements about how it is felt. Such an analysis must, of course, be regarded as essential to the aim of this work. How, simply by speaking about a memory and past behaviour which are fraught with guilt, can a person experience feelings of assuagement and deliverance? That question seems to encompass the entire problem of what psychological factors are in operation during the act of confession. Thus, by proceeding from this question and the answer to it, we should be able to fit together the elements in confession described above, to place them in an organically connected whole where each part has its inherent place and function.

Evidence is received from many quarters in psychiatry about the sense of release that comes from recounting certain memories, and how important it can be in curing psychic disorders. We shall now study such evidence and also the explanations that psychiatry can supply for the feeling of relief which coincides with the recovery of mental health : in other words, we shall see how the curative process can take place at the same time as concealed memories come to light by being divulged to a doctor. The findings gathered here should be useful in answering our question about the psychological factors involved in the act of confession. It seems the more likely that they will because, we may notice, the conditions we described for confession reappear where psycho-therapy is concerned and are of decisive importance to its entire result.

It was in his lectures of 1884-85 that J. M. Charcot, professor of clinical disorders at La Salpêtrière hospital in Paris, presented the results of his research work on hysterical paralysis. According to Charcot, the symptoms of paralysis were not due to an injury received in an accident but derived from memories of what had occurred. This theory was supported by others engaged in research on the subject—Pierre Janet foremost among them. Janet has provided an account of Charcot's researches in his work *Les Médications psychologiques*; he there reported his own adherence to the theorty of his teacher, and also how he gave wider scope to it. He said that he had carried out "an amplification of this idea and proved that neuropathic troubles of the same kind could occur as a consequence of more ordinary incidents which did not cause a physical injury but only a psychic feeling".[1] Recollection of such an incident remained in the mind along with the sequence of emotions it produced, and this memory developed the symptoms of mental illness : hysterical paralysis, blindness, dumbness, loss of memory, and so on.

Janet gave an example. He said that loss of memory by one of his patients, a thirty-four-year-old woman, was caused by the violent shock she received when one of her intimates had, as a joke, shouted in her ear that her husband was dead. Janet could establish that her amnesia and all her attacks of delirium were a direct consequence of that incident and her recollection of it.[2]

The theory that Janet had worked out while collaborating with Charcot in about 1890—that the memory of a distressing event is

---

[1] P. Janet, *Les Médications psychologiques* (Paris, 1919); vol. II, p. 205.

[2] *Ibid.*; p. 206 f. A number of similar cases are described in the same work, p. 205 ff.

the determining factor in the origin of many neuroses—was confirmed by his further observations over the years. And the investigations of others supported the view. That ominous recollection, lingering on like an unhealed wound in the psyche, was designated by Janet a "*souvenir traumatique*".

It is not always easy to uncover the patient's unfortunate memory. Janet spoke about the care and attention with which the patient's accounts of the past must be followed, how assiduously significant movements must be watched, in order to gain real enlightenment about the nature of the memory. Often the patient himself is completely unaware of what is sought. The memory has its own existence in a region of the mind not accessible to wakeful consciousness. In such case, the patient should be encouraged to speak of what he remembers from various periods of his life. If his reserve on a certain point, his gestures or expression raise a suspicion that he is leaving something out, an investigation must be made to see whether dreams, a somnabulistic state or automatic writing can bring forth the hidden memories. In some cases, the recollection will not emerge unless the patient is put under hypnosis. According to Janet, it is highly probable that exactly the unconscious nature of the memory makes it cause disturbance. The memory exists apart from consciousness: as a force withdrawn from it. Janet called the memory a psychological system: it is a collection of images and movements which has been able to elude control of the person's consciousness because he suffers from diminished mental strength; his psychic tension is too low to encompass more than may be contained by extremely limited awareness.

Those mentally-sick people who are dominated by traumatic memories have been arrested in their development. They remain fastened in the experience that gave them their shock. Consequently, they cannot get over it. They have not been able to assimilate it with their consciousness. Janet gives an illustrative example.[3] Irène, a young woman of twenty, has taken care of her sick mother with extreme devotion. When the mother dies Irène cannot grasp that this has really happened. She behaves in unseemly fashion at the funeral and has to be taken away. She shows no sorrow and refuses to wear mourning. Moreover, she will not replace her mother in taking care of

---

[3] Janet, *op. cit.*; p. 269 f   .

the home. If people ask her about her mother's death, she does not know what they are talking about. She has lost recollection of the three-month period when her mother was ill. Other abnormalities appear : she cannot work or decide on any matter; she has scarcely a normal feeling; nothing in her surroundings arouses her interest. Meanwhile, she displays various hysterical symptoms. She falls into states of violent crisis which last for hours. At such times she re-enacts with minute precision scenes from her mother's illness and death. Apparently she wants to help her mother, for she takes up positions beside her mother's bed, makes the same gestures and speaks the same words as when her mother lay ill there. Otherwise, when in a wakeful state she shows such symptoms as contractions and hallucinations.

Treatment in cases like that of Irène should be directed at freeing the mind from the unhappy past event. And doing so is primarily a matter of getting the person to relate what has happened. It is notable that in a good many cases simply talking about the experience is enough to clarify it and assimilate it to normal consciousness. Return of the dissociated memory there effects a reintegration of the personality. The experience can thereafter be held in check; it does not slip off on a course of its own, apart from consciousness. Usually, however, it does not suffice to relate the experience *once*. Indeed, such a method of treatment—which aims at achieving inner adjustment to a disastrous incident by getting the patient to see it in the clear light of reason—is often difficult and prolonged. Nevertheless, it was recommended by Janet as the best and surest way of re-establishing the patient's mental balance. It led to cure with Irène. In cases where relating the perilous memory a single time brings recovery very probably rational sense has worked effectively upon the recollection, and this explains the speedy result.

But Janet went deeper than that explanation in his attempt to elucidate the healing power involved in narrating a traumatic memory. In its essence such a memory is highly charged with emotion. Of course, it is precisely for this reason that the experience cannot be controlled by the patient. Fundamental psychic forces are aroused and follow courses outside the person's normal sphere. The personality is thus burdened with what it cannot command. The patient's nervous symptoms are, to be sure, manifestations of those ungoverned forces.

If we take such a dynamic view of emotional life, it is natural to assume, as Janet did, that what takes place when the patient relates his emotional memory is a release of the "charged tendencies" or emotions connected with it. Janet gave various illustrative examples which permit such an interpretation.

Another of his cases may be cited here. For fifteen years he had been treating a woman—now aged forty-five—for severe depression and obsessional crises that lasted for months. The crises came on every second or third year. On each recurrence Janet used mainly a persuasive method of treatment; and, through a rational approach to her obsession, she could overcome it and assimilate it to her normal consciousness. This obsession of hers derived from a guilt-fraught, or traumatic, memory of a moral lapse. From this, too, came her fixed idea that her husband was not the father of a child born to her. Janet's treatment never succeeded in entirely counteracting the memory and neutralizing it. Finally, however, she recovered without in a sense having treatment. It happened like this. In order to consult Janet, the patient made the long journey to Paris from the place where she lived. As he would point out later, the journey must have been very trying for her because of her mental condition. On her first visit to him, the doctor asked her what was troubling her, and she began to weep and moan. "You know very well what's wrong with me. It's always the same thing. I've told you a hundred times". Janet answered : "I'm afraid I've forgotten". "You know, all right. You wrote it down". "I can't find my notes. Help me out and explain again !" But, in spite of great efforts, she could not bring herself to to tell him once more, and she left in a state of despair. It took two or three visits before she could induce herself to confide the pathological memory. The confession was very painful to her. Her feelings found uncontrolled expression. She burst out in fits of laughter and had tremors; she made mimetic gestures; it all ended with her weeping abandonedly. Afterwards, she felt numbed and exhausted, but also unutterably happy. She was soon better, and, remarkably enough, she remained cured: she did not again suffer any of those relapses which had occurred regularly before.

Janet ended his account of the case with a question which, though of a rhetorical kind, contained his theoretical explanation of such "miracle" cures. "Might one not say that the tendency created by the memory had been charged anew, but that the journey, the painful efforts to reach confession and the labour of expressing this, discharged the tendency ?"[4]

---

[4] Janet, *op. cit.*; p. 297.

It is rather uncertain how Janet thought of these tendencies and
the psychic forces connected with them : the forces and tendencies
of which he spoke in order to explain the origin of traumatic memories.
While the *tendances* evidently correspond to what other psychologists call "impulses" or "instincts", the *forces psychiques* would
seem to be very much the same as strong feelings or affects. In the
case of the middle-aged woman the intended explanation seems to
be that she had an inclination both to flee from guilt arising from the
past and to get rid of it by confessing the unhappy incident. Though
she succeeded for a time in suppressing the memory, this re-emerged
into her consciousness with great power. Her affects of remorse were
the psychic forces which once more highly charged the tendencies;
her nervous symptoms resulted. In her confession to the doctor, those
forces were brought forth. The patient then underwent a powerful
emotional experience. We have seen how Janet compelled her into
this by getting her to overcome her resistance and submit to an
extremely painful confession. The forces—affects—were released, or
discharged, during the confession by the movements with which
she expressed herself, her tremors, grimaces, weeping and the words
she spoke.

Janet wished to do full justice to the concept of such release (*décharge*)
which he had taken over from psychoanalysis. He well knew the
reality of what was implied. For him the concept showed that danger
to mental health lies in the forces at the disposal of those tendencies.
And this illuminates the value of work to investigate the patient's
past experience. The release afforded by painful confessions weakens
the strength of the tendencies which are beyond control of the psyche,
and this facilitates the process of assimilation.

Producing affective release may be regarded as an advisable method
of treatment in the majority of cases. And the method is frequently
used in psychiatric clinics. Janet pointed out that one can often
observe how patients who for hours have suffered violent attacks, with
delirium, convulsions and so on, then show a certain fatigue but
also manifest an extraordinary calmness. They are much happier
and, in fact, more normal than before their crises.[5]

However, when it came to using methods for abreaction and assimilation of dissociated memories in the treatment of *all* neurotic
cases, as advocated by the psychoanalytical school, Janet took a

---

[5] Janet, *op. cit.*; vol. II, p. 300.

reserved attitude. That Freud and his followers were for this was, in Janet's view, connected with the fact that for them all neuroses derived ultimately from traumatic memories. He found the methods effective in more than fifty cases of traumatic hysteria. And he said that if their use was extended to other forms of neurosis as well, a greater number of cases where patients gained relief and abreaction from such treatment could easily be counted. Also, especially with young people not yet fixed in their mental disorders, the method led in many cases to complete recovery.

We have noticed that at times Janet placed himself in opposition to psychoanalysis when propounding his theories and methods; but, in fact, he was eager to point out what he had in common with Freud and his school. Indeed, he went so far as to consider that he had supplied the concept behind Freud's theories. He drew attention to the circumstance that Freud had come to Paris at exactly the point when he himself was making his observations and presenting his views on traumatic hysteria. And Freud had taken much interest in these discoveries. Also, before Freud (in collaboration with Josef Breuer) published his first study of similar cases, Janet had described his findings in print. The observations of those two in their work *Studien über Hysterie* were regarded by Janet as splendid confirmation of the opinions which he had published himself on the origin and treatment of traumatic hysteria.[6] But when Freud proceeded further and extended his system, Janet refused to follow him. And we

---

[6] Janet, *op. cit.*; vol. II, p. 216. "*Nous sommes heureux, disais-je à ce moment, que MM. Breuer et Freud aient vérifié récemment notre interprétation déjà ancienne des idées fixes chez les hystériques*". (We are happy, I said at the moment then, that Herr Breuer and Herr Freud have recently verified our interpretation, already old, of fixed ideas in hysterics.) To be sure, they had changed the terminology, but the basic ideas remained the same : "*Ils appelaient 'psychoanalyse' ce que j'appelais 'analyse psycholo- gique', ils nommaient 'complexus' ce que j'avais nommé 'système psychologique' pour désigner cet ensemble de phénomènes psychologiques et de mouvements soit des membres soit des viscères qui reste associé pour constituer le souvenir traumatique; ils baptisaient du nom 'catharsis' ce que je désignais comme une dissociation des idées fixes ou comme 'une désinfection morale' ! Les noms étaient différents mais toutes les conception essentielles... étaient acceptées sans modification*". (They called "psychoanalysis" what I called "psycho- logical analysis"; they gave the name "complex" to what I named "psychological system" in order to designate the whole group of psychological phenomena and of movements, whether of the limbs or the viscera, which remain associated together and thus constitute the traumatic memory; they christened "catharsis" what I designated as a dissociation of fixed ideas or as a "mental disinfection" ! The names were different, but all the essential conceptions...were accepted without modification.)

have seen that this occurred in the first place when Freud generalized
and (in Janet's opinion) considered all neuroses to be caused by
traumatic memories; as he recommended clarification of such memories and bringing them to consciousness, that had to be the sole objective in treatment of neuroses. About Freud's attitude here, and his
vague imprecision in other matters as well, Janet said : "He transformed a clinical observation and a therapeutic procedure, based on
definite and restricted indications, into an enormous system of medical
philosophy".[7]

However, Freud sharply rejected Janet's claim to be the originator
of his system.[8] According to him, the primary suggestion and virtual
foundation for psychoanalysis came from Josef Breuer, the Viennese
doctor already mentioned here. As Freud asserted this so energetically,
there is really no cause to doubt his word; it is probably true, nevertheless, that the study he gave to the French psychiatrist's investigations lay behind his getting Breuer to publish an account of his
subsequently well-known hysteria case; and Freud there added himself the observations which agreed so closely with those previously
made public by Janet—as that psychiatrist would point out.

Let us now examine Breuer's epoch-making case and the theories
connected with it. His method of treatment accorded with Janet's,
but on at least one point the two differed in theory, Breuer there
being much closer to later psychoanalysis. We find in Breuer's work
the origin of the psychoanalytical theory on emotional repression.
And we meet again—though now called "catharsis" or "the cathartic
method"—Janet's method of emotionally discharging, and thus
assimilating, memories dissociated from the normal psychic sphere.
Studien über Hysterie,[9] the work where Breuer reported his observations and propounded his theories, contains in purified form, as

---

[7] Janet, *La Médicine psychologique* (Paris, 1923); p. 41.

[8] In his paper *"Zur Geschichte der psychoanalytischen Bewegung"* (S. Freud, *Gesammelte Schriften*, vol. IV : Leipzig, Vienna, Zurich, 1924; pp. 411-480) Freud said of this
(p. 439) : *"In Paris selbst scheint noch die Überzeugung zu herrschen, der auf dem Londoner
Kongress 1913 Janet so beredten Ausdruck gab, dass alles, was gut an der Psychoanalyse
sei, mit geringen Abänderungen die Janetschen Ansichten wiederhole, alles darüber hinaus
aber sei von Übel. Janet musste sich noch auf diesem Kongress selbst eine Reihe von Zurecht-
weisungen von E. Jones gefallen lassen, der ihm seine geringe Sachkenntnis vorhalten
konnte. Seine Verdienste um die Psychologie der Neurosen können wir trotzdem nicht
vergessen, auch wenn wir seine Ansprüche zurückweisen".*

[9] Leipzig and Vienna; 1895.

it were, much of what is relevant to the psychology of confession in later psychoanalysis.

Breuer's patient, Anna O., was a highly gifted young woman. She was also very energetic and strong-willed, with a marked vein of sympathy for the sick and the poor. She often vacillated between intense joy and deep dejection. The sexual element in her temperament was, according to Breuer, surprisingly undeveloped.

This abundantly high-spirited girl led an extremely monotonous life with her Puritan family. She brightened her existence with daydreams. She had romantic adventures in her imagination as she was accomplishing her daily tasks. She carried out her household work irreproachably, nevertheless. Thus she led a double life, and this predisposed her to neurosis.

When her father, whom she greatly loved, fell ill, she became his nurse. She devoted herself with all her energy to looking after him, and when two months had passed her strength was much depleted. She suffered from anaemia and could not eat; finally, she had to be banned from taking care of her father. As immediate consequence of this, she was seized by nervous coughing. Soon a great need to rest overwhelmed her in the afternoons; along with this came a somnolent state, followed by intense agitation. And a series of nervous symptoms now appeared : she squinted and had contractions; she had anaesthesia in certain limbs and so on. When in this condition, she came under Breuer's treatment.

It became evident that his patient lived in two completely different states. In one of these, she recognized her surroundings, was sad and anxious, but relatively normal; in the other, she had hallucinations, was *ungezogen*, threw pillows at her visitors and was unmanageable. She resisted all treatment, and she suffered severe hallucinations. Also, she had peculiar difficulties of speech. After being completely dumb for a fortnight—unable to utter a sound in spite of great efforts— she regained her voice through Breuer's influence. "Here the psychic mechanism of the disorder first became plain. She had, I knew, been much angered by a matter but decided to say nothing about it. When I guessed this and forced her to talk about it, the inhibition disappeared".[10] But, curiously enough, she could not speak her mother tongue and expressed herself in English, apparently without realizing that she was speaking a foreign language.

---

[10] Breuer and Freud, *Studien über Hysterie*; p. 18 p.

The death of her beloved father was a grave psychic trauma for
her. She began to have peculiar trouble with her sight, as if her field
of vision were enormously reduced. She could quite simply not see a
medical colleague whom Breuer called in for consultation. But she
recognized Breuer himself, and for the most part was happy and
conversational in his company. Gradually, the various psychic states
she experienced during the day could be mapped out. In the morning
she had hallucinations and was in a state of anguish; in the afternoon
she was overcome by sleepiness, and later in the day she fell into a
deep hypnotic sleep. While in that state she could relate her hallucinations. After such descriptions she awoke happy and relieved, and
then worked until four o'clock in the morning, when she went to bed.
Breuer believed that this periodicity derived from the time when she
had nursed her father.

It proved that simply talking about her grievous hallucinations
was an alleviation for her. Unless she had what she termed a "talking
cure" or "chimney sweeping" (a form of treatment found by accident),
her condition worsened; this became very evident when Breuer
was unable to visit his patient for a time. He now made the surprising
discovery that her serious hysterical disorders disappeared if he
could get her to talk about memories and hallucinations deriving
from the incubation period of her disturbances. Here is his account of
the incident that provided the discovery.

There had been a period of very hot weather during the summer,
and the patient had suffered from thirst but could not get herself
to drink. Nor was she able to give any reason for this odd refusal. But
once, while under hypnosis, she began to speak about her hired
companion, an Englishwoman whom she did not like, and she related,
with every sign of disgust, how she had gone into the companion's
room and seen how that woman's dog, "the loathsome creature",
lapped water from a glass. She had refrained from saying anything
then, not wishing to be impolite. "When she had given further em-
phatic expression to her supressed anger, she asked for a drink,
unrestrainedly drank a great deal of water, and awoke from hypnosis
with the glass at her lips. The disorder therewith disappeared for
good". All her other symptoms were cured in a similar way. This
finding—that such symptoms vanished when a patient described
under hypnosis the events that had caused them—suggested "a
therapeutic, technical procedure which left nothing to be desired in
the way of logical consequence and systematic application". Each

particular symptom was taken by itself. Everything that gave rise
to the symptom was described, and this account continued on to the
point where the disorder appeared for the first time. If the patient
got so far and related what had occurred with all the intensity of the
original emotional experience, the symptom disappeared for good.
The patient was thus completely restored to mental health.

It now remained for Breuer and Freud to explain why the "cathartic
method" can effect a cure. Of course their answer depended on how
they supposed that hysteria and traumatic memories originate.

We have noted already Janet's assertion that the method and
theories of Breuer and Freud conformed closely with the method and
theory he advocated himself as regards traumatic hysteria. Concerning
their method of treatment, the agreement is plain. Janet also alleged
that Breuer and Freud had—though they expressed this in a different
way—taken over what was essential to his theory. And the theoretical
similarities are fairly clear. For Breuer and Freud, too, traumatic
hysteria meant that the person's mental strength was subjected to
over-tension. Because of this, a mental dissociation occurred which in
turn caused certain psychic forces to become separated from normal
consciousness, to follow their own independent and unconscious
courses, and to manifest themselves in the symptoms of hysteria.
In holding this dynamic basic concept, Breuer and Freud accorded
with Janet.

Nevertheless, on essential points differences existed between them;
and Janet obviously did not pay sufficient attention to this fact.
They differed foremost in their view of what consitutes the hysterical
character. They were also at variance about the physiological background of hysteria and mental life as a whole.

Janet regarded mental dissociation as being caused by a weakness
present in the psychic constitution itself. For him, the main psychological notion was that of "*la tension psychologique*". A person's
mental strength could be gauged by his psychic tension. Hysterical
and mentally-sick people suffering from psychic dissociation had
possessed feeble psychic tension from infancy and could never be
able to withstand the strains of life. The events that befell them
became too much for them. Because of their weakness, they could
not hold their experiences together nor place them in a personal context and control them.

In opposition to Janet, Breuer and Freud denied that a weak
psychic constitution was an element behind hysteria. They believed

that Janet had arrived at such a view because the subjects he studied were all patients of a psychiatric hospital. Incisively, they expressed negation of Janet's opinion : "Dissociation from the consciousness does not occur because the patients are feeble-minded (*schwachsinnig*), but they seem to be feeble of mind because their mental activity is divided and only a part of their capacity is at the disposition of conscious thought".[11] The number of hysterics does not include only backward and poorly-endowed individuals. On the contrary, it contains "those brightest in spirit, of strongest will and firmest character, the most critical people". Saint Teresa was cited as an example of such highly gifted hysterics. Then, too, the hysteric was of somewhat unusual intelligence in the case described by Breuer. It appears that he and Freud were right : to regard hysterics as being in general mentally ungifted individuals, and their disorders as depending on their weakness, is to take too limited a view.[12] The explanation that Breuer gave for the phenomenon of hysteria seems to do greater justice to cases which are placed in the hysteric category.

In this explanation Breuer started from the physiological background and proceeded to certain psychic phenomena. There, too, he differed from Janet, who regarded all reasoning of the kind as loose and hazardous. However, precisely by such argument Breuer seems to have provided a good explanation for the fact that in many cases the discharge method can effect recovery. And it is reasonable enough to suppose that the psychic tension does have its causes in physiology. For that matter, of course Janet himself was playing with a term that derives from the sphere of physical science when he spoke about psychic "tension". Breuer in his attitude on this point came close to modern psychiatry, which usually asserts the affinity of mental processes to physiology. A psychiatrist of standing, Max Nachmansohn, accorded Breuer special commendation for attempting to provide the phenomenon of hysteria with a biological background.[13]

---

[11] Breuer and Freud, *op. cit.*; p. 202.

[12] Cf. Tor Andrae, *Mystikens psykologi* (Psychology of Mysticism : Uppsala, 1926); p. 480 ff. Mrs. Baker-Eddy, as well as Saint Teresa, was here adduced as a good example of a strong-willed and purposeful hysteric (p. 483 ff.).

[13] M. Nachmansohn, *Die Hauptströmungen der Psychotherapie der Gegenwart* (Zurich, 1933); p. 129 f. : "*Abschliessend möchte ich über die Hysterielehre Breuers nur sagen, dass sie die wesentlichsten Momente der Krankheit mit grosser Schärfe herausgestellt hat, wobei es Breuer besonders hoch anzurechnen ist, dass er auch die körperliche Seite genügend berücksichtigt hat*".

Breuer said that the central nervous system has two extreme states : complete wakefulness and sleep, and in between there are many degrees of consciousness. While we are asleep we are unable to transform an idea into action. But we can do so when in an alert state. The difference in activity of the wakeful and the sleeping psyche is determined by tonicity of the brain and its tension-generating energy. This intracerebral tension exists in various degrees.[14] It reaches a high level when we are prepared to carry out a difficult task and are waiting to begin. The fact that, at length, such an expectant attitude becomes very tiring shows how much energy it requires. If we are "tense" when faced with some action or event, in order to reduce the strain we commonly indulge in ostensibly meaningless behaviour : we jump up, run about and make a "nervous" impression. If the abnormal supply of energy is not released by performing the expected action, it must be got rid of somehow. The tendency of the brain is to maintain a state of balance, and thus it strives to equalize an excess and a deficiency of energy. As Nachmansohn pointed out, the old Greek ideal of wisdom—sophrosyne—appears here to be the psychological and ethical expression of a biological law.

Often, where chronic affects (worries, grief) and acute ones (anger, terror) are involved, the increase in tension cannot be levelled out because the course of imagination is inhibited and the reflection paralyzed by the affect. Generally, however, in the normal psyche an equalization does gradually take place : people get over their grief or their anger. But even there abnormal reactions may occur.

The physiological mechanism of hysteria is now explained by the fact that the excessive tension of energy in the brain, caused by an affect, breaks out of the course which the response normally follows and manifests itself in inadequate reactions. When the same affect comes up again, the abnormal reaction takes place in the same way. This now pursues a path rendered increasingly accessible by the repeated stimulus. The tension has found an outlet in inadequate reactions : hysterical symptoms.

What is it, then, which stands in the way of natural, adequate reactions and prevents them from fulfilling the biological law of balance ? What, in other words, are the *psychic* reasons for the appear-

---

[14] It is of interest that this theory has received brilliant support from modern experiments with an encephallogram, for example in the study of dreams.

ance of hysteria ? Breuer and Freud mentioned two different groups of causes.

The first of these comprises cases where the nature of the trauma—its *contents*, that is—precludes normal reaction. Examples here are profound grief, the loss of a beloved person, or cases where the normal reaction would be incompatible with the social circumstances involved, or cases where the patient wants to forget a matter concerned, purposely excludes it from the conscious mind and represses it. Of these banned memories it was remarked : "Exactly such painful matters are found by hypnosis to be the basis of hysterical phenomena".[15]

The other group of causes includes cases where an emotional experience is rendered pathological by *the psychic state* with which it has coincided rather than by what the trauma itself contains. Such psychic states are those of a hypnoid kind, of autohypnosis and daydream, or states where a violent affect—panic, for instance—has paralyzed mental activity. The psychic paralysis which occurs at moments of panic is comparable with that arising in hypnoid states. Breuer called it *"ein Schreckhypnoid"*.

Of course, the reasons for hysteria may combine causes from the two groups : both what the episode has held for the person and his condition when it took place.

Breuer's patient, Anna O., was cited as a typical example of hysteria produced by strong affects experienced by someone whose psyche happened to be in a hypnotic state. Her condition before the disorder set in had been prepared by her way of living. She had led a double life : a life of dreams which gave nourishment and satisfaction to her imagination and emotions, and a life in the real world, where it was her duty to carry out certain household tasks. This situation forced her to mobilize all her mental strength : she showed a hypertrophy, or *"Überleistung"* of such strength. In her case there was no question, as with Janet's patients, of too weak mental tension or strength.

The double quality involved, the division in her mental life, became greater when she took care of her sick father. Her anxiety for him caused an extraordinary concentration on him; this finally turned into autohypnosis and complete forgetfulness of what she experienced in her hypnotic state.[16] Such a state severs the connection between

---

[15] Breuer and Freud, *op. cit.*; p. 7.

[16] Breuer pointed out that the patient found herself in a situation particularly

emotional experiences which may take place at such hypnoid moments and normal psychic activity. In consequence, the affects and the cerebral tensions that arise from them are prevented either from taking the normal courses of reaction or from wearing off through assimilation with the normal complex of experience. Thus, a memory that conduces mental illness is formed : in other words, the trauma, with its suite of physical phenomena. Pathological symptoms appear.

It now seems clear why, by recounting the affective experiences that took place during the incubation period of her disorder, Breuer's patient was cured. She recovered quite simply because she reacted to the emotions which she had undergone while in a hypnoid state. She experienced the emotions afresh as, during her treatment, she narrated to the doctor the events and memories that had produced her symptoms. Breuer attached great importance to the patient reliving such episodes with all their original intensity. The powerful psychic and cerebral tension that ensues from this is released by the movements which the patient then makes and what he says. The confined, and therefore dangerous, affects are freed; and a discharge or abreaction takes place. The abnormal reactions, manifested by hysterical symptoms, cease when a patient has been relieved of affects in this way. The memories involved lose their dangerous emotional charge; they are neutralized, transmitted to consciousness and assimilated in the normal context of experience.

Cure is explained in the same way where the other kind of hysteria is concerned, the kind not caused by the patient's hypnoid state but dependent on the nature of the trauma or its content. For example, the trouble might be a profound grief to which the patient has not been able to react normally, and which he cannot get over. We are reminded here of what Janet called "tenacious symptoms". This form of hysteria includes cases where the reaction may not have taken place because of the person's social situation or because of his principles in life, the ethical standards he has set up for himself. This repression, which induces pathological symptoms because psychic tension must somehow find an outlet, is imposed by action of the will, in contrast to the completely automatic repression in the other, hypnoid, form of hysteria. The act by which such voluntary inhibition

---

conducive to autohypnosis : "*Die Krankenpflege stellt durch die äussere Ruhe, die Concentration auf ein Object, das Horchen auf die Athemzüge des Kranken, geradezu dieselben Bedingungen her, wie viele Hypnotisirungsmethoden*". (*Op. cit.*; p. 191.)

is enforced is called *"Abwehr"*: it was Freud's studies that persuaded Breuer to accept use of the term. We may note here the presence in embryo of the *Verdrangung* concept later to appear in psychoanalysis, with the difference that repression then would be thought to occur unconsciously.

It is obvious with this form of hysteria why discharge is effected by talking to the doctor. A willed repression of the affects has of course taken place. The person in question has kept his great grief to himself; he has not wished to speak about his severe temptations or his offences against the moral code. The powerful feelings mobilized round the memory have accumulated into a dangerous underground centre of tension and mental disorder. The constrained feelings are released in the doctor's presence by the patient's gestures and, above all, the words spoken. Breuer and Freud attributed great importance to language as an instrument of discharge. They believed that it may serve as surrogate for the actions which would perhaps be the most adequate expression of the affects. The aim of treatment is to give the affects precisely their adequate expression instead of the inadequate reactions which the patient's symptoms represent. And language does not always need to be regarded as a surrogate; it can in fact be the adequate reaction, "as lament over, and utterance of, a painful secret (confession !)".[17]

We have dwelt so long specifically on Breuer's theory and his cathartic method because, on the one hand, his theory seems to be the best and most feasible explanation of why a "talking cure" can effect recovery in cases of traumatic hysteria;[18] and because, on the other hand, his theory and method have been of great significance in the history of psychiatry. His teachings were taken over directly by other psychiatrists, and they formed the very basis of Freud's system, which would in turn so greatly influence modern psychiatry. Later here, we shall have occasion to discuss somewhat more fully both the cathartic method and the theory attached to it. First, however, let us study how the method has been used by other psychiatrists and

---

[17] *Ibid.*; p. 6.

[18] Cf. Max Nachmansohn's opinion of Breuer's theory, already quoted here. Nachmansohn continued : "*Was er* [Breuer] *aber positiv gelehrt hat, scheint mir auch jetzt grossenteils haltbar, und soweit seine Ausführungen hypothetische sind, sind sie doch sehr gut begründete Hypothesen*". (*Op. cit.*; p. 130). Cf. also Freud's statement, quoted in Chapter VII, p. 94 f.

observe how it survives in psychoanalysis, even if the theory involved assumes a different aspect there.

Among psychiatrists who have most emphatically asserted the usefulness of the cathartic method and the soundness of theories attached to it, attention may be called to the Englishman, William Brown.[19] During the First World War, he worked at a nerve clinic in France and took care of countless "shell shock" cases : ones where psychic disorders were believed to be caused by the explosion of shells, land mines and other events of the kind. These breakdowns were often very severe. The men afflicted showed a number of hysterical symptoms : amnesia as regards everything connected with the accident, deafness, dumbness, paralysis, and so on. Having placed his patients under light hypnosis, Brown tried to get them to recall the episodes they had forgotten; he wished thus—supported meanwhile by such aids as rest, persuasion and interpretation—to achieve cohesion of their split consciousness. The pathological symptoms had a tendency to disappear as the forgotten memories were brought to light. A re-association, or synthesis, of the psyche was effected, and the forces which had caused the symptoms could be controlled in the process. Brown soon discovered that if he made a particular effort not only to bring forth the forgotten memory *but also to induce the strong affect connected with this in all its original vividness and intensity*, the hysterical symptom disappeared. While the patient was under hypnosis, it could be observed how he relived the traumatic event down to the slightest detail : terror was reflected on his face and expressed itself with the same power over his physical motility as before the symptoms appeared. After the patient had been allowed to give as complete outlet as possible to his emotional reaction, Brown suggested to him that in a wakeful state he should remember what he had talked about; the hypnosis was then broken off. In the great majority of cases, this treatment led to complete recovery.

The method of treatment here may be recognized immediately as that in the *Studien* of Breuer and Freud. Brown confirmed brilliantly the usefulness of the method in certain cases of hysteria. And

---

[19] William Brown, *Psychology and Psychotherapy* (London, 1922; 4th ed., 1940). The review in *The Church Quarterly Review* (1939; p. 151 ff. : the reviewer being Frederic Hood) of Brown's book *Psychological Methods of Healing* described the author as a leading contemporary psychiatrist. In his later works, Brown retained the basic concepts reported above.

he acknowledged his debt to Breuer and Freud as regards the theory he followed. It was psycho-catharsis or abreaction which took place in his patients. The affects produced during the accidents that befell them had overpowered them and not found expression through normal means of reaction; instead, they were suppressed and inhibited, and manifested themselves in pathological symptoms. The patient's memory of the event in question, also the affect connected with this, led a shadowy life apart from normal consciousness; the symptoms called attention to their existence. If the mental dissociation was brought successfully to an end by having the patient regain the memory while under hypnosis, and if the affect was allowed the normal outlet it could not take before, then the patient recovered. Abreaction went together with re-association, with synthesis of the split psyche. The healing factors were the same as those indicated by Breuer and Freud.

Although Brown achieved excellent results with the psycho-cathartic method, he emphasized its great limitations. He used the method only in cases where neuroses showed fairly severe symptoms and the aim was to achieve speedy results. He believed that in the ordinary circumstances of civil life it should be used with much caution. Other methods were preferable in such conditions: suggestion, persuasion and analysis (autognosis).[20] The cathartic method had a weakness: hypnosis was an important element in its practice. And hypnosis could not be used on all patients. Brown believed that it was possible to induce hypnosis only if the patient had a definite psychic dissociation, and that receptiveness to hypnosis disappeared when this was cured.

Similar treatment of combat neurosis was carried on during the Second World War. In his book *Peace of Mind*,[21] Joshua Loth Liebman reported on this from a study called "Men under Stress". The treatment aimed at getting airmen who suffered neurosis during and after combat to re-experience their shock and abreact to it. But evidently this process was not always sufficient to effect a recovery. A deeper and more comprehensive analysis was needed, and the therapist had also to let the patient relive conflicts from his previous life: from boyhood and youth.

---

[20] Brown, *op. cit.*; p. 100. Brown pointed out, however, that even in the customary analysis of a neurotic's experiences abreaction usually takes place during accounts of emotional memories. (P. 103.)

[21] (New York, 1946); p. 90.

A leading argument against Breuer's method—perhaps the most usual objection—has been mentioned : it cannot be used on all patients. Another argument is that some patients cannot abreact under hypnosis, so their condition remains unchanged. But, primarily, limitation of the method becomes plain when we consider that it can be used with good results only where purely traumatic neuroses are concerned. There, isolated experiences are brought to light; this can, as we have seen, restore the patient to mental health. However, a different situation is presented when the real cause of disorder is an inhibited instinct or drive. Basically, the symptoms are then manifestations of the conflict between the instinct and the element repressing it. In cases of the kind, abreaction alone is of no avail. Only the outward symptom will be affected, not the underlying pathological centre. This will simply find expression in another symptom when one symptom is removed. Instead, the aim must be to end the inhibition by drawing it into the light of consciousness; it is thus possible for the instinct to be controlled by the will. Abreaction does take place during the process, but not under real hypnosis, and it is by no means the principal function of treatment. Already here, we enter on Freudian lines of thought.

The objections noted to use of hypnosis in the cathartic method indicate a fundamental reason for Freud's separation from Breuer. Another cause was the stress that Freud placed on the part played in the etiology of mental illness by the instincts, above all the sexual intsinct. Let us now look summarily at Freud's basic ideas.

Instead of using hypnosis, what Freud tried was to get his patients to speak about their traumatic memories while they were in a normal state of consciousness. He had learned from the great figure in the therapy of suggestion, H. Bernheim of Nancy, that what the patient relives while in a hypnoid state has not genuinely been forgotten. If he is assured emphatically enough that he can find the memory which causes his trouble, he can be got to relate it while normally conscious. In other words : the doctor can extract the memory by suggestion. Freud discovered in due course the unnecessity of forcing patients during this procedure. Without pressure, the doctor can get to, and uncover, the heart of the trouble by the method of free association. "In the expectation—at first altogether unproved, later confirmed by abundant experience—that all thoughts which come to the patient when he starts off from a definite idea must possess an inner relation, the technique presented itself of training the patient to

refrain from any critical attitude and of using the material provided
by what comes to his mind in order to discover the connection sought
for".[22]

This method became the new technique of psychoanalysis, and it
has since been increasingly developed and improved. The treatment
involved usually begins with the patient being asked to describe an
episode in his life which might be thought to bear a relation to his
disorder. Another important way of starting off is to have the patient
relate his dreams. Meanwhile, much weight is attached to the fact
that the patient should not, for one reason or another, conceal anything
in his narrative. Precisely what may seem to him unpleasant, trivial,
meaningless or irrelevant gives the doctor vital information about
the causes of his symptoms. Freud said : "We instruct the patient to
induce a state of calm, unreflective self-observation in himself, and
to report everything he then notes—feelings, thoughts, memories—in
the sequence they come to mind".[23] For his part, the doctor is to
follow this introspective activity with "attention evenly suspended" :
which is to say that he must "surrender himself to his own unconscious
mental activity, avoid as far as possible being reflective and having
precise expectations, and not seek particularly to remember anything
of what he may hear; in this way his own unconscious mind is to
apprehend that of the patient".

Both patient and doctor should thus find themselves on a psychic
level from which clear, ordinary thought and logical understanding
appear to be banished, this to encourage the passive recording of
how obscure mental forces manifest themselves reflexively. To an
uninitiated observer the method must, incontestably, seem rather
mysterious. And in practice probably the doctor does not remain
so completely passive and impartial as that during a certain portion
of the analysis. Of course he must take careful note of all the patient's
reactions during treatment in order to interpret afterwards, on the
basis of his observations, the significance and deeper meaning of the
associations and symbols. The fact is that a patient's associations can
be shown to have a definite tendency. The doctor's task is simply
to fit what he learns together. By applying the language of symbols

---

[22] Freud's summary of psychoanalysis in *Handwörterbuch für Sexualwissenschaft*
(Vienna, 1923)

[23] S. Freud, "*Vorlesungen zur Einführung in die Psychoanalyse*", in *Taschenausgabe*
(Vienna, 1926); p. 297.

and from careful observation of the patient's free association, he establishes the cause behind the symptoms.

Gradually, the doctor gets the patient to discover this cause for himself, and thus also to perceive the connection between a conflict and his disorder. Achieving that end is the essential aim of analysis. In other words, the goal is to render the unconscious "complex" conscious, for the disastrous ability of the complex to bring on mental illness lies precisely in its unconscious character. The idea involved here is a basic factor in the psychological system that Freud took up from Breuer.

A conflict that engenders neurosis arises in the following way. The sexual instinct or "libido" (to which Freud attached a fairly wide significance and which is not to be identified merely with the reproductive instinct) strives to attain satisfaction. The object at which the libido is directed varies with the person's age. Opposition comes from instincts of the "ego" (*Ichtriebe*) and these prevent the libido from expressing itself in the original directions.[24] This inner authority—the censor—which restrains the libido is regarded as standing like a guard between the unconscious and the conscious (or preconscious). Another term for the censor is the "superego" (*das Überich*) : it is the person's conscience as developed by tradition and upbringing, the moral authority within him. Demands of the libido are suppressed, submerged in the unconscious, if they are not compatible with assessments of the superego. Here, it should be noted, the entire operation is believed to take place unconsciously. Repression—*die Verdrängung*—belongs to the *Unbewusst* system.

Now, the strong sexual instinct does not allow itself simply to be inhibited. Because in the normal psyche the libido possesses "plasticity", the instinct can be transferred to definite non-sexual objects : a "sublimation" of the libido occurs. But a condition for successful sublimation is that the psyche must have at its disposal a measure of free, adaptable libido. And the sexual instinct shows a certain *Klebrigkeit*, a tendency to remain attached to certain objects which have appeared in the person's development from earliest childhood : the libido is fixed on these.

The procedure here is like that of an army during an expedition of conquest. The army moves constantly onward into enemy territory, but it must leave forces behind to encircle and occupy important

---

[24] Freud, *Vorlesungen*; p. 367 f.

positions along the way. So, in development of the sexual instinct, particularly if the person has a nervous disposition, there is an inclination to leave too much of the libido behind at certain points. This has a weakening effect and renders the person less fit to respond normally when the ego prohibits demands made by the libido. The sexual instinct is in itself too feeble to break through the barrier, and too much of it remains at stages passed through for it to be formable and allow sublimation. The instinct retreats to the places where it has left much of its power. This movement is called "regression". The patient retrogresses to phases of his life where his libido had greater opportunity of receiving satisfaction—which usually means to childhood.

We might consequently expect the neurotic to relive his childhood infatuations, or expect his libido to find expression through "partial instincts" that existed separately before being merged with the reproductive instinct in the process that marks commencement of a person's normal life as an adult. But it is characteristic of the neurotic that he does not revert entirely to what was in the past (that would be prevented by the censor); instead, he unconsciously creates a compromise between the old course and the present cause of his neurosis. The symptoms which then appear can be related to the symbols in his dreams : these symbols are a peculiar conglomeration of elements from real emotional experiences and elements supplied by the patient's imagination. The symptoms are a substitute which the patient has created for expression of his instinctual drives; they provide the libido with satisfaction of a kind in a form acceptable to that severe watchman, the censor. Thus, the symptoms are a compromise solution to demands coming from the libido—"the pleasure principle"—and from the opposition which in actuality these encounter because of "the reality principle".

For the patient the connection between the symptoms and their deeper, underlying causes is completely unknown. The entire drama takes place beyond his consciousness. For example, a person suffering from compulsive neurosis is certainly aware that he performs strange actions which always seem to follow the same stereotyped pattern, but he does not understand *why* he performs them.

The psychoanalyst must help him to gain the knowledge of *why* which will lead him to mental health. We have already looked briefly at the therapeutic method employed here. One would think that, as the patient desires to recover from his disorder, he would be ready and willing to co-operate in the analyst's attempts at getting him to reveal the connection between the cause of his ailment and the symptoms from which he suffers. But, on the contrary, the patient puts up stubborn resistance to the analyst's endeavours. He is capable of using every possible expedient that may get the doctor to abandon his interpretations. The doctor's most substantial task during the analysis is to overcome this resistance from the patient. Precisely such opposition indicates to the analyst that he has reached the crucial point in the patient's unconscious and touched on the complex from which the pathological symptoms derive. The tenacity and power of the patient's resistance are explained by the fact that they originate from the same element that caused the inhibition : from the censor, which refuses entry into the consciousness of the disastrous affect and the ideas connected with it. As the disorders have arisen because the complex is severed from normal consciousness, it is easily perceived that the analyst's efforts must be directed at conquering both the resistance and the inhibition, thus to bring the pathogenetic complex into the patient's consciousness. In accomplishing this task, the doctor's best ally is the phenomenon of "transference"—*die Über-tragung*.

Freud excluded the use of hypnosis from his treatment, and he gave up the simple suggestion therapy of Bernheim. He did not, nevertheless, abandon suggestion. That is included in transference. The process there consists simply of the libido and sexual affects— which, by being repressed, induced the conflict that caused mental illness—being transferred to the doctor. Usually, transference manifests itself by the patient becoming infatuated with the doctor and entertaining feelings of tender affection and admiration for him (in positive transference, that is); more rarely the patient may show feelings of an opposite kind and take a rancorous and aggressive attitude (which is negative transference). It is significant of how central a part transference plays in psychoanalysis that only patients who are capable of it can be subjects for psychoanalytical treatment. The neuroses they suffer from are called "transference neuroses" or "psycho-neuroses", and are various forms of hysteria and compulsion neuroses. From these Freud distinguished the so-called actual neuroses : neurasthenia, anxiety neurosis and hypochondria, which like the real psychoses are inaccessible to psychoanalytic treatment.[25]

---

[25] Freud, *ibid.*; p. 406 ff.

Positive transference is the analyst's best aid in leading a patient to discover the connection between an unconscious conflict and the symptoms manifested. This is because the patient's emotional involvement with the doctor makes him very ready to accept the doctor's instructions and interpretations. Freud said that the patient "surprises the doctor by the certainty and swiftness of his explanations, and the doctor can feel only satisfaction in observing how willingly a patient adopts new psychological findings which usually arouse the bitterest response among healthy people out in the world".[26] But transference may at the same time prove somewhat awkward for the analyst. The aim for him is to get the patient to perceive that feelings being directed at him are really intended for another. In other words, what happens to the patient during transference is a re-experiencing of the conflict which produced his psychic disorder. But no exact copy is involved of the infatuation earlier repressed. Rather, what appears is a new version of the old attraction, based on it but given another character by being directed at a new object : the doctor.[27]

In this fresh variation of his conflict, the patient may behave as he did before, or perhaps as he unconsciously wished to do when the old conflict was created; but, with the doctor's assistance, he can now solve the problem. It might be said that the aim is to effect a reconciliation between the ego and the libido, the libido having previously freed itself from domination by the ego and, through its uncontrolled existence, given rise to the patient's disorder. The libido must be returned to command of the ego and must conform with its organizing power. For this to occur, a change is required in the ego itself : the change takes place during treatment, and it implies that the ego becomes master over the unconscious centre of disturbance, thus gaining the ability to dominate the forces which caused the disorder. When the conflict that engendered this is brought into the clear light of consciousness, the patient has the ability to solve the

---

[26] Freud, *ibid.*; p. 467.

[27] This can be illustrated by a statement from the psychoanalyst Gion Condrau. According to Condrau, Freud himself confessed to having previously believed that a conflict can be cured merely through being rendered conscious. Such is, of course, not the case. It is the patient's resistance which holds the conflict down in the unconscious, and it is by conquest of his opposition and through his *action* during the analysis that something takes place. "It is not primarily as recollection that the analysing reproduces what is repressed in the patient's life history, but as *happening*". (G. Condrau, *Angst und Schuld als Grundprobleme der Psychotherapie*; Berne, 1962; pp. 125-126.)

problem in a new way. The doctor exerts strong influence on this process, just as he has done in tracing the unconscious conflicts. With the part played by the doctor in mind, Freud described the entire psychoanalytical cure as training of the patient with the aid of suggestive influence from the doctor.[28]

In solving a conflict which has engendered neurosis, various courses may be followed. The ego, having now acquired greater maturity, can overcome the unconscious desire that has survived from childhood and simply ban it as an absurdity. Or opportunities may be offered to sublimate the libido. A third possibility is that of paying heed to the demand of the libido and granting it natural expression within due limits.[29] The entire treatment must aim at attaching the libido, previously constrained by the complex, to a new object; and this is accomplished through the person's conscious efforts. The libido must not remain fixed on the doctor after transference; it is to be directed further, along the lines already indicated. This liberation of the patient from his tie to the doctor, and his acquiring a new object for his libido or overcoming it in some other way, constitutes a principal element in treatment. When the unconscious centre of disturbance is thus neutralized, the psychic disassociation ends and the patient is restored to mental health.

During the process outlined here, abreaction—the emotional discharge we know from Breuer, Janet and others—has really taken place by and through the phenomenon of transference; for transference of course implies that affects adhering to unconscious recollections of the original conflict are transferred to the doctor. Freud did, in fact, attach great importance to having what the patient re-experiences resemble as closely as possible his conflict as originally experienced. The patient is to behave as he did when the conflict arose.[30] The abreaction involved appears to go together with the process of rendering the pathological experience conscious. The constrained affect receives expression; the dangerous tension it has brought is released. Re-occurrence is prevented, for the libido and its affects have been placed under the sway of consciousness and gained a conscious object.

---

[28] Freud, *Vorlesvngen*; p. 480.

[29] These three possibilities are stated by Freud in *Über Psychoanalyse, Gesammelte Schriften*, vol. IV (Vienna, 1924); p. 403 ff.

[30] Freud, *Vorlesungen*; p. 484.

Freud's view of mental life in general may be deduced from the above summary of his basic ideas on the origin and cure of neuroses. What takes place when neuroses are generated is merely the development and action of the normal psyche gone astray. Fundamentally, the same lines are followed as in normal psychological development. The unconscious element, the activity of the libido and repression, are here revealed primarily by inadequate acts and dreams. The latter especially are regarded as symbols, comparable with the neurotic symptoms, of the conflict between the pleasure and reality principles. Freud said : "Thus the healthy person is also virtually a neurotic, but the dream appears to be the only symptom which he is in a condition to form".[31] The dream is considered to be a wish fulfilment in symbolic form. During sleep, the censor's pressure ceases; this allows the libido to force its way up from the unconscious, and, by means of what remains in pre-consciousness of the day's experiences (*"die Tagesreste"*), it creates the composite images of dreams. Through interpreting the symbols in dreams, the analyst can gain knowledge of the deepest forces and desires existing in a normal person. He may also do so by analysing the person's inadequate actions and a great many other unconscious actions and movements.[32]

---

[31] Freud, *Vorlesungen*; p. 487.

[32] Cf. Freud's *Zur Psychopathologie des Alltagslebens* (Vienna, 1901).

CHAPTER SEVEN

CRITICISM AND VALUATION OF THE PART PLAYED BY ABREACTION AND ASSIMILATION IN PSYCHIATRY

In the preceding chapter we described a method of treating traumatic memories—what Breuer called "the cathartic method". We there observed that an essential element of the method is the discharge, or abreaction, of affects by having the patient talk about the traumatic event he has gone through. When memories have thus been relieved of their emotional character, they are neutralized; they can be submitted to rational examination and fitted into the patient's normal context of experience. This stage of treatment is called "assimilation" or "re-association". Another thing we have noticed is that these two phases are concurrent in the process of effecting a cure.

Of the two factors, Breuer and Freud in their *Studien* laid special stress on abreaction rather than assimilation; and after them Brown and others took the same attitude. But Freud's later, completely worked-out system gives special prominence to assimilation : to bringing the patient's previously unconscious complex, the cause of his trouble, into consciousness and integrating it with his experience. Abreaction remained, however, an element in treatment for Freud.

Janet gave good examples of how simply discharging an affect can bring about a patient's recovery. But at the same time, he strongly emphasized the important part played by assimilation. Janet's evidence deserves special attention because he proved convincingly that abreaction has a beneficial effect on various types of neurotic patient even when it is not an element in "cathartic" therapy. This means that abreaction is not limited to use in Breuer's and Freud's cathartic method—which of course Janet practised, too. Thus, criticism of that method does not at all affect the psychotherapeutic importance of abreaction. It is evident that William McDougall had the general occurrence of abreaction in mind when he said that "catharsis" is a general factor of mental hygiene rather than part of a psychotherapeutic method.[1] Here we should simply like to object that, even if abreaction is such a factor, it can be considered to form

---

[1] W. McDougall, *An Outline of Abnormal Psychology* (London, 1926); p. 479.

part of a therapy which aims at establishing, or restoring, mental health!

In examining general discussion on the cathartic method, we may observe how the function of abreaction in treatment is commonly underestimated to the benefit of work with the patient's consciousness : of assimilation. McDougall's criticism of the method, primarily as practised by William Brown, provides an instance of this tendency.[2]

Pierre Janet considered that during the painful and difficult narration of a traumatic memory the "forces" surrounding that memory are discharged; and he asked : "How does it happen that the traumatic memory, after it has been discharged by confession, is not immediately charged again ?"[3] In his opinion, recharge does not take place because of the high tension aroused in the patient by his emotional excitation during treatment. An *"opération de haute tension"* occurs; this brings assimilation of the dissociated memories and re-establishment of mental unity. Advocates of the cathartic method also hold that when the patient speaks of his traumatic memory he experiences mental tension which is brought to a high pitch and given full expression. But for Janet such tension meant a general state of excitation in (according to his theory) poorly endowed hysterics with low psychic pressure. During confession of the memory, all the concealed powers of these people are mobilized at once and there is a concentrated rallying of strength : this feat, unusual for them, produces release and assimilation of dissociated elements in their psyches.

It is evident that the cathartic method brings cures in many cases of neurosis precisely because of the abreaction which it includes; it is clear, too, that abreaction, even when unconnected with that method, has a great function in psychiatry. Here the experience of psychiatrists speaks for itself. And, in our view, the theory presented by Breuer to explain the effect of abreaction—a theory adopted in the main by Freud—is the most satisfactory one.

As token of the appreciation that has come to Breuer, the following hot-and-cold judgement of Freud may be cited : "Many opponents to psychoanalysis are in the habit of recalling casually that of course

---

[2] In a discussion printed by *The British Journal of Psychology* : Medical Section (Cambridge, 1920); pp. 16-33.

[3] P. Janet, *La Médicine psychologique*; p. 221. Cf. *Les Médications psychologiques*; vol. II, p. 297.

the science of psychoanalysis does not derive directly from me : it comes from Breuer. Naturally, they do this only if their attitude allows them to find something worthy of consideration in psychoanalysis; if their rejection is too complete for that, then psychoanalysis is always indisputably my work. Never in my experience has Breuer's great share in psychoanalysis brought him a corresponding measure of insult and censure".[4] This statement is scarcely fair to critics of the two men. When the pros and cons of psychoanalysis have been weighed in the balance, Freud has usually received his due share of credit. Nevertheless, his words have their significance, for they show a frequent inclination to accept that much of what is valuable in psychoanalysis was, in basic outline, already complete in *Studien über Hysterie*. Of course it is obvious that, if people object to the theories and fancies enounced by Freud over a long succession of years, they will regard the earlier stage of the new psychology and art of mental healing in a more favourable light. This does not mean that Freud's later, more profound study of trauma psychology has failed to win him proper esteem.

What Freud has been reproached with by temperate and influential critics are his bias and dogmatism—even if those qualities have been more characteristic of his imitators than of the master himself. Such critics cannot lend support to his one-sided way of determining a person's instinctual life : this is regarded as too narrow and caused the epithet "pansexualism" to be applied to his outlook. The same critics readily accept that the sexual instinct is of great importance and that Freud's permanent achievement lies in the attention he drew to this fact, which prepared for an unprejudiced discussion of sexual psychology; but they object to his view that the sexual instinct is altogether dominant. They call particular attention to the unreasonable element in his conception of infantile sexuality, with the Oedipus complex as the central and dangerous trauma of childhood, even though they are prepared to admit that in some cases incestuous infantile desire is of disastrous consequence. Freud has been criticized, too, for his opinion on how mental phenomena are determined by unconscious forces, this being regarded as a generalization that overlooks the import of conscious mental actions. It follows that criticism has also been directed against his interpretation of symbols, which is considered to be frequently too laboured and fanciful, neglect-

---

[4] S. Freud, *Zur Geschichte der psychoanalytischen Bewegung*, in *Gesammelte Schriften*; vol. IV, p. 412.

ful of simpler explanations that lie closer at hand. But where criticism seems to have been applied with most effect is to his attempts at psychoanalysing spiritual and cultural life.

We find, meanwhile, that psychologists and psychiatrists who are critically disposed towards Freud have made statements in which they readily acknowledge his significance. McDougall, for instance, said : "In my opinion Freud has, quite unquestionably, done more for the advancement of our understanding of human nature than any other man since Aristotle".[5] And Arthur Kronfeld, an eminent psychiatrist who was critical of Freud in many respects, declared : "There is no doubt that with psychoanalysis a new era was initiated in understanding of the neurotic and psychotic way of experiencing and responding".[6] It may be said of Freud's importance in general that his teachings on the interplay of needs and instinctual impulses behind mental reactions occupy a dominant position in modern psychology of personality, and that his dynamic view of mental life and so-called "deep-psychological" outlook do the same. Even when people criticize the Freudian system for its biasses, they are often willing to perceive the value of its basic concepts and prepared to show their appreciation of many ideas there. The attitude commonly taken in psychological literature may be represented by the following observation from the American psychologist Joseph Jastrow, who was none the less a sharp critic of psychoanalysis : "Freudian psychology is a *depth* psychology, including the submerged or suppressed unconscious; it is a *libidinal* psychology, referring behaviour to basic urges; it is a *sublimation* psychology, tracing the course of the psyche from the primal trend to the final form. If a subscription to this programme as a vital one entitles one to be ranked as a Freudian, I claim that appellation. Such depth psychology is peculiarly the proper study of mankind".[7]

More recently, detailed studies have been devoted in America and Europe to the influence of Freud and psychoanalysis on psychology and psychiatry.[8] And many leading researchers in the field have acknow-

---

[5] W. McDougall, *Psychoanalysis and Social Psychology* (London, 1936); p. 17.

[6] Arthur Kronfeld, *Psychotherapie* (Berlin, 1925); p. 156.

[7] Joseph Jastrow, *The House that Freud Built* (London, 1933); p. 137.

[8] See, for example, R. S. Woodworth and M. Shehan, *Contemporary Schools of Psychology*, 3rd ed. (New York, 1964); D. Shakow and D. Rapaport, *The Influence of Freud on American Psychology* (New York, 1964); and Dieter Vyss, *Die tiefenpsychologischen Schulen*, etc. (Göttingen, 1966).

ledged that their own theories are similar to those of Freud or are dependent on his. Two men may be mentioned here : Curt Lewin and Henry A. Murray.

Lewin has elaborated the concept of psychic energy : he speaks of "systems of tension". He comments on the similarities between his outlook and Freud's, and the correspondences involved are on altogether essential points.[9] As for Henry A. Murray, it is doubtless sufficient to quote this statement by an authoritative reviewer : "Murray has been recognized as one of the first to attempt a large-scale reconciliation of psychoanalytic theory with the concepts of academic psychology".[10]

David Rapaport, the well-known psychoanalyst of moderate views, takes a particular interest in the formation of psychological theory, and he too has attempted to establish the influence which psychoanalysis has exerted on essential points of general psychology. He finds "convergence"—in Piaget, among others—where ego psychology and the outlook on development of personality are concerned. He sees agreement also on the psychology of learning and memory, and above all as regards motivation and the personality. Finally, about the influence of psychoanalysis on medicine and psychiatry, Rapaport states : "The convergence of psychoanalysis with medicine in general and psychiatry in particular, though only too obvious, is practical rather than theoretical".[11]

But the following seems a good comment on the hazard involved in tracing and proving the influence of psychoanalysis : "It is difficult to epitomize the meandering course of Freud's influence on the birth and development of motivation theories in psychology. One can only be amazed by the intricate intertwining of influence and by the unpredictable channels through which influences are effected. What appears highly probable, however, is that the passage through a stage of 'acceptance', which amounts mainly to taking the specificity out of concepts and turning them into vague conceptions, is unavoidable in the historical process."[12]

Where we are concerned here, it is of special interest that such scientists of psychology willingly and often acknowledge the service

---

[9] Shakow and Rapaport, op. cit.; p. 131.

[10] Woodworth and Sheehan, op. cit.; p. 363.

[11] D. Rapaport, A Structure of Psychoanalytical Theory (New York, 1960); p. 138 f.

[12] Shakow and Rapaport, op. cit.; p. 159.

psychoanalysis has rendered in showing the importance to a person's mental state of personal conflicts and emotionally charged memories : showing how these memories can be repressed from consciousness and yet maintain an unconscious tension which may affect the conduct of the person's life in many ways, and produce mental disorders in certain individuals with tendencies to them.

In accepting the theory of dynamic tension in the psyche and that of repression, many have perceived the import both of abreaction— the action by which tension finds an outlet—and of the assimilation of now-clarified memories which takes place at the same time.

Arthur Kronfeld has already been mentioned here as a representative of the psychiatrists with a tempered attitude towards Freud's theories on neurosis and psychotherapy. We return to him because he had interesting views on the section of psychoanalysis relevant here.

One of Kronfeld's chief complaints against Freud was that he did not give sufficient post-therapy training to patients under his treatment. Of course, Freud could not devote any great thought to that factor for reasons of principle, the idea behind his theory and treatment being that the patient is transformed and mentally healed when unconscious memories are brought to consciousness. But Kronfeld said that Freud added to this idea his concept of how inhibited libido energy is liberated, of "abreaction", which concept is of extraordinary significance to psychiatry and "insofar as the analysis is in its service...undoubtedly of therapeutic power". Kronfeld was also prepared to admit that psychoanalysis is particularly well adapted to bringing about abreaction of inhibited affective tension at a profound level. He gave his own, independent analysis of emotional discharge : all the affectivity attached to the experience that produced conflict exerts pressure towards discharge. "From the purely motor aspect, emotional discharge is possible merely through the spoken word".[13] The immediate consequences of abreaction are an equalization of tension and mental calm. By being put into words and brought through into consciousness, the complex has broken out of its previous isolation and entered into the context of consciousness; on doing so it gradually loses its affectivity and disappears.

As a logical consequence of this, Kronfeld took up Freud's teaching on repression, which he regarded as "perhaps the greatest benefit

---

[13] A. Kronfeld, *op. cit.*; p. 136.

rendered by Freudian investigation". The therapy he recommended for repression was moderate psychoanalysis. This should "be taken at least far enough for the doctor to gain a picture of the inner connection between [the patient's] tendencies and experiences in early childhood, and for this to be made clear to the person afflicted. It is, moreover, to be carried so far that fundamental abreaction can take place at all junctures of treatment".[14] Certain people are inaccessible to such treatment, according to Kronfeld. But he considered that, in general, psychoanalytic investigation and treatment are fruitful in all cases of "psychic-responsive" and psychogenic disorders of function, especially where conflict disturbances of an inter-personal kind are involved.

As for Ernst Kretschmer, like Freud he stressed the enormous part played by instinctual drives in psychic development.[15] A person's normal action is a component of different motives (instincts) which struggle to determine that action at a given moment. Inhibition is a normal phenomenon. Most neuroses arise from conflicts between the instincts. Complexes lie "in the sphere of consciousness" (Kretschmer's term for the unconscious), and the tension they produce causes disorders—that is, the usual hysterical symptoms. Moreover, Kretschmer took up Freud's concept of a *Konversion ins Körperliche* when explaining the origin of many symptoms. But he extended the idea of conversion and made it cover as well the symptoms of anxiety neurosis. He, too, said that the affective energy in complexes can be neutralized through abreaction. This may take place through an emotional action—an outburst of anger, for instance—or effected by providing the complex with a *"psycho-motor outlet"* of any kind. All such actions can diminish, or may end, the painful affective stagnation. So an exhaustive talk with the doctor or with an intimate often produces a favourable result—"That is what people call confession". In consequence, Kretschmer recommended the cathartic method for use in suitable cases.

In the survey of contemporary psychotherapy provided by Donald Ford and Hugh Urban, the authors speak appreciatively about certain aspects of psychoanalysis which have a bearing on our investigation.[16] They have this to say about the "talking cure" : "S. Freud,

[14] A. Kronfeld, *ibid.*; p. 177.

[15] See : E. Kretschmer, *Medizinische Psychologie* (Leipzig, 1939).

[16] *Systems of Psychotherapy* (New York, 1963).

as is known, widely developed the phenomenon of 'talking cure'. The entire field of individual verbal psychotherapy has been built upon his initial work". Though later systems vary technically and theoretically, "all of them are constructed around Freud's basic discovery that if one can arrange a special set of conditions and have the patient talk about his difficulties in certain ways, behavior changes of many kinds can be accomplished". (Page 109.) And, later (page 177) : "But in spite of these variations [in modern theories and practices] the fundamental medium is speech, the therapist operates primarily upon his [the patient's] speech... Verbal psychotherapy as it is conducted to-day is not remarkably different from that which Freud conducted in the early 1900's".[17]

Much is said, too, about Freud's "brilliant observations" : his theories about the repressions, the symbolic language, the relation between the therapist and his patient and his psychology of the child. Finally, it is said of "his assumption that all behavior has to be started by a reservoir of energy, which exists in the individual, which becomes attached to various responses and which can be expended by greater and greater attachments, thereby impoverishing the individual's behavior", that this "seems unreasonable in the light of to-day's knowledge". (Page 178.)

Another extremely critical examiner of psychoanalysis, N. S. Lehrman,[18] considers that its greatest service lies in the perception it offers of how decisive inter-personal relationships are both in engendering neuroses and their cure : "Perhaps the greatest contribution by Freud to psychiatry : his recognition that mental illness arises from distorted interpersonal relationships beginning with the family of origin". And, later, "the most potent tool there is in the field, a tool scientifically defined by Freud's genius" is "the emotional interaction between patient and doctor". Still further on : "I believe the science of interpersonal relationships which Freud founded can, properly modified, lay open the causes and nature of functional mental illness. I believe that only psychoanalysis has forged the scientific tools able to overcome the effects of man's inhumanity to man, perhaps the prime cause of human fear and mental illness.

---

[17] Cf. Gregory Zilboorg in *Psychoanalysis and Religion* (London, 1967); p. 175 : "The clinical empirical system of Freud seems to stand very well the test of time and experience".

[18] In Thomas Millon's, *Theories of Psychopathology* (Philadelphia, 1967).

Fortunately, despite the negative trends mentioned above, psycho-analysis is far from dead, e.g. Ferenczi's demonstration that the analyst's warmth is a necessary condition for cure". (Page 241.)

Theologians and psychologists of religion, as well as psychiatrists, have taken up many of Freud's ideas. Of course it is natural that people concerned with the theory and practice of the cure of souls should interest themselves in Freudian psychology and be eager to discover whether it has anything to teach them. They level criticism, as a rule, against Freud's biassed conception of sexuality as the dominant instinct, and against his view of people being dominated in general by their unconscious, instinctive life. As regards the latter criticism, we must not forget, that of course Freud in no way denied the ability of normal people to govern and direct the demands of their sexual instincts. This is shown by his theory on sublimation and on the natural attachment of libido energy to objects. The reason why he appeared to advocate an outlook that stresses the overwhelm-ing strength of the instincts—their power to prevail against all obstacles erected by consciousness and society (the censor, *das Überich*) —is connected with his having started off from study of neuroses where the conflicts give rise to psychic and psycho-physical disorders because of the emotional intensity and abnormal force in previous libido fixations. Behind criticism of Freud's view as to how dependent people are on their instincts, there lies a desire to make defence against a concept of human beings as plainly and simply creatures of instinct; for that belittles the "ethical personality" which, after conscious and rational reasoning, arrives at decisions. But the ques-tion may be asked if something else is not to be deduced from Freud. Actually, he assumed the conscience to be founded on what he called the *Ichtriebe*, and this should serve to protect the ego against effects of unrestrained expression on the part of the sexually directed libido.[19] To base the conscience in such a way on people's profoundest forces hardly seems to indicate too low a conception of human beings. But we shall have occasion later to return to these trains of Freud's thought.

Here, we should mention a group of psychiatrists—the "ego-analysts"—who, by building on grounds supplied by psychoanalysis,

---

[19] See Freud's *Vorlesungen*; p. 367, ff. The ego instincts are accepted without any very close analysis of their nature. They serve the instinct for self-preservation, and their encounter with the sexual instincts can produce dangerous conflicts.

have developed it in a certain direction. The psychotherapists in question give serious consideration to the behaviour of normal Man and to its causes; these are seen as highly conscious and rational, formed in accordance with demands of the environment. Thus, Man is not merely an "it" impelled by his instinctive drives. "Interaction with situational events is not something forced upon Man, he actively seeks it. He does so not only because he is impelled towards them by innate psychological energies but also because his biological evolution has provided him with behavioral equipment, such as vision, which responds to the environment, independent of the internal psychological energies. The social milieu and the environmental circumstances surrounding a person are powerful behavior elicitors and modifiers above and beyond the primary psychological energies (drives)."[20]

And later on : "One criterion for an effective and significantly growing theory is that its proponents continue to modify and develop it so as to encompass new ideas and new evidence as it becomes available. By this criterion, Freudian psychoanalysis as modified and elaborated by the egopsychology theorists is still a lively and growing theory".[21]

Theodor Müncker, the Catholic professor of ethics, devoted a chapter in a large work on the psychology of morals to "Restraints on Experience and Decision by the Conscience", and he there submitted psychoanalysis to examination.[22] "Pan-sexualism" was rejected; so were Adler's equally one-sided conclusions about a person's instinctive life; so, too, were "the attribution of volition to causal mechanisms of a mental kind, the underestimation of that which in an independent mind is capable of consciously taking measures, above all unconditional responses, to direct and determine the course of events, and of guiding the mental mechanisms by spiritual volition".[23] But Müncker could not, in spite of such criticism, deny Freud's great contribution. He was prepared to admit that even the conscious personality which maintains its independence in relation to the instinctive life may be taken unawares and humbled when complexes and inhibitions disrupt the normal scheme of life. He stressed how

[20] Ford and Urban, *op. cit.*; p. 182.

[21] *Ibid.*; p. 210.

[22] Theodor Müncker, *Die psychologischen Grundlagen der katholischen Sittenlehre* : *Handbuch der katholischen Sittenlehre*, ed. by F. Tillmann; vol. II (Düsseldorf, 1934); p. 189 ff.

[23] T. Müncker, *op. cit.*; p. 189.

important it is that educators and spiritual advisers should be able to discern unfortunate developments of such kind and dispel them. Müncker made use of psychoanalytical terms and data without much criticism. He took up the theory of repression and defined the phenomenon as a "general psychological means of dealing with experience, where everything felt to be unpleasant is concerned".[24] He endorsed also Freud's theories on the formation of complexes, on affective tension and abreaction. The advance made by Breuer and Freud lay in their observation that "completing blanks in the memory by bringing to consciousness what has been repressed, and discharging the inhibited affect, can remove psychogenic (disrupting) phenomena and inhibitions".[25] Müncker said that such discharge of affects, along with assimilation of withheld or unconscious memories, may occur during Catholic confession as well. But he declared the connection between psychoanalysis and Catholic confession to be very limited in scope. For, primarily, the effect of confession depends on "the sacramental expunging of sin". One of his chief criticisms of psychoanalysis was the same as that levelled by other theologians and even certain psychiatrists : it does not provide the patient with any post-therapy training and, on principle, avoids influencing his values.

Usually, very strong emphasis is laid in Catholic quarters on the differences between sacramental confession and what occurs during the "talking cure" of psychiatric treatment. Nevertheless, psycho-analytical terms are often used on the Catholic side and psycho-analytical points of view taken with regard to psychotherapy and the profane conception of Man.[26]

A Swedish theologian, Arvid Runestam, proceeded from the Christian outlook and concept of humanity in his discussion of psycho-analysis.[27] His criticism aimed, in consequence, to show that the view which psychoanalysis gives of mankind is unwarrantably restricted, also that it is unable to offer values which can profoundly liberate the individual, and which can create personal responsibility and awareness of guilt. Psychoanalysis turns the human being into simply a creature of instincts, and it regards the interaction among

---

[24] *Ibid.*; p. 193.

[25] T. Müncker, *op. cit.*; p. 191.

[26] See also, for instance, A. Snoeck, *Beichte und Psychoanalyse* (Frankfurt am Main, 1960).

[27] *Psychoanalysis and Christianity* (Rock Island, 1958).

his instincts as the source of his conflicts; he is not himself responsible, and the feelings of guilt which he may feel are explained away; by this means his complexes and inhibitions are removed, and harmony among his instincts—his mental health—is restored. Psychoanalysis is a psychology without a soul in the real meaning of that word : it lacks any ethical gauge or authority creative to the personality. It can elucidate the deeper levels of mental life, but it offers no help to people in their profoundest need : that which derives from the absence of anything or anyone to believe in or make the object of devotion. However, Runestam gives psychoanalysis credit for stressing such human need through its theory of transference and for making that theory a mainspring of its therapy. In transference the doctor serves as object for devotion. But he can be only a surrogate, more particularly so because the analyst refuses to influence his patient by directing attention to higher, imperishable values. The instinct for self-surrender can be turned to positive account only if it forms the psychological basis for the redeeming and regenerating power of Divine Will.

Though Runestam is principally interested simply in comparing the psychoanalytical and the Christian outlooks on life and the world, he does find space in which to acknowledge the merits of psycho-analysis in itself. He is willing to concede that it yields results in the treatment of neurosis. All Runestam's own reasoning is characterized by a dynamic basic view of mental life. He makes use of psychoana-lytical terms—even if he readily alters their meaning. He accepts the claim that psychoanalysis reveals the unconscious mind and that it is a depth psychology—though he believes that there are truths which it does not uncover, or which it overlooks. In principle he accepts, too, the concepts of transference and repression. But, exten-ding the latter term, he applies it to the thrusting aside of forces which inwardly direct people towards morality and religion. (We shall have occasion to return in a later chapter to this idea.)

When Tor Andrae, another Swedish theologian and historian of religion, examined psychoanalysis,[28] he rejected its dogmatism, also its pretensions to universality and those of a philosophic nature. But for him the primary aim was not to compare the Christian outlook with that of psychoanalysis but to investigate what deeper under-standing could be gained from the new psychology on how the human

---

[28] In his *Psykoanalys och religion* (Psychoanalysis and Religion : Stockholm, 1927).

spirit manifests itself. Andrae was fully aware of the very important contribution made by psychoanalysis to our understanding of mankind on the whole, of its particular service in drawing attention to the significance of childhood experiences in the development of a personality. The interpretation of dreams he regarded as of great value because it reveals forces acting in the unconscious—though he commented on absurdities involved. The theories of repression (understood "in the broadest sense") and affective tension won his approval. In consequence, he perceived the value of psychoanalytical techniques and methods, of the action which takes place in affective discharge and in assimilation, of the part played by the doctor's personality in producing those effects and in the final resolution of conflicts. He made a fruitful comparison between such processes in a psychoanalytical cure and confession. "The new psychology", he said, "has evidently rehabilitated confession".[29]

It may be noted that in books on pastoral psychology the cathartic effect of confession is spoken of without analysis of the effect. For instance, in his great work *Psicologia pastorale*[30] Roberto Zavalloni speaks simply about confession as discharging an inner tension— "*Il soggetto ha la possibilità di liberarsi dalla tensione interna*"—on which a cathartic effect ("*valore catharchico*") is elicited.

Our survey of Freudian criticism will no doubt have stressed further the view that abreaction and assimilation are of great therapeutic consequence; it will have emphasized, too, that we may seek in their action a good deal of the explanation as to why the methods described in the previous chapter could lead to cure in many cases. The same people who at times take an extremely critical attitude towards Freud often seem quite prepared to admit the value of his method precisely to the extent that the functions of abreaction and assimilation are allowed to take place. In acknowledging appreciation here, logically they either draw closer to psychoanalytical theory on essential points or they adopt it in principle. Acceptance is given to Freud's idea concerning the repression of instinctive impulses which are in some way unsuitable or unpleasant to the individual and the repression from consciousness of complicated experiences; though at the same time there is a wish to modify the concept with regard to the extent

---

[29] T. Andrae, *op. cit.*; p. 59.

[30] (Rome, 1965); p. 399.

and breadth of the process. Along with the idea of inhibition and repression, the theory of withheld affective tension is taken up, also of the complexes from which this derives: the unconscious *Fremd-körper* and the way in which they make their existence known to consciousness through the obscure language of symbols. We might add that, while examining the reasoned and dispassionate criticism of Freud, we have gained the impression that the portion of Freud's system outlined here constitutes what is most accepted in the modern psychology of personality.

We have dwelt in the foregoing particularly on the function of affective discharge, partly because this is sometimes overlooked or underestimated, but primarily because it seems able to make an important contribution to the analysis of psychological factors in religious confession. In order to illustrate further the significance of such discharge in religious confession, we shall now, in conclusion, draw special attention to the value which is ascribed to *spoken words* as an instrument for discharging an inhibited affect. We have noted that Janet regarded the words spoken during a patient's confession as an instrument of the kind. Breuer and Freud did the same, along with all other advocates of the cathartic method. Those two perceived that speech can function as a surrogate for the action which would be the adequate expression of the inhibited affect. And, where a secret is involved, one kept deep within the patient and perhaps dangerous to his mental health because of its unconscious character, revealing it in speech constitutes in itself precisely the adequate expression. Breuer believed that during confession—using the term in its real meaning—such an adequate expression of a previously repressed and emotionally charged secret takes place. Furthermore, we have seen that Kronfeld and Kretschmer—to give two examples— considered words spoken, especially when forming part of a confidence to someone regarded with trust, as a "psycho-motor outlet" for an inhibited affect. And the psychiatrist A. Muthmann declared that, as a medium of discharge, "the muscular process of speaking" can produce abreaction equally well as other kinds of muscular movement.[31]

Of course it is a generally known fact that strong feelings often find expression in "a stream of excited words". Language as simply the ability of speech to release feelings has been interestingly illustrated

---

[31] A. Muthmann, "*Psychiatrisch-theologische Grenz-fragen*", in *Zeitschrift für Religions-psychologie*, 1908; p. 61.

by the psychology of language. Herrman Gutzmann was a psychologist who devoted exhaustive research to such matters. [32] He remarked that language is by origin nothing else than the discharge (*"Entladung"*) of an inner tension. It is expressive movement, and thus primarily an instrument of discharge. To begin with merely a means of expressing emotions, it developed into a way of communicating thought. "In spite of that", said Gutzmann, "throughout the whole of life emotional stimulus (*Erregung*) remains stronger for manifestation in language and has far more influence than the stimulus which arises through imitation or that which accompanies thought". The primary part played by emotion becomes apparent when we consider the psychological development of children : crying is their first expression of feeling. It emerges, too, from an examination of speech disorders. In dumbness or aphasia, the sounds or small words (interjections) uttered have proved to express strong affects : they are all that remains of the ability to speak. "Emotion is the father of language". And language is particularly suited to serve as a kind of safety valve for inner affective tension because of the muscular apparatus which it sets in motion. Gutzmann maintained that the various parts of the speaking apparatus constitute the best and most utilized means of expressing affects. This applies particularly to the respiratory and mimetic muscles and the vocal cords.

From Gutzmann's analysis into the original nature of speech and the way it manifests powerful feelings, excellent support is provided for the idea adopted in psychiatry that confession discharges affects which create tension. The speech apparatus is surely in itself one of the most natural means of expressing affects. This fact confirms the belief that we must regard affective discharge as an important element in the act of confession, and we thus make a considerable advance towards answering the question of what causes the feelings of relief which people so often say that they experience after confession.

As our next task here, we shall attempt to shed more light on the part abreaction plays in confession.

---

[32] H. Gutzmann, *Psychologie der Sprache* : *Handbuch der vergleichenden Psychologie*, ed. by G. Kafka; vol. II (Munich, 1922). Cf. O. Dittrich, *Die Probleme der Sprachpsychologie* (Leipzig, 1913); p. 10.

PART THREE

APPLICATION OF PSYCHIATRIC TEACHINGS
TO THE PSYCHOLOGY OF CONFESSION

CHAPTER EIGHT

AFFECTIVE DISCHARGE IN CONFESSION

In our survey of the need to confess and receive absolution, we witnessed evidence that confessants often find themselves in a state of great tension before making their confessions, also that by submitting to confession they gain release from their tension and enjoy feelings of relief and joy. In our view, the release experienced confirms the previous state of tension. We shall here study the tension more thoroughly; we shall observe how it manifests itself before and during confession, and try to throw further light on how it is created. In giving an explanation of how it can be dispelled, we shall try to apply what psychiatry has taught us about abreaction.

In the investigation by Georg Wunderle (described in the first chapter here) concerning the psychology of repentance, good examples are provided of how devout Catholics feel towards confession and their responses to it. The thirty subjects used in that survey had to answer a questionnaire where, essentially, the questions aimed at establishing how remorse sets in, how it shows itself during the special examination of conscience which precedes confession, and what means are offered to restore the penitent's peace of mind.

Naturally, when examining the answers we should bear in mind what belongs to the spiritual exercises which a pious Catholic undertakes before confession, and we should be attentive to the fact that suggestion may be received from the question itself by the person answering. But even when regarded with such reservations, a good deal in the answers appears to be of great value. In many cases, the distinctive and expressive phrases used make it clear that genuine and spontaneous experiences are involved. Most of the subjects explain that their compunction over fairly serious moral lapses sometimes amounts to true anxiety and depression. For instance, No. 8—who alludes in his answer to a period of scrupulosity, and who is evidently of a highly sensitive nature—says : "The real worry ends in depression but reappears now and then as veritable anxiety— namely, when occasioned by outward causes : spiritual reading, and so on". The anxiety lingers until the person becomes tired out. And No. 17 speaks about worry and dejection that last for days and weeks.

These feelings are often accompanied by definite physical symptoms which recall those characteristic of certain neuroses. Most of Wunderle's subjects say that they feel a kind of oppression with constraint across the chest, palpitations, agitation and irritability. No. 6 speaks about nervous perturbation accompanied by poor appetite and sleeplessness. And No. 8 describes his physical symptoms in the following way : "It is, with the veritable anxiety, as if my blood retreated; it's like a fading away and inward trembling; a depression comes on, at the first moment almost like stinging, like a blow on the heart. There is a jolting, an alarm of the entire organism : this shows in the face, by paleness, by woe and melancoly in the gaze and on the features". And mental powers are seriously impeded : "Everything stagnates; I become monosyllabic, absent-minded; my imagination and memory are as if paralyzed, inert; my thoughts are impoverished". And everything he undertakes requires the strongest effort of will. Here, an extraordinarily sensitive person has been speaking, a man with the ability to give his feelings nuanced and vivid expression. No. 24, a nun, answers in a similar way : "My physical condition is greatly altered by remorse". Her symptoms are "nervous agitation, shortness of breath, conspicuous paleness, lack of appetite". She says : "It is like a kind of paralysis of my physical and psychic forces".

And during the special act of contrition which, according to Catholic confessional practice, is to precede the confession itself, the remorse of many subjects involves intense feelings.[1] Thus, No. 2 relates : "Really, I always feel at least a strong commotion of the mind, which often expresses itself in weeping and consequently I try to hide it". And No. 17 : "The thought of the impending confession exhausts me mentally and physically, and, because of great spiritual distress over certain lapses, I am even inclined to weep".

Wunderle's material contains some further examples which show what a strain the self-examination can be for a devout Catholic and indicate that he finds himself under great tension at this stage. But he may also experience that the special act of contrition brings feelings of relief and consolation, results in calmness, as if the burden of sin were lifted from him. In a number of cases, the examination of conscience entails a discharge of guilty and remorseful feelings. But it

---

[1] See the answer to Question 14. Some things asked here are whether any distinct sensations occur during the act of contrition, if the thought of the approaching confession arouses particular feelings, and whether there is a disposition to give remorse outward expression, for instance, by weeping.

is fairly significant that many of the people who state that they have such experiences after the exercise in question do not, in any case, feel wholly pacified before they have gone through confession. Probably, No. 9 can be regarded as a rather typical representative of those who gain a beneficial effect from self-examination. He says that repentance taxes him both mentally and physically, and that it can also calm him temporarily. He adds : "Without the good, concluding confession, however, I wouldn't be completely tranquil". The fact that contrition can produce such an effect of relief at all is evidently connected with its being part of the penance sacrament; as such it is undertaken on the natural assumption that it will be followed by confession and absolution.[2] One receives the impression that the contrite penitent carries his remorse on from the examination of conscience to his confession, where it manifests itself anew. Of course his repentance must be clearly evident in the presence of his confessor for the confession to be accepted at all.

It seems to be very usual in Catholic quarters for the decisive discharge of feelings to come during the act of confesssion itself, and there find outlet in words and gestures. Half the subjects of Wunderle's survey expressly state that confession is the best means of restoring them to calm and peace of mind after the anxiety and dejection produced by remorse. And the fact that confession is thus regarded as a fundamental method of regaining tranquility and ease of conscience allows us to suppose that it involves expression of powerful remorse, and that a discharge of psychic tension takes place thereby. This assumption is confirmed by direct evidence from a number of Wunderle's subjects. No. 3 gives a very forceful account of the tension he feels when facing confession; and he tells how it is dispelled during the act of confession : "I can describe my state best if I say that there is a prickling in all my fingers. I want to stretch,

---

[2] The answer given by No. 26 to Question 5 seems typical (p. 44). He says that a certain remorse and anxiety remain "until I have worked myself up to the decision to confess in just a certain way. This decision, which sometimes comes only after a couple of days, is joined with unquestionable trust in God's mercy and gives me back my ease of conscience even before the confession takes places". But evidently No. 22 does not agree at all to the difference between remorse before and during confession. She answers : "For the most part, a sense of relief begins *after the confession*". The experience of the remorse having a liberating effect goes together with the dogmatic outlook. Saint Thomas's view was that absolution and sacramental grace are efficacious with *contritio*. So contrition anticipates absolution.

to move in all directions, as if my clothes were too tight".[3] Also : "Weeping and similar outbursts very seldom occur before confession; they come easier in the confessional and after confession". Another subject, No. 15, says that she does not undergo the stress of her situation as penitent sinner until during the act of confession : "Actually, I feel oppressed and nervously upset first when I have to confess my moral lapse in confession". And No. 17 expresses in a direct way how much it means to speak about guilt-laden memories in confession; she says that the worry and depression caused by remorse— which with her may last for days and weeks—can never be stilled unless she is able to speak completely about what lies on her mind or confess it.

Thus, to Catholics confession presents itself as a reliable means of gaining peace in struggles of conscience. Penitents who go to confession with powerful feelings of guilt find that the psychic tension caused by these subsides. Many of Wunderle's subjects provide evidence of this.

One of them says : "Confession gives the awareness that now everything is removed again, however and whatever it may have been". That awareness, with the relief and reassurance it brings, is always present in the understanding, for the most part also present to the emotions (in the form of calm and peace)". And another declares : "After a good confession I am in the best conceivable spirits, almost overflowing with peace and happiness". All the physical sensations resulting from remorseful nervous anxiety disappear. No. 22, for instance, says : "The feeling of relief that begins after confession promotes physical well-being".

The subjects we encounter in Wunderle's survey are convinced and pious Catholics who go habitually to confession. To a great extent, their devotional lives are ordered in accordance with this religious exercise performed at regular intervals. If we take the quantitative view of sin which prevails in Catholic moral theology, we may in general assume that the quantity of serious sins which must be accounted for at every confession can hardly be very great. Indeed, it is apparent from a number of answers given in the survey that people go to confession without being sure that they have any serious sins at all to confess. This naturally does not prevent a devout person from having a strong sense of general moral inadequacy during

---

[3] G. Wunderle, *op. cit.*; p. 18.

the penance sacrament; the rule applies that piety strengthens feelings of this kind when a person is faced with the demands of Divine Will.

It is obvious, however, that with so-called general confessions, covering the entire previous lives of penitents, we may expect greatly increased remorse and a powerful manifestation of repentance for sins committed; this is particularly the case if the general confessions are made by people who have newly turned to the Church or who wish to enter it as converts. In the over-all examination of their previous lives, penitents of this kind often find that a multitude of guilt-laden memories precipitate over them, forcing them to undergo the limit of what they can endure. As a result of their new faith, they see life in a different light, and their feelings of guilt are thoroughly aroused as consequence. But they now see, too, that it is possible to get rid of their intolerable burden and the strong psychic tension it entails. And they know a liberation and a happiness of which the intensity and vividness seem to come in direct proportion to their previous tension. As a typical example of such experiences gained from Catholic confession, we shall take the penance of the French writer Joris-Karl Huysmans, described by himself. His case may appear rather too extreme to be called typical, but what is regarded there as extraordinary emotional excitation seems to illuminate more clearly essential features of a serious confessional experience.

In his novel *En Route*, Huysmans gives a description of his conversion and return to the Catholic Church of his childhood. The principal character in the novel, Durtal, is Huysman's *alter ego*.[4] As the author was of the naturalistic school, we have particular reason to expect that his portrayal of penance should be faithful and realistic; and in fact it is profoundly marked by the author's own experience. Durtal-Huysmans went, on the recommendation of a priest whom he had consulted, to a Trappist monastery to become a fully practising Catholic. There, he was faced with having to make a confession. He immediately recoiled from the requirement, but nevertheless he prepared for the penance enjoined on him, with its compulsory examination of conscience. In the course of this, he saw his life pass in review. He was tortured and laid low by the immense burden of guilt by which he felt beset. And he was seized both with terror and shame at the

---

[4] For a more thorough account of Huysman's literary position and personal development, see J. Calvet's *Le Renouveau catholique dans la littérature contemporaine* (Paris, 1931); p. 53 ff. As regards Huysman's identification with Durtal of *En Route*, see p. 59.

prospect of having to confess everything to another person—of having "to relate all the disgusting things to another man, to confess his secret thoughts, to relate what he didn't dare repeat even to himself".[5] Anguish took hold of him : he felt loathing for himself and for his whole life. "He was hammered by grief at having lived so long in the sewer; he was doubtful of foregiveness, and did not so much as dare pray for it any longer, he felt so base". He was torn between the demand that he must confess and the impulse to withdraw, simply to abandon penance altogether and flee from the monastery. His conflicting emotions continued to dominate him until, at the appointed time and place, he sat waiting for his confessor. And when the priest had entered the confessional, it was very difficult for him to begin. "Durtal wanted to be dead and thus spared having to speak. But he managed to control himself, to suppress his shame; his lips parted, but nothing came from them. He was still overwhelmed, had his face in his hands; he tried to hold back his tears, which he felt burst forth". With a desperate effort, he finally managed to begin. But he did not get far. He succeeded in giving only a few general intimations of his sins. Then he was completely crushed by his sense of shame; his throat contracted, his body shook, and tears streamed down.[6] Crying to the confessor "I can't! I can't!", he broke off the confession. The priest consoled him, urging him to come back next day and go on with the confession.

Huysmans-Durtal was more collected the second time; he managed to get started on his confession by first enumerating what he thought were minor and rather common sins : "insufficient love for his neighbour, calumny, hatred, hasty judgements, injustices, falsehoods, vanity, anger and so on". Thereafter followed more serious sins and those peculiar to Durtal himself—and with these he obviously came close to being overcome, as on the previous day, by his feelings. He had great trouble in controlling himself and holding back his tears. "Durtal was about to be suffocated by his disgust; the confession of his nefarious actions cost him a terrible effort". When he believed that he had confessed everything and felt for a moment that he could breathe freely, he was struck by still another dreadful memory:

---

[5] *En Route* (Paris, undated : prefaced edition dated August, 1896); p. 219. The description of preparations for confession and the confession itself are in pp. 216-239.

[6] "*Il s'étrangla et les larmes contenues partirent; il pleura, le corps secoué, la figure cachée dans les mains*". (He choked, and the restrained tears sprang forth; he wept, his body shaking, his face hidden in his hands. Page 220.)

how he had once become guilty of sacrilege by taking part in a "black mass". Yet again he was laid low, but finally, with great exertion, he stammered forth confession of that crime, too. When the confessor considered that, through his questions, he had gained a full confession, a penance was imposed on the sinner and then absolution granted, at last. Raising his arms, "his eyes lifted towards Heaven", the priest pronounced "the powerful phrase that breaks bonds; and the three words *Ego te absolvo,* uttered in a slower and louder voice, fell on Durtal, who trembled, his head deeply bowed". The penitent felt "incapable of collecting himself, of understanding himself; he knew only one thing but that very clearly : Christ was personally present, was there close to him on that seat, and he found no words to thank him and wept, bent under the great sign of the cross that the monk made above him".

It might be objected that this description by a practised writer of what he had gone through personally contains literary additions and improvements, and is a dramatization of what was in fact a simpler experience. But the account of a tormenting conscience and great tension during the act of confession has unmistakable veracity, and there seems every reason to take all the details as emanating from something genuinely lived through.

In Catholic circles it is regarded as very unusual that devout people give so complete an account as Huysmans did of what they have undergone during confession. Reverence for the Blessed Sacrament would seem to impose certain restrictions. It is more usual to receive from the recently-converted evidence of a rather general kind about what confession has meant to them—even if this, too, is not provided very often. But such statements, intended to show that confession has brought feelings of relief and spiritual exaltation, possess great value. They are tokens of the taut state in which penitents have previously found themselves and denote the emotional strife that their effort to settle with the past has entailed.

Charles de Foucauld exclaimed "What a blessed day !" at thought of his first confession to Father Huvelin : it signified for him the beginning of his life as a devoted Catholic. It marked the end of his struggle to acquire firm faith and be done with his life outside the Church. And his confession obviously took place under strong emotional tension.[7]

---

[7] Charles de Foucauld, *Écrits spirituels*; p. 82 : "*Quel jour béni, quel jour de bénédiction !*"

Catholic converts often regard their first confession as Foucauld did his. The Danish author Johannes Jørgensen, for instance, spoke of his first confession as his real conversion. He felt eased and transformed when he left the confessional. In his diary he wrote : "Sensation of happiness. Fullness of faith. Long turn in the sunshine". He had shed his old life like a worn-out garment; he felt renewed and filled with strength.[8]

Oxford Group confession is comparable to that of newly converted Catholics because again there is question of submitting the confessant's previous life to general scrutiny. Much evidence has been given of the beneficial effect produced by confession. In Harold Begbie's book we find the sense of relief described as an almost physical sensation : "The feeling of this [confession] was not, as I should have thought, one of shame and disgrace..., on the contrary, it was one of tremendous relief. That in itself surprised me. I had the distinct sensation that one gets in dropping a heavy load from the shoulders— a feeling of expansion and lightness".[9] Kitchen made a similar report on the experience gained from the confession which he and his wife made to each other. "When, however, we told each other fully and freely the kind of people that we really were—the kind of things we really did and thought—when we took off the masks we had worn through seventeen years of married life and stopped pretending to each other to be something that we were not—we each directly felt an acute and actual sense of physical release, as though some thousand pounds had fallen from our shoulders".[10] But also emanating from Oxford Group quarters come statements of exhaustion. For instance, a convert—"formerly a soldier under Ludendorff"—said of his reactions after confession, in a book relating conversions through the Oxford Group movement : "From that moment I was noticeably relieved, though also physically worn out".[11] The amount of psychic

---

[8] J. Jørgensen, *Mitt Livs Legende* (The Legend of my Life : Copenhagen, 1918); vol. IV, p. 82. And an eminent Swedish convert, Claes Lagergren, related of his feelings after his first confession : "I was not the same man. Joyous, unutterable happiness flowed through me. I had never felt so happy—and I would never know later such wonderful, liberated happiness as I felt that morning". (C. Lagergren, *Mitt livs minnen*— Memories of my Life : Stockholm, 1925; vol. IV, p. 270 ff.)

[9] Begbie, *op. cit.*; p. 98.

[10] V. C. Kitchen, *op. cit.*; p. 100.

[11] *Ermatinger Tagebuch*. A similar example can be cited on the Catholic side. Stating with force his experiences of confession, a French writer of the seventeenth century,

energy expended shows what exertion the emotional struggle during confession has involved.

Our description of the mental tension experienced before and during the act of confession, also of the relieved feelings which follow it, plainly reveals that the discharge of a pressure or a tension is involved in Christian confession. That brings us to psychotherapeutic abreaction and what we have learned on the subject. In the act of confession, too, a discharge of emotionally intense memories appears to take place. Here the painful memories are designated as sins by confessants—which is to say that they are offences against the code of behaviour founded on religion. Their emotional charge can, as we have seen, be very strong. Affects here are described as guilt feelings or remorse. They may be attached to isolated memories in the past. But they may also be directed at an entire previous way of life and its values. Very often the two tendencies seem to combine, so that remorse for separate deeds spreads to include the whole trend of the will involved, and the sins are then considered to spring from this.

Affects of guilt or remorse appear to call for closer examination. By careful analysis we should gain a somewhat clearer insight into the nature of different tensions and a better understanding of how they drive people to make confession and even incite the change of heart which then appears.

The character of remorseful affects can vary greatly. According to prevailing Catholic theology, true remorse—*contritio*—is defined by the phrase established at the Tridentine meeting : "suffering of the spirit and detestation of the sin committed, with the intention not to sin further".[12] Of the three elements here, the particular aim with the first two is to state what the emotional properties of remorse are : pain and disgust. And the aim with the last is to emphasize that the will enters into remorse. According to Catholic theology, this is the principal thing in *contritio*; indeed, contrition should be regarded as wholly an act of volition.[13]

Pierre Grenier, said that he left the confessional "weak and staggering" from the wounds, he had received from the devil ("*du démon*") but filled with a true and earnest desire to remain faithful to God in the future. (Bremond; vol. IX, p. 117, note 1.)

[12] "*Contritio*...animi dolor *ac* detestatio *est de peccato commisso cum* proposito *non peccandi de cetero*". (Denzinger, *Enchiridion*; No. 897, p. 294.)

[13] See, for example, the Catholic definition of remorse in the article on "*Reue*" in *Lexikon der Pädagogik*, edited by E. Roloff (Freiburg-im-Breisgau, 1915); vol. IV. Wunderle, too, strongly emphasized the part of volition in remorse and called special

Clearly, the Catholic definition just given hits on essential factors in genuine remorse. This is shown by Wunderle's survey, for one thing—even if the affects reported there are of greater variation and cannot be fitted entirely under the headings of pain and disgust. For instance, fear and anger are advanced as remorseful feelings.[14] In any case, one might object that it is scarcely remarkable if Wunderle's subjects, being pious Catholics, should adjust their remorse, and their answers to the investigator's questions in accordance with the criteria for *contritio* established by the Church. But this objection in no way prevents us from regarding the answers as essentially the expression of genuine and spontaneous remorse. That they must be so is confirmed by the simple reflection that the Church's definition of contrition naturally has at its core a long experience of how genuine remorse truly manifests itself. Then, too, of course the spontaneity of statements about guilt feelings is shown by the circumstance pointed out : they will not fit completely into the authoritative definition of remorse. On only one point can the regularizing effect of this on the subjects be said to emerge clearly—on the demand for a special resolution not to sin further. Here we may observe how the statements comply with the norm, and in an outward, sometimes almost reluctant way. The requirement that a conscious resolve should be made, that it should be a detached and particular element in penitence, does not really correspond to the actual experience of remorse; it is evidently added for pedagogical reasons. The special resolution has the character of a solemn promise made by the penitent before the highest authority, a promise which is to give him support in his future way of life. But statements from a number of Wunderle's subjects confirm that the resolve truly is part of, or included in, remorse. For instance, Subject 16 says : "Remorse and resolve are so much a part of each other that usually I especially consider the resolution once more *solely for the sake of form*".[15] And Subject 21 states : "In my remorse I am aware that my will turns against the sin committed; however, I always make particular further statement of this in the

---

attention to the resolution as an act in itself, concluding the entire spiritual process. "*Mit ihm ist die conversio, die Bekehrung innerlich zum vollkommenen Abschluss gebracht*". (Wunderle, *op. cit.*; p. 5.)

[14] In answer to Question 14, Wunderle's subjects give an account of their feelings during repentance. These are somewhat undefined ones of uneasiness, dissatisfaction, dread, and also chiefly the following : pain, shame, repugnance, disgust, terror and anger.

[15] Wunderle, *op. cit.*; p. 34. Our italics.

good resolution". And Subject 29 makes the following reflection : "Remorse and resolve do not really seem two different things, for a person cannot return to God without turning away from sin".[16] Of special interest, too, is a statement of Subject 30 : "For the most part, after a moral lapse has been committed the reproaches of conscience remain so fixed in the mind that, besides the feelings mentioned, an opposition of the will comes to consciousness, when this is still unexpressed in the good resolution".[17]

These statements show with all desirable clarity that remorse itself contains the urge to an act of volition directed against sin.[18] The strong affects in remorse—pain or grief aroused by the sin and detestation for it—have an active tendency which is the driving force behind the act of will. This force, existing in the affects and impelling towards a definite goal, has been given particular illustration by the English psychologist A. F. Shand.[19] He considered the so-called simple emotions, such as sorrow and disgust, to be each a system consisting of three elements : there is the quality of the emotion itself; there is factor of knowledge, even if this be vague; and there is at least one instinctual drive which seeks to attain its goal by means of a certain behaviour. The emotion here serves to support the instinct and promote its aim. Shand said that grief involves an instinct to seek aid. In origin, wailing and weeping have the instinctive purpose of summoning help when people are hard pressed. Loathing contains the instinct to thrust aside what is unpleasant, to get rid of what causes pain. It follows that sorrow is the more passive emotion, merely signalling that the person is in distress and cannot extricate himself from the situation; detestation is more active, an expression of the person's attempt to struggle out of his dilemma by himself. The grief in remorse is concentrated on the sin committed. Thus, it is often directed against the person's own ego, and it evinces itself as self-dissatisfaction because of the incapacity or weakness which has brought a betrayal of the ideal that the person has set up for himself or at least caught sight of. Grief may give place to loathing

---

[16] G. Wunderle, *op. cit.*; p. 48.

[17] *Ibid.*; p. 50.

[18] Cf. the paper by Martha Moers "*Zur Psychopathologie des Reueerlebnisses*" in *Zeitschrift für pädagogische Psychologie*, 1926; p. 257 ff. The same view is there asserted.

[19] A. F. Shand, *The Foundation of Character* (2nd edition London, 1926). Cf. J. Elmgren's article "*Emotioner och sentiment*" in *Psykologisk pedagogisk uppslagsbok*, I (Stockholm, 1943).

and anger, and with this the remorse becomes more actively concentrated. The loathing here contains an instinct to remove what has caused the affects, and the anger includes a strong tendency—aggressivity—to struggle against the reasons for regret and what causes the anger itself.[20]

Naturally, with some people the passive aspect of remorse may predominate, and with others the active side is to the fore, depending on their temperament. In passive cases we encounter depressive states; in active ones there are excitations. A singular vacillation between extremes in either direction appears to be characteristic of revivalist movements with an ecstatic tendency, such as Laestadianism.

In that movement, as in all those where preaching lays down the law and emphasizes punishment, dread plays a great part in the situation of the repentant sinner. And in Catholic theology it is a minimum requirement that the sinner should have developed a feeling of dread. A lesser form of remorse, *attritio*, derives from fear of punishment in Hell. It is obvious that such fear, which here drives people to confess, is by no means the equivalent of real remorse; but it can give rise to this and, as we have seen from Wunderle's survey, may also be included as a factor in more developed remorse. Dread, with the instinct to flee which it entails, has in it an impulse to move away from punishment of the sin; thus it impels the sinner into an attempt at eliminating what there is reason to punish : the sin itself.

Our investigation of the confessant's reactions before and during confession and of the affects which govern him will have made it clear enough that great similarities exist between confession and the elements behind it, on the one hand, and, on the other the abreaction of withheld or confined affects which we have seen is of crucial importance in certain cases under psychotherapeutic treatment. The reason for the effect of abreaction is, in our view, that it releases an affective tension which arose because certain highly charged experiences or memories had been repressed or otherwise removed from the control of consciousness; the affects were thereby hindered from finding

---

[20] The French psychologist Georges Dumas has commented on a type of grief which is close to anger. He distinguished between passive and active sorrow. In the latter, reactions appear which are characteristic of anger. They express revolt against causes of the affliction. (G. Dumas, "*Les Emotions*" in *Nouveau traité de psychologie*, Paris, 1932; vol. II, p. 421.)

normal expression, or the memories prevented from gradually losing their emotional quality by the action on them of consciousness or assimilation.

In our opinion, what takes place in confession and the confessant's situation is of a similar kind. The confessant very often experiences a tension caused by remorseful affects; these are attached to the sins, or to the memories of culpable deeds, which he knows that he has committed. Recollection of the sin, along with the remorse bound to it, may have been repressed from consciousness and formed a kind of affective memory which, from the psychological point of view, is similar in nature to those traumatic memories whose existence and ways of working we know of from psychiatry.

Developments leading to the confessional situation may be thought to have come about as follows. When the person had committed the action later to be avowed in confession, he regretted it and felt an impulse to make amends and efface the matter by seeking pardon. But the affects of remorse, which may have declared themselves with force, were not allowed expression. The moral attitude or norms then governing the person would not permit it. So the feelings of remorse, together with recollection of the event, have, figuratively speaking, been shoved down to a lower level of the mind, where the "complex" has been more or less isolated from consciousness. But the repression has not been completely successful. In a good many cases the affective memory has asserted itself by giving rise to nervous anxiety and tension, perhaps without the person being aware of what caused them, or the memory has made itself felt by emerging now and then as twinging of conscience; it provides an element of worry, latent but easily brought to life and then requiring great effort to restrain. It will have become apparent from examples given of mental tension before and during confession, and not least from our analysis of the various affects in remorse, that those affects often act as very strong psychic forces. In connection with confession, the affective tension can come to the fore in real earnest. It is thus possible to bring the more or less unconscious memories properly into view, present them clearly, and let remorse have full scope. This may take place systematically as in the Catholic examination of conscience, or in a more formless way as with non-Catholics who experience a great need to confess; but it occurs above all during confession itself— which is proved by the often exceedingly evident way emotional intensity there manifests itself.

The opposition usually erected against remorse—against bringing it to the surface and confessing the guilt-laden memories—has been overwon because the religious object in view, which is at the same time the highest moral authority, has come so close to the person, has appeared at once so inviting and so liberating; the person could not withdraw. The memories charged with affects of remorse are brought forth; often while the person is in a state of crisis, his tension reaches a culmination and is discharged, being vented through his movements and words as he confesses. The "congestion" in his emotional life (caused by the repression of memories), which has produced the latent centre of tension and anxiety, gains an outlet.

Thus far, the parallel between psychiatric abreaction and confession seems valid. But a factor appears in confession which is peculiar to it, one connected with its religious-ethical character. In the psychotherapeutical methods, discharge was thought to concern only the affects attached to certain experiences in the past. In confession, however, it seems to concern also remorse not originally attached to the experiences but developed only at a later stage. We might very well think that a misdeed involved produced very little feeling of guilt when it was committed, and that the feeling was aroused by later influence on the person. In general, as regards true Christians and people with sensitive consciences, we can establish that actions in conflict with the moral code leave guilt-laden memories behind. But with others, whose consciences are deadened or shrunken, we may assume that a lesser and perhaps very slight affective burden is suffered. When their consciences are awakened under religious-ethical influence, remorse over certain actions in the past should be created; it will find expression and as a rule extend to cover a whole tendency of the will. But in general there is probably question of remorse for previous deeds being developed and of the guilt feelings attached to them—feelings of which the person has earlier been unconscious or only dimly aware—coming to the fore. Naturally, even when the the remorse is of recent creation, strong affective tension is aroused. This constitutes an important element in the crisis-filled process of conversion, and it presses to gain an outlet.

Whether the guilt feelings and remorse expressed in confession were originally attached to certain recollections, or whether the remorse over past deeds has for the most part been created recently by new experience and a new attitude (a distinction that may be assumed to exist but which is not usually very sharply defined), the affects of remorse are discharged during the act of confession. As we have seen, those affects may often find eruptive expression there—for instance, in the form of weeping and wailing. By such means and especially through the words spoken in confession—speech being, as we could observe, a particularly sensitive instrument for the discharge of emotion—the high tension in remorse is relieved. A feeling of liberation, ease or joy comes on, and fatigue occasionally sets in.

CHAPTER NINE

RESTORING PSYCHIC UNITY: ASSIMILATION

In the previous chapter we tried to go some way towards explaining the sense of relief felt after confession : we did so by giving an account of the emotional discharge which then takes place in confessants who seriously suffer effects of remorse and the mental tension aroused thereby. It has seemed of importance to emphasize particularly that side and function of confession because people may not always have their eyes open to it. Cases can be found of people who interpret the so-called cathartic method as narrowly intellectualized and who therefore criticize the psychoanalytical method on the grounds that it does not sufficiently admit affective discharge, or abreaction; similarly, it appears that people sometimes want to construe confession in a too rationalized way and to regard it, apart from its purely religious function, as primarily an excellent means of gaining clear perception into the confessant's personal problems—as a way to self-knowledge. Of course, confession also serves that purpose. True self-knowledge ought indeed to result from it. But while establishing this, we must not disregard at all the nature of confession as an instrument for discharging the great tension in affects of remorse.

Actually, the two functions—abreaction and the winning of clarity and insight—run parallel to at least some extent. The intellectual function involved strengthens the value of the emotional discharge. We encounter here a similar psychic activity to that met with in psychiatry under the name "assimilation" : dissociated elements in the psyche reassociate; mental unity and harmony are restored. With the action of assimilation, the person again achieves mastery over himself and is once more in a condition to control personal experiences, tendencies and inclinations which previously, having withdrawn from his conscious personality and his will, pursued an independent course damaging to his mental health. In this chapter we shall give an outline of how psychiatrists believe that the assimilative process takes place, and we shall attempt to apply our analysis to the psychology of confession.

What there is question of here can be made plain by a simple illustration. When a well-balanced person finds himself somewhat troubled because of a grief or worry, or because personally offended, he may feel severely depressed for a time, but he gradually gets over his misfortune. He overcomes it by submitting the matter to sound reason. He "talks sense" to himself and can master his trouble. In the course of daily life and work, what is injurious to him in the experience wears off; the recollection becomes integrated with the normal context of his mind, becomes neutral and does not disturb his peace. If such a well-balanced person should be the object of, for instance, a personal affront, he will not react with a reprisal; his good sense places the event in perspective and tells him that the offence is unjust, incompatible with what he knows to be his own worth. Thus, he can very well endure the attack, which does not strike home, and he regards it as "beneath his dignity" to reply in kind. Here an experience, perhaps affect-laden at the initial moment, has had its force dissolved by the influence of reasoning, has become the object of associative reworking.

As we observed, it is characteristic of the neurotic that he cannot perform such a mental task. For him an experience may have so strong an affective charge that he cannot get over it. Janet spoke about "fixation symptoms". The neurotic remains fixed in the affect-laden experience. He begins over and over the work of adjusting himself but never succeeds in getting past the starting point. We saw an example of this in Janet's case of the girl who was struck by grief on her mother's death—or, more accurately, refused to be struck by grief and instead remained fast in the situations that immediately preceded the fateful event. Her symptoms consisted of the actions, constantly repeated, which she had carried out when her mother lay dying. In the case of Breuer's Anna O. we may regard the symptoms as having been similar. She did not emerge from her emotional experience. Her symptoms revealed that, unconsciously, she still felt that she was nursing her father. The cases described by Brown showed the same pattern. In Freud's view, mental illness and the formation of symptoms do not originate merely from fixation on an intrusive experience; there is also a return to an earlier stage in the development of the personality, to childhood with its unconscious incestuous desires.

It is now believed that when a doctor attempts to remove such a fixation on an event in the past, to nullify the tension arising from it and resolve the dissociation in the patient's mental life, a curative effect is achieved by rendering conscious the unconscious reasons for mental illness. Along with the affective discharge which then occurs, the experience must be rationally worked through, so that the dissociation will be ended for good. All the psychiatrists cited here agree on this. They maintain, too, that the work of bringing what is hidden to consciousness and that of logical reasoning must be carried out by the patient himself. Janet placed strong emphasis on this psychic activity in the patient and on the healing that can be brought about by mobilization of rational powers. Freud likewise was most anxious to stress that the patient himself must discover the connection between his previously unconscious experiences and his symptoms. The patient is thus, one might say, induced to build anew his tumbled down moral edifice, incorporating there stones that have fallen from the walls. In other words, the treatment must achieve assimilation of the experiences severed and repressed from consciousness : it must re-establish mental wholeness and unity.

Attention should be drawn in this connection to the well-known "client-centered therapy" of Carl Rogers. Of its essence an authoritative survey has said : "An effective therapist does not change the patient, the patient changes himself". It was further remarked : "The learning that occurs in therapy is self-discovery".[1] (We shall have occasion to return later to Roger's method.)

Evidently, in Christian confession, too, assimilation may occur of previously unelucidated experiences from the past. The sins confessed can of course be regarded as such experiences. But before we draw a parallel between psychiatric assimilation and what occurs in confession, we must answer the question : Do we really encounter unconscious memories in confession, as is assumed by the psychiatric methods which we have got to know ?

As regards this question, it should first be noted that a difference of conception clearly exists between the psychoanalytical school and other psychiatrists as to the degree in which memories that engender mental disorders are unconscious. Freud and his followers have regarded complexes as entirely isolated from ordinary consciousness. All the devices that their method provides are required in order to summon the complexes up to consciousness. However, according to other psychiatrists—it was the view of Pierre Janet, for instance—the pathogenic memories do not necessarily exist in such complete confinement as the psychoanlysts imagine. The memories may be more or

---

[1] Ford and Urban, *op. cit.*; p. 400.

less conscious. The difficulty of bringing them to the surface is related
to the degree to which they are unconscious. Naturally, it is also
possible that an experience with pathological result may be entirely
conscious.

Can the assimilation of previously unconscious memories take
place in confession ? Scarcely, it would seem, if the term "unconscious"
is interpreted in the psychoanalytical way. But if by "unconscious
memories" we mean memories that are certainly not present in the
confessant's mind when he decides to make his confession, yet ones
which may be called up by his concentrating thoroughly on the past,
then we can evidently speak of unconscious memories arising during
confession itself or during the scrupulous examination of conscience
connected with it. Claes Lagergren, the Swedish convert mentioned
earlier here, was doubtless reporting a common experience when he
wrote of the self-examination before his first confession : "I had made
the examination of conscience. No, I couldn't relate all that. Why
had my memory become so good ? I recalled everything—all that I
had done since I was a child. All that was banished for ever to the
darkest corner of oblivion had wakened up and was reaching out
pale and ghostly hands towards me".[2]

Speaking from his own experience, the Danish psychiatrist H. I.
Schou said about discovering unconscious memories : "Perhaps a
person is aware of an elementary sin or mistake. But during confession
unconscious sins which have exerted pressure come forth. It is as in an
operation : a simple abscess is found, but more abscesses lie behind
this—until at last the centre of infection is found".[3]

The relationship between confessor and confessant, with the feeling
it should have of attachment, provides a favourable atmosphere
for self-examination. Charles E. Curran says on this : "It is in a way
the counselor's striving to understand that intensifies the client's
own efforts to understand himself and to communicate and share
with the counselor what he slowly and sometimes torturously is
discovering about himself. As another client puts it, 'Because you are
trying so hard to understand me, I am urged all the more to want to
explain myself clearly to you and to myself'."[4]

---

[2] C. Lagergren, *op. cit.*; p. 270.

[3] H. I. Schou, "*Skriftemaalets Betydning humant og kristeligt set*" (The Significance of
Confession, from the Human and Christian Points of View), in *Kirke og Kultur*, 1933;
p. 584 f.

[4] "The Counseling Relationship and Some Religious Factors", in *Journal of Counseling Psychology*, 1959; p. 267 f.

We learn from the psychology of memory that what we recall comes to us in accordance with the laws of association. Our memories are bound to those laws, and the process of recollection follows them. But the memories, associatively joined together, do not as a rule emerge in a simple, mechanical way. The associations involved tend in a definite direction, and this is guided by the person's will and attitude. A decisive part in the reproduction of facts which the memory contains is played by need and interest. We saw earlier how modern psychology stresses the function of need in psychic developments. Emphasis has been laid there by, not least, the *gestalt* psychological school. A leader of it, Curt Lewin, stated with reference to our particular question that an association possesses in itself no vital force impelling reproduction. Preparation must be made for its operation, and this depends on an instinctual drive or on an act of will. The eminent French psychologist H. Delacroix has also drawn attention to the function of the person's activity in recollection, to his personal attitude and interest. "The activities dominant at the moment or over a period direct it [recollecting]. It follows changes in the character and variations in the personality".[5]

Similar views are put forward, and illustrated by experiments, by Edward J. Murray in his work *Motivation and Emotion*.[6] Summarizing there, he says: "Thus, it can be seen that motivation and emotion affect how and what we remember and forget". (Page 16.)

We see, then, that the psychologists confirm scientifically the universal experience that recollecting follows the occupations and interests which currently engage the person and by which it is inspired. Concentration on the task at hand and the desire to carry it out arouse the associations required. This general law for mnemonic reproduction applies in confession. A powerful need drives the confessant to get rid of his sins, to reveal everything in order to clear away the old and begin anew. The concentration incited by need or interest provides the confessant with extremely favourable conditions for discovering, during confession, guilt-laden memories which he may long since have forgotten. Naturally, these may also appear during the careful examination of conscience before confession; or the penitent may come on new things after the act of confession which he has not included there.

---

[5] H. Delacroix, "*Les Souvenirs*", in *Nouveau traité de psychologie*; vol. V (Paris, 1936), p. 353.

[6] (New Jersey, 1964); pp. 15-16.

To make clear the power that lies in the concentration of people who come seriously to accounts with themselves as they repent and confess, it should be pointed out that an important psychic factor is in action : the tendency of affects to direct ideas in a definite direction For instance, a person who is struck by severe grief can think about nothing but his sorrow and its cause. Everything that goes through his mind revolves about them. Both his memories and his present experiences are placed in relation to the matter over which he grieves; they are attached to it by what may often be peculiar trains of association. We can assume that, in the same way, affects of remorse which have profoundly moved the confessant compel his ideas to revolve about his guilt-charged memories; thus, he is forced as it were to concentrate on those memories, and also he is enabled to supplement and elucidate them.

From what has been said it is probably clear that the confessant's state facilitates the emergence of forgotten, guilt-charged memories; and we may assume that these come up during confession or in connection with it. But what confessants primarily and most frequently relate are of course their conscious memories, indeed in many cases memories that so fill their consciousness that there seems to be no room for anything else. When the confessant speaks about these memories he obviously performs an intellectual operation of great importance if he succeeds in mastering them and assimilating them in the general context of his mind.

To shed light on what takes place here, we might turn to an analysis of the assimilation process undertaken, in an interesting investigation that attracted much attention, by the American psychiatrist Samuel D. Schmalhausen.[7] His analysis was directed at psychoanalytical treatment and constituted an attempt to explain the psycho-therapeutic effect of assimilation. Schmalhausen did not himself belong to the psychoanalytical school, but as an objective assessor he plainly had a sense for what is of value in its method. He asked himself why the

---

[7] S. D. Schmalhausen, "Is Consciousness Curative", chapter of *Our Changing Human Nature* (New York, 1929); p. 297 ff. Of the investigation by Schmalhausen referred to here, Joseph Jastrow said in his work *The House that Freud Built* (London, 1933) : "This so fundamental query [why bringing to consciousness is a curative process] which gives the turn to the entire practice—namely to bring out the complexes into the light of day and dispel them like ghosts—has, so far as I know, not even been raised by psychoanalysts within the fold, but is admirably discussed by Schmalhausen, a practising psychologist distinctly hospitable to Freudian concepts rationally formulated".

process of rendering matters conscious is curative, and he came to the conclusion that this results from certain elements which he gave as follows : "dramatic objectification, analytic dismemberment, release of tension, realization"—the last being the action whereby a clear general view is gained, an understanding of the whole situation in the mind and the proportions that events assume there.

Objectification means that while under analysis the patient achieves a certain distance from his painful experiences. This he attains by relating the experiences. He describes them again and again during analytical treatment, until by repetition they acquire the character of historical facts and are thus free from their previously strong emotional force. Abreaction is obviously implied here. But there is something more than that to objectification. Language does not serve only as a channel of discharge. It also enables the patient to control his affects through the intellectual function it fulfils in giving a name and supplying definition to an often vague and diffuse experience. By investing what the patient has gone through with words, it gives him insight into what his experiences really signify; and he then has the possibility of struggling against them and mastering them. The term "analytical dismemberment" as Schmalhausen used it denotes the same process, the difference being that with it he wished to draw attention to the distinct positions occupied by individual details in the larger complex. He said that the patient must learn to divide up his emotional situation into small parts. Each part is to receive a name, a linguistic label : it thus acquires the character of a tangible fact and becomes an object in the patient's intellectual sphere. The psychoanalyst helps the patient to achieve a system of linguistic expression which drains away what was originally emotional in his experience and therefore of unpredictable effect. By dominating his experiences intellectually, the patient is able to relax his tension. His conflict, which is a manifestation of tension between different instinctual drives and motives, can be solved by this dramatic objectification and by intellectual analysis. But a new appraisal of values is usually required, and this comes in the course of treatment; it may arrive through the patient's intellectual understanding but also through direct influence from the doctor. He conveys new assessments to the patient and may even turn him into a new personality. This is what psychoanalysts call "after-education".

Successful psychoanalytical treatment leads to "realization" : the gaining of insight, the elucidation of an obscured emotional

situation through understanding of its context and the re-establishment of mental balance. Schmalhausen said that a neurotic mind
contains a living context of experience where all is completely undif-
ferentiated. The whole mental situation there consists of a crowd of
irrational associations. Events, people and things are inextricably
woven together and held fast by a memory of fear, shame or failure.
In such a position, the person must feel that he is the victim of his
emotional memories. As no logic exists in his mind, he cannot bring
to order all that pursues its own course there. He needs help from a
doctor who, by means of technical instructions and judicious advice,
can enable him to gain understanding of his situation; it thus becomes
possible for him to neutralize his painful experiences so that they
interfuse, or are assimilated in a normal, related whole.

It may be remarked of Schmalhausen's reasoning that he seems to
pay very little attention to the fact that the essential work of the
therapist in carrying out a psychoanalytical cure is to get the patient
to remember. According to psychoanalytical theory, of course it is
precisely because memories are unconscious that they are dangerous
and produce the symptoms of mental illness. If this theory is strictly
adhered to, then bringing unconscious memories to consciousness is
itself the curative element in treatment—which Freud certainly
believed. With Schmalhausen, what seem primarily to be at issue as
factors generating neuroses are more or less conscious memories.
Evidently, in his reasoning danger comes not from the unconsciousness
of memories but the lack of balance, of understanding and logical
connection brought on by the affective experiences involved. Of course,
other psychiatrists as well as Schmaulhausen have assumed that
conscious memories, too, can induce mental illness. Because Schmaulhausen's investigation reflects this view, it is of special value in
elucidating the psychological factors that operate when the confessant
speaks about the remorse-filled memories which, even if blurred and
confused by the force of emotion, are more or less conscious.

Obviously, with the memories revealed by a confessant there is
question of "objectification" in the sense worked out by Schmalhausen.
Narrating a guilt-charged and troubling memory to the confessor
serves to clarify this; it becomes a palpable fact which can be regarded
and assessed in the clear light of reason. The thing at issue during
analytical treatment may be conveying to the patient new points of
view on his personal problems, giving him a new gauge of values;
by means of this he can appraise his personal situation and reach a

better solution to his problems than the one which he sought previously and did not attain. The condition required for this new solution is that the patient has gained understanding of his problems and thus views them clearly. In other words, the "objectification" spoken about is demanded. In the same way, for a confessant to reach self-understanding and lucidity a condition is the objectification of his guilt-laden memories and of the deeper motive forces which these manifest. His insight then aids him in solving his problems and difficulties. We shall in what follows illustrate more closely some points that show how such objectification may be regarded as obtainable in confession or joined with confession.

Schmalhausen wished to make repetition a hallmark of psycho-analysis; at the same time he used it to explain how objectification takes place. The patient reiterates again and again his account of the disastrous events which led to mental illness; he thereby divests them of their emotional force and acquires a clear view of their background. Repetition will very probably occur in a similar way during confession. There a description of the same thing may be given from different standpoints. This can be done at the same confession or at successive ones. Obviously, the tendency to repetition is dictated in normal cases by a natural need to allow remorseful feelings further release, also to present still more clearly to rational understanding the circumstances in which the sin was committed. An earlier narration is supplemented as the confessant gives details that he did not happen to think of before and which might shed new light on the previous telling. Or memories that were unconscious or forgotten before have become conscious and require confession.

Both Catholic and Protestant confessors can attest to the existence of this need to reiterate, and add to, a confession already made. The need makes a common appearance in Catholic confessional practice, as could be expected in view of the careful examination of conscience which is strictly demanded both before and during confession, also because of the extreme penalty that an irresponsibly-made confession entails. As was pointed out in a previous chapter, constant preoccupation with sins and brooding over them may easily foster scrupulosity in people of delicate conscience. Such people find it hard to be content with the absolution granted in the penance sacrament; they must drag in doubts about their candour and conscientiousness in a past confession. That noted confessor Charles de Condren wrote to a penitent of the kind : "Be sincere and simple in your confession, and when it is made think no more about how it was made".[8]

But it is certainly false to adjudge all confessants who want to repeat or complete a confession as unhealthily scrupulous. Indeed, instances may be found of confessors who have shown by their practice an understanding that many penitents satisfy a natural need in repeating their confessions. Saint-Cyran got penitents who had particularly grave sins on their consciences to come to confession a number of times before he gave them absolution. And he did this at their own request.[9] He was severe as a confessor, and his penitents evidently had a strong feeling of their own shortcomings in his presence. He compelled them to make an extremely detailed examination of conscience. Faced with his demands here, they felt a need to relieve their guilt further, to search more thoroughly in their memories for sins and become clearer about their entire spiritual situation. The Protestant Blumhardt also sensed a need in his confessants to repeat their confessions. As a rule, he had sinners confess three times. We previously interpreted this arrangement as a means of inculcating the seriousness of confession. But doubtless we are not mistaken in regarding it from this point of view, too : as indication that Blumhardt perceived a need in his confessants to reiterate their confessions so as to investigate their recollections properly and be sure about their spiritual condition.

A further element in the objectification of guilt-laden memories should be noted with regard to the exposition by Schmalhausen. He speaks of "dramatic" objectification in analysis. And it was observable from the report on how William Brown treated war hysteria that objectification may truly take highly dramatic forms of expression, for he allowed the soldiers to act out their affects and dramatize the shocking combat experiences that caused their nervous disorders. Naturally, objectification becomes as dramatic as that only in exceptional cases, but a kind of dramatization is very often involved when a person relates his memories because he gives theatrical emphasis to his own part in the emotionally charged events that he recalls. The mentally ill have a need to act out their personal dramas as on a stage. Schmalhausen plainly believed that here a natural instinct finds its self-evident expression. But the instinctual drive may

---

[8] Bremond, *op. cit.*; vol. III, p. 405 (note 2).

[9] Bremond, *idem*; vol. IV, p. 144 ff.

assume too great proportions and serve an excessive craving for self-assertion. What the patient's self-portrayal then amounts to is self-glorification; this can be construed as compensation for a powerful sense of inferiority.

We may observe the same phenomenon in confession : both a natural self-portrayal and a kind that tends to self-glorification. The latter sort of self-display on the part of a confessant very frequently manifests itself as a need to exonerate himself, perhaps making excuse by laying blame on other people, on circumstances and environment; these have been too much for him, and he implies that he could not have overcome their influence with the best will in the world. François de Sales cited a number of such impure motives that might be found in a penitent, all of them having as purpose to place him in a more favourable light.[10] Saint François said that a penitent may put the mistakes made by others into his confession so as to give himself excuse. Or he can deliver an imposing speech to the confessor and relate a fine story in order to gain esteem and make the confessor believe that he is a person of attainments. Or, while putting up a semblance of scrupulously examining his conscience, he may conceal genuine and serious errors. In all these ways, confessants will surround themselves as with a veil; thus camouflaged, they wish to remain intact, invulnerable, and meanwhile they explain away sins as matters that do not really concern them. The penitent declares his sins to have been caused by a course of events over which he has no influence, and so he himself has no responsibility for them.

All confessors certainly encounter such cases. A Norwegian clergyman, E. Berggrav, gave examples in his book *Fångens själsliv* (The Prisoner's Spiritual Life). He wrote there of prisoners who were seized by emotional religiosity and talked at great length about their sins, thereby seeming to prepare for the expression of great contrition. But when the chaplain agreed that they really were such sinners as they declared themselves to be, they reacted against his interpretation of what they had told him and claimed that they probably were no worse than other people. Berggrav said that they lacked probity. It was as if they had no hold on their personalities and were hiding behind a show of piousness. All their religion, and their confession of sins along with it, was false and empty. They did not want to pass judgement on themselves as earnestly repentant people do; they

---

[10] See J. Viollet, *La Confession* (Paris, 1929); p. 136 f.

resorted to religion merely to obtain a solacing emotional intoxication that lulled their consciences.[11]

Arne Fjellbu, another Norwegian clergyman, reported similar experiences in his work *Själavård* (Cure of Souls). While some of the people concerned here directly excuse themselves, others dissemble their true selves behind a conventionally devout way of talking. Fjellbu said of the former, excusing type : "Another day, we stand before a person who wants very much to talk with a minister of religion, but not about his own sins and guilt. He wants to talk about other people's lives, what others are responsible for. All sinfulness and guilt lie with others".[12] People of the apparently devout type come to the clergyman or priest and speak in a pious manner about their sins, as did certain prisoners of whom Berggrav was chaplain. They talk about their sins in general without stating any definite one. And, evidently, this type is not very uncommon. "All spiritual advisers know from their work many cases of such people who chatter about their great sinfulness without meaning anything by it".

If, in the former type, we meet with a simple form of self-assertion where the person gives himself a prominent position at the expense of others, what we seem to encounter with the latter type is an attempt at getting an official stamp, so to speak, that the person is a believer : hence the superficial and conventional show of piety. In both types there is no genuine remorse or awareness of guilt, and consequently no serious confession can be made. Instead of revealing their true personalities in confession, these people hide themselves by presenting fictional identities which they seek to establish as genuine by inducing the confessor to believe in them.

But there also exists in confession what we may call a normal and legitimate form of self-presentation. What we have then is an account of the part played by the ego when sins were committed, a depiction that does not aim at self-exculpation but manifests the person's natural instinct to evoke vividly his experiences, and his actions and behaviour in connection with them. That such self-dramatization may often come to the fore both in a psycho-therapeutic cure and in confession derives from the fact that the person seeking help is more or less invited to play a rôle.[13] He is given to feel that his listener

---

[11] E. Berggrav, *Fångens själsliv* (Uppsala, 1929).

[12] A. Fjellbu, *Själavård* (Uppsala, 1934); p. 201.

[13] Janet made an interesting comment which is of value from the point of view

has an interest in him, is concerned with his problems and trying to help him. This means that he is freed from his previous isolation and establishes a sense of community with another person. In their fellowship, he is asked to speak openly about what oppresses him. He is permitted to assert himself insomuch as he feels that consideration is being taken of him as a person. He often does this verbosely, repeating himself, twisting and turning his problem in order to analyse it from different points of view, both for his own benefit and the confessor's. Rather frequently, there seems to be a failure both among doctors and the clergy to appreciate an element here that is certainly essential in confession. They speak prematurely; perhaps this is from a misguided desire to uphold their own authority and that of their position. In any case, because of deficient insight into the psychological background of the patient or confessant they prevent him from giving the spontaneous description of his difficulties which would have been of extraordinary, indeed perhaps of decisive, importance in restoring the disharmonious and agitated person to unity and tranquillity. H. I. Schou heavily underlined the mistake and declared: "Most people who receive a confession speak too soon. To listen, listen and again to listen is the point in all mental healing, also in confession and not least there. Young doctors and clergymen speak too soon. Old ones as well, at times; I must practise daily the art of keeping quiet. A train of thought is broken off in the person confessing; an account, long thought through and reasoned out during hours of the night, is interrupted. We must not believe that it is our words which are of significance. The confession itself is a therapy. It is a treatment for a person to vent what lies within to the man who holds his confidence. If we could just learn that and not constantly forget ourselves".[14]

Both the need discussed here to repeat what has been said, to confess over again what is already avowed, and the factor of self-dramati-

---

taken here. It has to do with explaining faith healings and the miraculous experiences of certain mystical religious figures. Janet claimed that the people involved have often lived sad and eventless lives, without interests and real aims, and they have been isolated from others. When a person of the kind is able to emerge from his isolation, when others direct their attention on him, take an interest in him and expect him to have a remarkable experience, then he does have such an experience; this is precisely because the interest centring on him and the role he is allowed to play have produced in him a desire to fill the part. A mobilization of his deepest powers takes place, and the miracle occurs. See Janet's *La Médicine psychologique*; p. 109 f.

[14] H. I. Schou, *op. cit.*; *Kirke og Kultur*, 1933; p. 586. Cf. P. Leo, "*Zur Frage der Seelsorge*", in *Monatschrift für Pastoraltheologie*, 1939; p. 143.

zation may be placed in a larger context and viewed together with the entire self-activity of the confessant. The importance of self-activity in the confessant's situation was stressed in our chapter on confessional method. Its value has, in fact, been emphasized by psychiatric experts. Repetition and self-dramatization are connected with the mobilization of mental powers which the confessant undertakes in order to achieve self-knowledge and inner transformation.

The objectification of affect-laden memories during analytical treatment should have as result that the patient comes to understand the real nature and significance of the experiences injurious to his mental health; and by so doing he ought to be in a condition truly to solve his problems. As we have observed, he may then recover his mental health and balance by himself, without any special intervention on the doctor's part. He has in that case talked reason to himself; his previously insurmountable difficulties have been solved by the arguments that he could summon up through working intellectually from his earlier experience and the bases of values at his own command. He has thus been able to incorporate the disastrous experiences into his personal background; the process of assimilation has taken place, and the unity of his personality is restored.

In other cases the course is not so simple. The doctor must there take measures: using all the personal esteem he has been able to gain with the patient, he must get the latter to solve his problem in a new way, a better way than that attempted before. Various lines may then be pursued by the doctor. The easiest method consists of trying, through logical reasoning, to induce the patient to place his earlier experiences in perspective so that he can effect the process of assimilation. This method may prove successful in some cases. However, for the most part, the serious and often lengthy process of re-training must begin. The work here is that called "after-education" in psychoanalysis. This is generally and rightly regarded as the crucial element there. The aim involved, that of re-training or changing the patient—which is to say, revising or improving his way of evaluating—applies for that matter not only in psychoanalysis but in all therapeutic treatment of neuroses. It does so because in such cases the solution of the patient's problems will as a rule depend fundamentally on his moral conceptions.

The result of objectification in confession proceeds in a similar way. Here it leads to insight into the nature of sins. In some cases perhaps efforts of the confessor—like those of the psychiatrist—must be

directed at getting the confessant to see his alleged sins in proportion.
But as a rule the confessor's efforts do not stop there. While the
ideal thing in psycho-therapeutic treatment is to bring the patient
as quickly as possible to a rational understanding of how his affect-
charged experiences should be placed in perspective—thus in a sense
causing his complex to be argued away—that is not usually the course
in confession; for natural reasons it cannot be what generally occurs.
The confessant himself impels forth an objectification of his sins
and of the instinctual drives from which the sins arise. His deepened
self-knowledge has as result the personal transformation that constantly appeared in his mind during his self-examination, and this
is perceived under the influence of the religious aim he has in view.
Here confession shows certain similarities with the more complicated
after-education of psychoanalysis : with the process that should lead
the patient to new valuations.

We shall see first in what follows how confession can serve to place
sins in their true dimensions; and we shall then study how more
profound self-knowledge is attained and how, where confession is
concerned, this manifests itself.

Confessional practice shows that in some cases the confessor is
justified in trying to induce the penitent to understand the real
nature of his sins and, by sensible argument, demonstrate their true
extent and importance. This is called for with people of extremely
sensitive conscience who are inclined to magnify their sins to an in-
ordinate degree. Catholic confessors have great experience of confessions made by these scrupulous people. In cases of the kind, Linus
Bopp recommended that the confessor should try to tone down the
penitents' remorse over their sins.[15] He said also that the confessor
should pay careful attention to the unconscious instinctual forces
which generally lie behind the exaggerated lamentations and impel
them forth. There may be question here of neurotics suffering from
depressions and compulsive notions. Though it is impossible to find
that they have committed any serious sins, these people feel themselves
to be absolutely worthless and rejected. Bopp believed that their
feelings are often based on a sense of inferiority; the unconscious
causes of this must be brought to light. Fjellbu spoke of the same
thing, but he agreed with Berggrav that the sense of inferiority is

---

[15] L. Bopp, *op. cit.*; p. 90 ff. Cf. O. Schöllig, *op. cit.*; pp. 338-341. Here practical
instructions are given on the handling of scrupulosity by the confessor.

motivated in a good many such cases by religion and originates in the person's humility as he stands before God and faces Absolute Holiness.[16] In such a situation, the confessor's concern must evidently be to comfort the overwhelmed person by speaking to him about God's grace and mercy. But such sources of consolation are sometimes of no avail, and then good sense on the confessor's part bids him—as recommended by Bopp—make an attempt to get the boundlessly disturbed sinner to see his alleged sin in perspective.

Where normal cases are concerned, however, the usual thing seems to be that the priest tries to establish an over-all view of the sin confessed and show its connection with the tendency of the will in the entire personality. The confession then serves to increase self-knowledge. Just as in a psychoanalytical cure the patient is brought to understanding of the instinctual forces that rule him and which are the deepest causes of his symptoms, in confession the penitent comes to true and clear knowledge of the sins he has committed and thereby also to understanding of the deeper forces of his nature that manifest themselves in his individual sins.

In evangelical circles criticism is levelled against the Catholic doctrine on sin and its practical application in the penance sacrament on the grounds that sins are atomized and that too strong emphasis is placed on separate ones, preventing the evangelical view of the whole. But, as in evangelism, the best Catholic confessors attempt to look behind the individual sins to their causes deep in instinctual human life. Bopp was anxious to stress this. Each penitent is examined in accordance with the Ten Commandments and the Five Commandments of the Church. And joined here is examination concerning the seven so-called Deadly Sins. The light shed by the last reveals for analysis the more hidden instinctual forces that lead to sin. "Actually, in the net cast by meditation on the seven Deadly Sins it is not difficult to catch all the movements and tendencies of many-faceted human ambition and there submit them to religious-ethical assessment".[17] And Bopp said that behind all the various impulses, thoughts and

---

[16] A. Fjellbu, op. cit.; p. 203. Cf. J. B. Pratt's portrayal of John Bunyan and David Brainerd in The Religious Consciousness (New York, 1921; pp. 140-147). The two spent an anguished time suffering a sense of general inadequacy and sinfulness; they periodically felt doomed and were harassed by severe compulsive ideas before they were allowed to experience Grace Abounding.

[17] L. Bopp, op. cit.; p. 73.

feelings there lies the person's vanity. All sins are to be regarded as resulting finally from the instinct to love oneself.

The same views were put forward by another Catholic writer, Jean Viollet. He also drew attention to the value of confession in giving a person self-knowledge. "Seen from a purely natural and human point of view, confession is valuable for the way it can help the sinner to know his faults better and can give him the additional force that enables him to change and improve himself".[18] Viollet strongly advocated frequent confession on the grounds that only thereby can true self-knowledge be gained—which is to say that, such confession alone makes it possible to discover the dark tendencies that govern what lies beneath the surface of the mind. "Christians who confess too seldom perceive only vaguely and mistily the multitude of deficiencies in their moral lives. They live, in a way, on the surface of their minds and are incapable of detecting the evil roots, the dispositions to egoism and pride, in the depths."[19] For Viollet, as for many other apologists of confession, not merely are self-love and pride discerned to be the profoundest sources of all sin; they are also, he declared, the basis of opposition to confession.[20] People cherish their prestige too much; they have no wish to reveal their true natures to others and thus humiliate themselves. Consequently they are against confession. Viollet considered—and others are of the same opinion—that the great merit of confession lies precisely in its overcoming a person's pride and forcing him to a humble self-confrontation and a change of heart.

Because confession does this, in principle the comprehensive view of sin is maintained in Catholic circles; but all the same there is no escaping that the minute division of sins often occurs in ordinary confessional practice. What the confessor has of course to do is examine each more serious sin and all the various circumstances involved, for he is deputized by the Church to pass judgement on every offense and, in the form of penance, impose the appropriate sentence. But if the confessor goes sufficiently to the bottom of things, even in ordinary, recurrent confession he can produce a comprehensive idea of the penitent's sins. If the confessant really takes confession in earnest he will himself impel forth such an over-all view. This is the

---

[18] J. Viollet, *op. cit.*; p. 106.

[19] *Ibid.*; p. 120.

[20] Cf. similar reasoning in the Oxford Group movement, cited here in Chapter I, p. 17.

purpose behind profound remorse. *Contritio cordis* must be developed, and this "contrition of the heart" necessarily implies that the person has gained insight into his sinful nature, because that is what he feels sorrow over. The comprehensive view should emerge with particular clarity in the Catholic general confession, where sins and evil tendencies of the entire previous life are taken into account. Not only are individual sins objectively put forward, but the confessant should meanwhile acquire an understanding of his own personality. There occurs completely here what Ernst Jahn called an "objectification of the ego".[21] Jahn believed that the value of psychoanalytical treatment resides in the fact that the ego there takes itself as an object—"that the ego, captured within itself, removes to a distance from itself". The patient is seeking a You (the analyst) and attains self-objectification in relation to that You. The same thing happens before or during confession : while examining himself in the confessor's presence, the penitent "settles accounts with himself" and perceives the shortcomings in his own character.

Johannes Jørgensen supplied an example here when he told of how he prepared for his first confession.[22] As he went back through his previous life, he reread old letters : they all seemed to belong to a stranger of whom he would now take leave. But first he had to get the stranger properly in view before him as a living figure with discernible traits. Jørgensen saw himself in his old life as "a monomaniacal egoist who withdrew himself from all accounting—a bad person, a good-for-nothing—*nichtsnützig, nichtswürdig*". And he added : "First now I looked at myself. At that time I had believed I was always right. Now I saw my wrongness, my ugliness, my baseness".

A frank and careful self-examination in search of one's different sins often results in similar feelings of inadequacy and worthlessness. In general these do accompany an earnest awareness of the various sins. We could observe that in the expressions of contrition and dejection studied earlier here. We then took from Protestant quarters what is certainly a rather typical example of how the ego may be objectified in the way now described : how during the very act of confession it can be placed at a distance, so to speak, and submitted to critical judgement. That instance was from the Oxford Group movement. A member there said of his first confession : "I shared

---

[21] E. Jahn, *Wesen und Grenzen der Psychoanalyse* (Schwering, 1927); p. 48 f.

[22] J. Jørgensen, *op. cit.*; vol. IV, p. 71 f.

everything that lay on my mind with a friend, I revealed my weaknest side to him, and he did the same to me. And while I was telling him what oppressed me, I suddenly realized what a worthless creature I actually was, how I valued myself too highly, loved myself". And then : "I talked and talked until there really was nothing more to tell that he didn't know and—I was free".[23]

Objectification is necessary for true self-knowledge. And self-knowledge is required in turn if a person of divided mind is to gain domination over his disrupting tendencies and his mind to be made whole.

During confession, and because of it, an assimilation takes place, a reassociation of the previously dissociated mental life. Here we seem well able to concur with psychiatric theories on the point. Certain neurotics have lost the ability to hold their experiences together because some among these are so charged with emotion that they are incompatible with their normal lives; likewise, the confessant of sensitive conscience has not been capable of governing, or getting over, his experiences in the past. He is burdened with a sense of guilt because of certain actions, or he feels himself to be generally inadequate and worthless. In many cases these feelings take the form of nervous anxiety, and consequently it is often difficult for the confessor to distinguish between people who possess what may be called a normal sense of sin and those who are in need of medical care. Even the "normal" sort of remorse frequently creates an agitation and a dissatisfaction that cannot be allayed before the sin is confessed. What occurs during confession is, then, that the guilt-laden memories— submerged, or suppressed from ordinary daily consciousness, or unexplored because of their affectivity—can emerge thoroughly into consciousness; they are there divested of their emotional charge, abreacted and investigated, and it then becomes possible to combine them with the general context of the mind. Tendencies and instinctual drives in the person's nature are drawn forth from behind and under his various sins into the full light of consciousness, whereafter they can be controlled.

A question now remains to be answered. What is the factor in confession which enables the confessant to take his new opportunity of creating and maintaining unity among the conflicting forces within

---

[23] *Ermatinger Tagebuch* (previously quoted here p. 48).

him, of truly dismissing the disquieting recollections of his various sins? In other words, what allows him to achieve psychic assimilation? Here we might again cast a glance at psychiatry and a similar issue which arises there. We noted how Freud was reproached for merely providing abreaction and rendering dangerous memories conscious—for considering that psychic unity and health can be restored by those functions alone. Their insufficiency was emphasized by, for instance, Kronfeld; he underlined that the doctor must actively influence the patient and supply new ways of looking at his problem, new norms: to put it briefly, the patient must be given a new upbringing. And many eminent psychiatrists have, after egressing from the psychoanalytical school, supplemented Freud's system precisely with programmes for after-education.

Such new values truly are conveyed in confession; that is what characterizes confession and ultimately what makes the confessant feel able to establish unity of mind. The great value here is religious: it is the Divine Will, with all that represents in the confessant's eyes. And the presence of the Divine Will is sensed not only during the act of confession but also before confession. It is a power present to the sinner as soon as he repents and decides to confess; in its light he undertakes his examination of conscience and self-objectification; he feels that he partakes of it in the remission of sins and absolution. Of course, in most cases the confessant's aim is to obtain such forgiveness, to be informed and assured of pardon: one thing that shows this need for assurance is the demand in some quarters to hear a formal absolution pronounced by an authoritative spiritual leader. Normally, when the confessant learns that his sins are forgiven or has made sure of this through some form of absolution, he feels relieved from the pressure of sin. The troubling and agitating memory has lost its power to give him a painful conscience, and it can thus be ranged in the background of experience—there, like other neutral recollections, perhaps to be forgotten.

But the experiencing of absolution in confession involves something more than the effacement of the different sins confessed. Absolution is given on the condition that the penitent has deliberately resolved to place his life under the domination of the Divine Will. He has had a change of heart or embarked on a conversion, and the pardon granted for his sins may be regarded as a sign or proof of the transformation in him. Later, the relation of confession to conversion will be the subject of discussion here; we shall now merely establish that a confession earnestly made is really a stage in conversion and that it can be considered the keystone in the process there. When the confessant places himself under the Divine Will, he perceives an instrinsic worth, and aided by this he feels able to govern the forces that incite him to sin—forces of whose existence and nature he has become clearly conscience through the self-knowledge gained during his examination of conscience and confession. Thus, it is the religious factor in confession which provides the power to create and maintain relatedness and coherence among conflicting forces in the personality; or it is this which really brings about the equivalent to psychiatric assimilation.

Earlier, we put forward a question regarded as fundamental in our investigation. How, we asked, is the feeling of relief after confession to be explained? We saw in the previous chapter that some part of the answer may be sought in the affective discharge that takes place during confession. However, it is evident that the sense of release there should be regarded also in the light of what has been dealt with in this chapter. The objectification of guilt-laden memories here described provides understanding of their true nature and background. What has been worked through and elucidated does not go on troubling the person as it did before. Having acquired a clear idea of what may have been only an obscure and diffuse element of disquiet, he can resist the memory involved with a greater chance of success. He has in fact gained insight into his own character, so he knows what forces he has to deal with, which tendencies and inclinations are to be overcome. Exactly the clarity here about his psychic state should aid in creating a certain calm and confidence, and this may be found to form part of the relief experienced after confession.

But such understanding alone does not help. That is itself reached by influence of the Divine Will and on the basis of a religious decision. Ultimately, it is the religious factor, the experience of absolution and certainty of it, which mainly explain the sense of relief; this is more especially the case as confession comes to signify and sanction the process of turning, or returning, to religious faith. Confession is now perceived to be the conclusion to a period of strife among tendencies, and as such it often leaves a strong sense of mental peace, of tranquillity and release.

CHAPTER TEN

THE PART PLAYED BY PERSONAL INFLUENCE IN PSYCHOTHERAPY AND CONFESSION

In the two previous chapters we directed our attention to psychological factors active in a patient who is undergoing psychotherapeutic methods of treatment, and we believed that we could establish the existence of similar processes in confession. Meanwhile, the matter of the rôle played by the doctor or confessor came time and again to the fore. The doctor's personality and actions are decisive for success in the assimilation of past experiences which are severed from consciousness and in the resolution of the conflict that caused mental illness. We have recently noted how Schmalhausen, for one, emphasized the part taken by the doctor: he pointed out that the doctor conveys new standpoints and new norms to the patient during treatment, thus changing him completely and enabling him to resolve the conflict from which he has suffered. C. G. Jung laid great stress on the dominant rôle played by the doctor; and on the subject of allaying the disturbance caused by traumatic memories he said: "The relived experience of the traumatic moment can nullify the neurotic dissociation only if the person's conscious personality has been so strengthened by his relationship with the doctor that he is consciously in condition to place the complex, which has become autonomous, once more under control of the will".[1] There is striking similarity here with the confessor's relation to his penitent. Consequently, we may expect the explanation offered by psychiatry and psychology as to the origin of the trustful relationship between doctor and patient, and for its effect on the patient, will be of value to us in our investigation of the psychological factors in the act of confession.

The explanation is contained in a definition of the conditions required for such a relationship. We shall try to demonstrate in the description that follows how similar the requirements are in psychotherapy and confession.

---

[1] C. G. Jung, "The Question of the Therapeutic Value of 'Abreaction'," in *The British Journal of Psychology*, Medical Section, October number, 1921; p. 16. The lines quoted are italicized by Jung.

The trustful relationship between patient and doctor is of basic importance in psychotherapy. That emerged from the statement by Jung just quoted. And the importance holds true not only for psycho-analytical treatment but for all therapy. The Swedish psychiatrist Bror Gadelius said : "A boundless confidence in the person who, in one form or another, deliberately or unintentionally, exerts psycho-therapeutic effect is thus a condition for obtaining favourable results".[2] And if a relationship of trust is to arise, certain requirements must be fulfilled both on the patient's side and on the doctor's.

In order for the patient to be susceptible to influence, he must *want* to be influenced; he must, in other words, desire mental health. This wish is the doctor's best ally during treatment. From it comes the patient's participation in the cure : his willingness to accept the treatment prescribed, his trustful feelings for the doctor. What corresponds in the confessional situation to the factor creating the patient's confidence is the confessant's need to escape from his oppres-sive burden of guilt, which becomes a need for confession and absolu-tion. Just as the penitent does not take his confession to someone at random, but to an officially recognized authority or at least to somebody in his environment who inspires trust, a person who is mentally ill generally goes to an accredited doctor. Here again a need for authority and guidance makes its appearance. A case that H. I. Schou encountered in his practice illustrates this.[3] He has related that a woman travelled from a distance to see him. She com-plained of headaches. He examined her but could not find that she suffered from any nervous ailment with an organic cause. "In the course of an hour the patient had talked about her whole life and her most private affairs." Her visit ended without his having taken any action. Nevertheless, it had the desired effect on the patient. She wrote to Schou after returning home and thanked him for his excel-lent "treatment". In his account of the case, he added that he could not recall having uttered "a sensible word during her confession, much less having given any directions".

This case—which is of course an excellent example of how merely talking, along with the emotional discharge and assimilation involved, exerts a curative effect—was construed by Schou as evidence that a

² Bror Gadelius, *Tro och helbrägdagörelse* (Belief and Faith-healing : Stockholm 1934); p. 9.

³ H. I. Schou, *op. cit.*; p. 580.

would-be confessant prefers to take his (or her) confession to somebody he does not know. But it seems rather to demonstrate the contrary : what simply going to a noted medical authority can mean to a disharmonious and perplexed person. The woman did not seek out just anyone in order to make her confession; she went to H. I. Schou, famous chief doctor of "Filadelfia", the largest Danish mental hospital. She expected to receive help from such a highly-regarded doctor. He played an entirely passive rôle during her avowals, but all she apparently needed was an opportunity to talk about her troubles : to abreact and examine her experiences by going through them logically in the presence of an authoritative person who, just by being there, forced her to put them seriously into order.

The patient needs an authority who has the qualifications to help him, and he expects to find what he requires in the doctor whom he goes to consult. Ernst Kretschmer said on this matter : "We see that the doctor cannot decide himself whether or not he is practising psychotherapy, since because of a catathymic (affective) constraint everybody expects and obtains psychotherapy from the doctor. He does not function as psychotherapist because he wishes to but because his patients want him to. He exercises an intense psychic influence on his patients..."[4] And a patient is often extremely anxious to make sure that the authority possessed by the doctor is maintained. Indeed, he would like to see this further increased. It is of course well known that popular opinion tends to increase the results of a successful doctor's treatments. The patient listens eagerly to tales about the doctor's wonderful feats, and if possible he contributes stories of his own. It is as if he wishes to assure himself that the doctor truly can help him. Thus, his strong desire for health both intensifies the need for authority and strengthens the authority itself. Here lies much of the curative effect observable in such cases as that described by Schou.[5]

The doctor, being well aware of what the patient's confidence in him means to the success of treatment, is anxious to retain the authority with which he is invested in the patient's eyes. We might note at this point that measures deliberately taken by the doctor are similar

---

[4] E. Kretschmer, *Medizinische Psychologie* (Leipzig, 1939).

[5] Cf. Kretschmer, *op. cit.*: "With medical and religious institutions which are encircled by a strongly suggestive fame, merely entering the building can be sufficient for the patient to become well".

to those which we have seen certain confessors use in order to affirm
their authority. He, too, can assert his presence by behaving in a decisive
manner that inspires confidence. The orders he gives create the impression that he has found the cause of illness and the means of curing
it. Insofar as possible, he avoids suggesting to the patient that he is
powerless against the malady. If he conveys the idea of helplessness,
he will no longer possess authority in the patient's eyes; confidence
will be gone, and with it he loses the best ally in his fight against the
illness. Kretschmer recommended that, to evade such an unfortunate
situation, the doctor should resort to a *pia fraus* and do something
even in cases which appear to be hopeless; he thus conveys to the
patient that an effort is being made. And the patient's trust must
be kept up to the very end.

Sigmund Freud, brilliant psychologist that he was, had a sense of
the importance which must be attributed to the doctor's authority,
and he asserted his own deliberately when dealing with patients.
He has himself given us an interesting example of how he could
inculcate proper deference in a disrespectful patient. Even if in this
case the patient's behaviour was unintentional, it revealed to the
trained eye of the analyst what stirred deep in the patient's mind.
Freud related[6] that between his consulting-room and his waiting-
room he had double doors which, for obvious reasons, were sound-
proof. Usually, a patient would close the doors carefully behind
him after being called into the consulting-room. But if the waiting-
room was empty when the patient arrived and when afterwards he
went in to the doctor, he might fail to close the doors. He then received
a sharp order from Freud to go back and shut them—for, said Freud,
"a person who behaves in such a way belongs to *hoi polloi* and deserves
an unfriendly reception". This judgement appears highly exaggerated
to the layman. But Freud saw deeper than people generally do into
the motive forces that underlie human life, and he believed his view
to be justified. To him carelessness with the doors revealed that—
according to "the psychopathology of everyday life"—the patient
took a negligent or sceptical attitude to the doctor and the cure he
was to undergo. Freud reasoned that such a patient was of the sort
possessing a ready desire to be dazzled and impressed by outward
show. Perhaps the patient in question had telephoned to inquire
when he could have an appointment. He imagined that the famous

---

6 S. Freud, *Vorlesungen*; p. 252 f.

doctor's waiting-room would be crowded with people—and the simply furnished room he entered was empty. This surprised him greatly, and he felt indignation : really, he was going to make the doctor atone for having inspired so much respect without actually warranting it. And thus when entering the consulting-room he did not close the doors behind him, quite unaware that this neglect was caused by his recent vexation and by diminished esteem. But Freud understood the reason, and he issued a reprimand in consequence. If this reproof was not given to the patient, then "during the conversation, too, he would behave in an ill-bred and disrespectful manner". It is therefore a concern of the doctor who practises psychoanalysis, as well as for other doctors, to create and uphold respect and deference on the patient's part, even if later during a cure he may establish relations with the patient that seem to efface the distance between them.

We thus see the great importance which the doctor's authority is acknowledged to possess in psychiatry. And, as where confession is concerned, this derives from perception of how valuable a relationship of trust is in achieving results. Of course the confidence is based on relations between two individuals. So the doctor's authority must not be regarded as of an impersonal kind. Here, as in confession, the personal element comes clearly to the fore. It appears plainly in the cases described by Breuer and Janet. Anna O., Breuer's patient, quite simply refused to tell her hallucinations to anyone but Breuer : in short, she rejected the "talking cure" which had such an excellent effect on her condition; and she did so in spite of having at hand another doctor whom she esteemed.[7] Janet regarded the part played by personal influence as a common and well-known phenomenon in suggestion therapy, and he gave as instance the case of a patient who suffered recurrently from contractions.[8] This woman could be put completely right by simple suggestion. But the therapy had little or no effect on her when not carried out by Janet himself. Though it was usually he who treated her, another competent person, fully initiated as to his handling of that particular case, tried to replace him; no results were achieved in spite of energetic efforts and the fact that the patient

---

[7] Breuer and Freud, *op. cit.*; p. 24. Breuer related that, after being away on holiday, he returned to find his patient in a much worse state, for she could not persuade herself to tell anyone else about the hallucinations she had experienced while in twilight sleep.

[8] P. Janet, *Les Médications psychologiques*; vol. III, p. 394 f.

had herself asked to be treated by someone else when Janet was not available.

As Janet alleged here, even where simple suggestion is concerned the personal element plays a decisive part. And, naturally, still greater significance should be attached to this element when patients place their deepest personal conflicts before the doctor. In fact, the opinion seems to prevail fairly unanimously among doctors that the essential thing in therapy is the doctor's personality. He must be able to inspire confidence in the patient and create a rapport that aids the patient's recovery and the unification of his divided personality.

Arthur Kronfeld thoroughly investigated what the doctor requires in order to exert a propitious influence on his patient during treatment; he claimed that much depends on the special aura surrounding the doctor, which causes people to attribute to him extraordinary knowledge and a particular ability to help them.[9] But that is not enough. Primarily, what lies behind his influence is the patient's impression that the doctor, with all that special aura, is genuinely taking an interest in him and his problem. Kronfeld said that the doctor must be able to induce a sense of deep and personal interest even when patients are acquainting him with the great number of unimportant details which they often produce.

The psychiatrist Karl Birnbaum concurred with Kronfeld's views here, and among specially important qualifications that a doctor should have he placed the power of *Einfühlung* into a patient's state and difficulties, also the doctor's "human devotion" to the afflicted. His image must be that of "the compassionate, understanding, readily helpful and thereby superior counsellor".[10]

Many similar statements could be cited, all affirming the importance of the doctor's personality. The methods employed are secondary to this. A psychiatrist should make a critical appraisal and not confine himself to a single method. The thing required is adaptation to the individual case concerned.[11] Janet, too, placed great weight on the consequence of personalized treatment. If the doctor is to exert

---

[9] A. Kronfeld, *op. cit.*; p. 135.

[10] K. Birnbaum, *Die psychischen Heilmethoden* (Leipzig, 1927); p. 23.

[11] See, for instance, Bror Gadelius (*Tro och helbrägdagörelse*; p. 4) on the various schools and methods. He declared that "*none and all are right*" and went on : "If the therapy is to be kept on a scientific basis, preconceived views must be avoided, and every case must be regarded as strictly individual". Kretschmer claimed that he availed himself of all demonstrably usuable methods in his practice.

influence, it is important that the patient should "feel understood" by him. Janet constantly heard this expression from patients. They said how happy they were that they had finally met someone who understood them and shared in their troubles. In order to arrive at a situation so favourable to therapy, the doctor must adjust treatment to the patient he is dealing with and not tackle every case with a routine method, the same for all. To the psychotherapist wanting his patient "to comply", Janet's advice was : "You must begin by conforming yourself to him".[12]

Carl Rogers has provided a model of the doctor-counsellor conceived in the spirit outlined. He there summarizes the doctor's behaviour by declaring that the counsellor says in effect : "To be of assistance to you I will put myself aside—the self of ordinary interaction—and enter into your world of perception as completely as I am able. I will become in a sense another self for you—an alter ego of your own attitudes and feelings—a safe opportunity for you to discern yourself more clearly, to experience yourself more truly and deeply, to choose more significantly".[13]

The psychoanalytical approach, in spite of its narrow method, seems to provide good opportunity for the personality of the doctor to make itself felt and for a relationship of confidence between him and his patient. Their rapport is of course a necessary condition for the success of therapy. The motto that François de Sales gave to the confessor, "Make yourself beloved", expresses a leading view on how the psychoanalyst should proceed. For only with the establishment of positive transference, containing love or unreserved admiration, can the patient's opposition be overcome and the method gain results.

Quite obviously, the psychoanalytical method is by its nature particularly conducive to feelings of love and admiration in the patient. To explain why this is so we scarcely need to bring up the theory about transposition of the libido from an object in the past to the doctor. It is enough to remark that the lengthy treatment involved in psychoanalysis—often lasting for months and years, and allowing the patient constantly to ventilate his most intimate secrets—

---

[12] P. Janet, op. cit.; p. 430.

[13] In Insight, 1967; p. 251. Cf. Rogers' The Therapeutic Relation and its Impact (New York, 1969), with its three cardinal points for the therapist's behaviour : (1) Genuineness, congruence with the patient. (2) Unconditional, positive regard. (3) Empathic understanding.

must create a feeling of confidential fellowship. And in this situation the critics of psychoanalysis have found a point where they can profitably make attack. Their reasoning is approximately as follows. The psychoanalysts regard their theories as confirmed by revelations which patients make during treatment. The symbolic language of dreams and of unintentional lapses, the flow of free association and especially the cessations of this—all evidently support the correctness of psychoanalytical premises. But the critics say that psychoanalysts are guilty of a dangerous mistake in basing their claims here. For the doctors have more or less directly let patients know what they want to emerge during analysis. They have influenced their patients by suggestion and lured forth material, excellent from their point of view, which can easily be construed to accord with their theories. The psychoanalysts usually counter this criticism—which does in fact present itself—by declaring that there can never be question of their instilling the interpretations of symptoms into patients' minds. If the cure is to have any success, the patients must come himself on the connection between his symptoms and his complex. But it may be asked how the patient is actually to do this. He can scarcely offer the desired interpretation *"auss der Tiefe seines Bewusst-seins"*. Of course it is inevitable that the doctor exerts influence. He cannot fail to indicate the direction that he wants the interpretation to take. Freud made a statement of significance here when he said that this indication should not be conveyed "before a fruitful transference, a genuine rapport, has been created with the patient".[14] The foundation is then provided for unopposed acceptance of the doctor's ideas. Freud believed that the patient's new understanding and the willingness with which he becomes absorbed by psychoanalytical interpretations results from an inward change, and this change in him is the beginning of his recovery. It follows that such alteration of the personality is due entirely to the doctor's intervention.

Psychoanalysts are well aware of the power they exercise over patients. It is a necessary requirement if they are to achieve results, but it is also a very delicate factor in treatment and must be handled with great care. Freud warned against its misuse. In actual fact,

---

14 Cf. Freud's words, cited previously here (page 90) concerning the patient's willingness to agree with the interpretation of symptoms, entirely as intended by the analysts, after transference has occurred.

treatment cannot be regarded as over before the affective relationship between doctor and patient has subsided and assumed a normal character. For both parties, release from it can often be a difficult process. But when the patient has truly freed himself and perceived that emotions intended for someone in the past were transferred to the doctor, then a genuine personal relationship commences. C. G. Jung made this perception the touchstone of an analysis.[15] After liberation has taken place, the doctor and his patient are on equal terms. Neither is any longer in a superior or subordinate position. And the patient can now leave the doctor; independently and using his critical sense, he has assimilated the doctor's views about the shaping of his future life. It may be seen from this, said Jung, that the psychoanalytical doctor—more than a psychiatrist who keeps to routine methods— must fulfil moral requirements.

We have dwelt at special length on the interconnection between doctor and patient in psychoanalysis so as to illustrate how a trustful relationship may arise there, also to show how far it may impel the patient into becoming dependent on the doctor. Extreme cases of such attachment are to be found in psychoanalysis. But similar dependence on the doctor appears in other forms of psychotherapy.

Concerning transference, Arthur Kronfeld has said that what the term covers in psychoanalysis—the affinity between patient and doctor, based on the affective tie that joins the former to the latter—is well known in psychotherapy generally. And it is indispensable to such therapy. "This transference enters into *all* psychotherapeutic procedures, and it brings success there; it is *not* bound to the psychoanalytical method nor directed with special ease by that method *as such*. If it does *not* take place, *every* psychotherapy fails".[16]

Janet likewise claimed that such involvement on the patient's part is very common; he said that it almost characterizes certain forms of mental illness—hysteria and various neuroses—if the sufferers receive regular treatment from the same doctor. He emphasized, as we previously observed, that the mentally ill become particularly attached to the doctor because they feel that he has understood them in a new way, as they have never been comprehended before in their lives. Their feeling of communion with him finds expression similar to that shown by psychoanalytical patients. They sense

[15] Jung, *op. cit.*; p. 21.

[16] A. Kronfeld, *op. cit.*; p. 175. (The italics are Kronfeld's.)

his presence as they go about their daily life; they believe that he watches over their every step; they even have hallucinations about him. He is made into their divine guardian. To give an instance, this is how a patient wrote to Janet : "I am like those believers who have sought solace in churches, and I carry my mainstay about with me as the faithful have with them their God. The lines I am scribbling down in accordance with your will, which you will probably throw away without having read, do me as much good as prayer does to the faithful". The writer continued, "I too have my guardian angel". And another said : "I turn continually to you as the believer turns to the priest who manifests God to him". And a third : "You govern all my thoughts, it seems to me, as if you constantly watch over me".[17] Janet added that not merely did they express devotion, they really followed the doctor's desires in all things; and they wanted to put everything they experienced before him so as to make evident the great part he played in all that happened to them.

Janet pointed out, as others have done, that the attachment of patients may often assume forms which are awkward for the doctor. Because of this, when he has made use of their personal devotion to influence them in the way desired, he must hasten with the task of releasing them from their dependence; the patient must be rendered a self-governed human being who no longer needs to stand on the doctor's authority in order to face the world and shape his life.

Again with such therapy as that of Carl Rogers, it is required that the patient should have respect for, and confidence in, his doctor, and also wish to regain mental health. Here once more it is clear that the success of therapy depends to a great extent on the doctor and his ability to "enter into the patient's world". Concerning this therapy, we learn with interest from the summary of Rogers' goals made by Ford and Urban that "the therapist should periodically tell the patient his understanding of how things look from the patient's vantage point".[18] And later on (page 942) it is remarked : "The point is that what happens in a therapy session is a function of what the therapist does. One set of operations elicits certain types of patient responses, another set induces still different behaviors". From this it is not difficult to understand what the doctor's rôle must be in such "client-centered" therapy.

---

[17] P. Janet, *op. cit.*; vol. III, pp. 396-399.
[18] Ford and Urban, *op. cit.*; pp. 430-431.

Generally speaking, then, psychotherapeutic treatment involves entrance of the patient into an intimately dependent relationship with the doctor. On this point striking agreement exists between the consequences of confession and of psychotherapy as experienced by distressed people. We saw earlier here, in Chapter IV, how similar forms of rapport between two minds occur in confession : for example, in Jeanne de Chantal's relationship with François de Sales, or that between "Greats" and Frank Buchman.

There are evident similarities between the methods in psychotherapy and in confession by which such propitious relationships are achieved. The likenesses emerge with special clarity when we consider the weight attached both to the doctor's and the confessor's personality. The method of treatment ought of course to receive its direction and its character from the doctor's personality; and to a considerable extent it is dictated by the need to create the relationship of confidence decisive for treatment. The doctor and the confessor must each engage himself in the person seeking help; each is to behave in an accessible manner, and listen willingly and tirelessly to what the person has to tell; each ought to show understanding for this person in his troubles, and should always be ready to supply help and advice. These mutual requirements obviously involve general methodological similarities between confession and a well-balanced psychotherapy. And, in fact, a comparison between the ideal Catholic confessional method as represented by François de Sales, for instance, and psychoanalytical method shows fairly detailed conformities. The outward arrangements for psychoanalysis, to begin with, resemble those that Catholics meet with in the confessional. Of course, a patient must be so placed that he cannot see the doctor, as he could be disturbed by the doctor's visible reactions. Then, too, the psychoanalyst must take care to let as much as possible depend on the patient's own actions and initiative. Interpretation of the patient's symptoms must not be forced upon him; as far as possible it ought instead to come from him. The doctor is to watch for the "inner change" experienced by the patient during treatment. He should guide this without issuing any orders or other-wise asserting himself. As we observed earlier, that attitude has been the leading principle in the method of François de Sales and other model confessors.

Differences are also obvious, of course. Psychoanalysis often makes use of techniques—for instance, experiments with association, hypnosis and similar states—which are alien to confession; this results from the fact that psychotherapy concerns itself with neurotics. Analyzing situations of conflict is a great deal more difficult in psychoanalysis because of the strong emotional charge suffered by patients, also because of the opposition they make to revealing unpleasant memories which may be forgotten or repressed to such an extent that complicated methodological devices are needed to draw them forth. But in spite of such differences it is remarkable how similarly psychiatrists and confessors look on the importance of the person who exercises therapy and of the general attitude he takes to people seeking help; from this resemblance it follows that many essential likenesses are to be found between the ways these people are approached and handled.

Thus, as far as requirements and operative factors are concerned, we have been able to establish that there is extensive agreement between religious confession and the psychotherapy employed for certain mental ailments. In both cases we have observed the same need to escape from oppressive psychic distress : on the one hand there is a desire to get away from sin, and, on the other, a wish for mental health; and there is the same consequent need to turn to an authority. We have observed, too, how the instinctual force involved is confronted by the authority, whether by priest or doctor, and how the position on which authority rests is built up. But, on either side, it is not enough simply to possess outward authority ; for if the authority is truly to be maintained the person upholding it must regard the person who seeks help as a fellow human-being and treat him so ; premises are thereby created for a relationship of confidence, and by use of a suitable method such a relationship can then be established and consolidated. Finally, through this contact of an ideal kind between the helper and the person seeking relief, either the latter recovers his mental health or a profound change takes place in him.

It now remains for us to see whether psychiatry can offer any closer explanation for the unreserved way the patient submits himself to the doctor and his emotional involvement in their relationship : such an explanation would cover more than may be found simply in a description of the premises on which that psychic relationship is based. "Suggestion" is a term often met with in attempts to explain the personal influence exercised by the doctor. If the term can be applied where the doctor-patient tie is concerned in psychiatry, it should also be applicable in the psychology of confession.

Let us take the definition given by William McDougall, one of the most reasonable offered during the many attempst to throw light on what is contained by the idea. "Suggestion", said McDougall, "is a process of communication resulting in the acceptance with conviction of the communicated proposition in the absence of logically adequate grounds for its acceptance".[19]

The merit of this definition is that it covers the commonest form of suggestion, which is the kind that arises in interpersonal relationships.

McDougall claimed that receptivity to suggestion depends on the following factors: "(1) Abnormal states of the brain, of which the relative dissociation obtaining in hysteria, hypnosis, normal sleep, and fatigue, is the most important; (2) deficiency of knowledge or convictions relating to the topic in regard to which the suggestion is made, and imperfect organization of knowledge; (3) the impressive character of the source from which the suggested proposition is communicated; (4) peculiarities of the character and native disposition of the subject".[20]

According to McDougall, the most important factor would appear to lie in the third point: the impressive character of the authority exercising influence. Even if the subject has the best possible knowledge of a field and his arsenal of ideas contains the most convincing arguments against what is conveyed, he cannot resist an opinion or a belief presented by an authority possessing value to him. McDougall called this form of influence "prestige suggestion". Examples of authorities exerting it are priests, who have a powerful church behind them, people in high social positions or who possess eminent intellectual gifts, or those who are of superior physical strength. All elicit what McDougall called the "instinct of subjection"; this may vary in force depending on the personal basis existing for it: on innate disposition, education and knowledge.

Of the theory here it may be remarked to begin with that the person influenced does not reflect at all—so one might easily think—on what is being proposed to him and accepts it without hesitation because of the authority behind it. But of course that is not what always happens. Very often, the person accepts what is conveyed after what he regards as thorough deliberation, and this confirms to him that he has the best possible reasons for acceptance. There is, he finds, total agreement between the proposals and beliefs presented and the conclusions which he has arrived at himself after mature consideration. He does

---

[19] W. McDougall, *An Introduction to Social Psychology* (London 1908); p. 98.
[20] *Ibid.*; p. 84.

not observe, or does not wish to observe, that his thinking proceeds from basic points of departure supplied by the authority.

Evidently, however, McDougall felt that personal influence always has a more or less salient suggestive effect. This depends on the suggestibility of the person being subjected to influence. We have noted that McDougall put forward several important prior conditions for suggestibility. But a factor involved has not yet received fully the attention it deserves. Though McDougall spoke about the instinct of subjection (what we have called "the need for authority" in this survey) as the basic explanation for what occurs in the person influenced, he laid no stress on the feelings which may best bring that instinct into play : the varying emotions of love, tenderness and admiration for the person who exercises influence—feelings which we have seen illustrated many times in psychiatry and confessional practice. It is obvious that the so-frequent emotional attachments to doctor and confessor are an extremely important element in explanation of how suggestion originates—as McDougall himself bore out when he said in another context that "almost any emotional excitement increases the suggestibility of the individual."

The import to suggestion of the strong emotional tie mentioned comes forth even more emphatically in the psychoanalytical theory on suggestion. In this, such attachment is made the sole explanation for suggestion. Freud declared that he abandoned hypnosis only "to rediscover suggestion in the form of transference".[21] Here the previously constrained libido is transposed to the doctor, and this means that a tendency to devotion and submission is aroused in the patient.[22] That states the most essential requirement for suggestion. What it in fact implies where the patient is concerned may be seen from the effect ascribed to transference : that the patient accepts the doctor's proposals and beliefs entirely because they come from him. According

---

[21] S. Freud, *Vorlesungen*; p. 475.

[22] S. Ferenczi, a leading psychoanalyst who concerned himself particularly with the theory of suggestion, gave the following definition of suggestions and hypnotism, formed along lines laid down by Bernheim : "*Das Suggerieren und Hypnotisieren wäre nach dieser Auffassung die absichtliche Herstellung von Bedingungen, unter denen die in jedem Menschen vorhandene aber für gewöhnlich durch die Zensur verdrängt gehaltene Neigung zu blindem Glauben und kritiklosem Gehorsam—ein Rest des Infantil-erotischen und Fürchtens der Eltern auf die Person des Hypnotisierenden oder Suggerierenden unbewusst übertragen werden kann*". (*Bausteine zur Psychoanalyse : Vienna*, 1927; vol. I, p. 56 f.) The words spaced out were emphasized by Ferenczi.

to the theory here, the doctor can lead his patient to mental health only if transference occurs and the patient surrenders to his authority. Even the critics of Freud's system attribute considerable suggestive effect to transference, as we were able to establish earlier when we stated the common criticism made against the interpretation of symbols during analysis. The merit possessed by the psychoanalytical theory of suggestion lies in its placing due emphasis on the part played by emotional attachment; but it goes to an extreme with this and presents such attachment as the sole and universal requirement for successful suggestion. The development of suggestion does not necessarily demand the intense manifestations of emotion which psychoanalysts have been able to note on the part of their patients. But the view taken in psychoanalysis about the importance of affective devotion does form an indispensable complement to McDougall's theory, which one-sidedly stresses that imperious authority and the need for submission are crucial in developing suggestion.

In relation to emotional involvement, another factor of consequence to suggestion may appear : this is the need for a feeling of community— and, incidentally, McDougall numbered "the gregarious instinct" among basic human instincts.

Erwin Strauss took up the need for fellowship and the experience of it when he wished to find the explanation of suggestion in what he called the "we-experience".[23] (The term seems to indicate a certain equality between participants which is by no means always present.)

Like McDougall, Strauss appears to have overlooked, or to have laid too little stress on, a fundamental factor producing suggestibility, one of great significance in the practice of doctors and confessors : that factor is self-interest.

The patient who obeys orders from the doctor inducing suggestion, or the weak and timorous sinner who follows what his confessor ordains, probably has no "we-experience" in the real meaning of that term. Then what makes each of them willing to surrender to authority ? Ultimately, the explanation of the patient's readiness to suspend critical observation, to submit come what may to the doctor and his treatment, seems to be the need for help in finding relief and recovering. We have seen how psychiatrits emphasize the desire for recovery as a suggestively operative element in treatment, that it induces

---

[23] Erwin Strauss, "*Wesen und Vorgang der Suggestion*", in *Abhandlungen aus der Neurologie, Psychiatrie, Psychologie und ihren Grenzgebieten*, 28 (Berlin, 1925).

great eagerness in patients to submit to cure, and how doctors consider
the factor to be both an aid in effecting a successful cure and a condition
for doing so. And in the confessant's psychic situation a similar
factor is active : the will to be released from sin.

Thus, self-interest appears to be of crucial importance in intensifying
suggestibility where the form of suggestion that we have most closely
under view here is concerned : what McDougall called prestige suggestion. The political demagogue or propagandist, no matter what
kind he may be, who really understands how to appeal to his listeners'
vital interests is sure to achieve the results he is after. His audience
will be disposed to agree with his proposals because he realizes so
well what is best for them. He becomes their authority and guide,
and they are prepared to follow where he leads them. In doing so,
they are of course promoting their own success. Criticism is prohi-
bited; they accept the leader's catchwords as if they had thought
these up themselves. They have at the same time subjected themselves
to their leader and entered into community both with him and his
other followers. And the more complete their subjection, the more
intimate is the communion they feel, the more willing they are to
obey the leader's authority and the more susceptible they are to
suggestion.

In psychiatry and confessional practice, the personal suggestion
exercised should evidently be understood in the same way. But,
while submission and the need for communion are both of importance in producing suggestibility, what brings them out seems primarily
to be the instinct for self-preservation—self-interest. This is a main
reason why the person seeking help invests the authority with the
most splendid qualities and entertains the fondest feelings for him.
When the authority is regarded in such a way, the personal relations
involved provide the most fertile soil for cultivating suggestion.
People subject themselves to the authority and accept what he says
as Truth itself. His statements are regarded as beyond discussion.
They are believed just because they come from him, and may or
may not possess objective validity. That is not a matter for reflection.

A characteristic thing about the confessant is his acceptance of
the whole background which the authority represents : that is, the
religious community with its beliefs and conceptions. In making
his confession, he wants to surrender himself completely and become
part of this context, to make its values his own. He is more inclined to
do so because of his perplexed and helpless state, and because he does

not see any possibility of extricating himself alone from his difficulties. He is in a condition that renders him specially disposed to accept without criticism what the confessor conveys to him.

Moreover, another of the factors which—as McDougall pointed out— develops suggestibility seems to make itself felt here : the lack of knowledge concerning a certain subject. Because of the general psychic disorientation in a person distressed by his sins, he is incapable of finding his own way out of his troubles, of acquiring the means to regain calmness and a peaceful conscience.

Similar views to those offered here are put forth by James E. Dittes; he asks in effect : How is one to interpret suggestibility as it is involved in, for example, conversion.[24] And he answers that, to begin with, suggestibility is due to "a kind of general personal weakness or frustration looking for support anywhere and finding it on occasion in such phenomena as revival, conversion, etc". He calls this type of personality a "weak ego".

In addition, suggestibility depends on a tendency to submit oneself to an authority ("a superego religion"), a tendency which we recognize from the previous survey here.

Dittes says that the receptivity to suggestion may depend further on a sort of conventionality. People are willing to subordinate themselves to a sanctioned religious system or religious community because it represents something established and permanent.

This last element is of course connected with the need for authority and the desire to fit into a community.

Our discussion of what lies in the idea of suggestion has indicated that one may properly speak of suggestion as existing everywhere that personal influence makes itself felt; and thus essential importance must be attributed to the phenomenon in religious confession. Suggestion may there vary according to the character of the relationship between confessor and confessant. The need for submission seems to reveal itself particularly in certain forms of confession where institutional aspects are stressed and where the priest assumes chiefly the role of a powerfully commanding authority—as in a number of cases we became acquainted with in the chapter on the confessor's authority (Chapter III). We have also studied how the need for authority can manifest itself with primordial force (in Chapter II).

---

[24] James E. Dittes, *Psychology of Religion*, in G. Lindsey & E. Aronson, *Handbook of Social Psychology*, V (Reading, Mass, 1968); pp. 602-659.

The need for communion and the experiencing of it are allowed greater scope when a relationship of personal confidence comes seriously into existence, as is ideally the case in Catholic and evangelical confession. We have, in the chapter on that relationship of trust (Chapter IV), seen examples of suggestively active relations between the two participating in the act of confession. How by his manner of procedure the confessor achieves an emotionally felt communion—and with it the most propitious situation for a suggestively operative relationship— has been given special scrutiny in the chapter on confessional method (Chapter V). It appears that in confession, as in medical practice, the driving force behind submission to the authoritative figure and fellowship with him is self-interest, the instinct of self-preservation, which expresses itself through the sinner's remorse, his will to escape from his sins, to reform and be converted : evidence of this was presented earlier here, mainly in the chapter on the need for confession and absolution (Chapter I).

There are two further factors to which particular attention should be drawn in the matter of developing, intensifying and fortifying the experience of communion during confession, and these are of great consequence in explaining the confessor's suggestive influence. The prior conditions for experiencing communion are, as we pointed out earlier, the confessant's need for community and his will to recover spiritual health—with, on the other side, the confessors' personal involvement and use of a well-advised method. But the experience gains its special character largely from the fact that what the confessant avows is an oppressive secret which he shares with a single other human being. It is a matter of common observation that a confidence entrusted to a reliable person creates a special bond with that person. No friends are so intimately attached as those who share their secrets. We noted in the first chapter here how Nikolaus Lenau declared to his friend Justinus Kerner, after making a confession to him, that Kerner now shared his burden. A confidence which a friend is obligated to keep engenders on his part a particularly close tie with the person from whom it comes. And the friend who confesses feels relief that he no longer bears his heavy burden alone; he is now aided in withstanding its weight.

We may well suppose that a sense of community is to be experienced with more intense feelings of happiness and gratitude by a person who has been able to unburden an onerous sin to another. The sin has in itself an inhibiting and isolating effect. We witnessed evidence of this when dealing (in Chapter VIII) with the powerful tension in a repentant sinner's state. Particularly with subjects of Wunderle's investigation, we saw how feelings of guilt decrease people's forces, hampering them and setting them apart. Powerful feelings of the kind produce a stagnation of the person's ability to devote himself to others and to his tasks. The confession itself can be experienced as an end to isolation, a release from constraint. Such may be the case when the confession is made directly to God, providing that He is sufficiently vivid in the sinner's mind.[25] And of course it applies also when the confession is made to another person. By talking about what has weighed upon him, inhibited and isolated him, the confessant yields himself to the person receiving his confession and feels that the person now shares his burden. This feeling gives his sense of communion a special character. An intimate bond is established between him and the receiver of his confidence, and the tie often endows that person with a higher value in the confessant's eyes than he previously possessed there.

In connection with the aspect just mentioned, a further factor enters here; this is what we may call the rehabilitation of the confessant through the confessor's understanding attitude. Perhaps the sinner has felt himself to be despised and rejected because of his sin. Not of course that he need actually have been so. But strong awareness of sin induces such feelings. Troubled by them, the sinner has construed the reactions of those in his surroundings—perhaps quite differently occasioned—as reflecting on his inferiority and bad character : this in accordance with the law that an affect binds the life of the imagination in the direction of its own object. It follows that the sinner feels increasingly disgraced and isolated. When in confession he now reveals himself to another person, he is able to experience community not only in the sense that we have already brought to attention but also a community that comes through recognition of him, by the receiver of his confession, as a fellow human being whose

---

[25] An often-cited example of this is contained in Psalm 32; verses 3-5 :

"When I kept silence, my bones waxed old through my roaring all the day long.

For night and day thy hand was heavy upon me. My moisture is turned into the drought of summer. Selah.

I acknowledged my sin unto thee, and mine iniquity have I not hid. I said, I will confess my transgressions unto the LORD; and thou forgavest the iniquity of my sin. Selah".

problem is to be discussed and solved. The rebuffed and isolated sinner is thus achnowledged and rehabilitated. Accepted anew, he enters into solidarity with another person.

We may refer again here to the therapeutic views of Carl Rogers. According to Rogers, the patient's difficulties are created by incongruence between him and his environment. So the most important condition for therapy must be "unconditional positive regard" on the doctor's part; and his relationship with the patient, the emotional interaction in the therapeutic situation will be decisive for success of the healing process.[26]

Thanks to the sinner's fellowship with the confessor and help from the confessor he is introduced into the larger community. The determining cause behind this development is his spiritual conversion, the change of heart brought on by the Divine Will, a change already on its way when he experienced affects of remorse before confession; through these and by the confessor's influence, the change has become clearly conscious and been confirmed. This means that the confessant reaches the highest feeling of communion : that with God Himself, which communion comprises and gives inspiration to union with his fellow beings. H. Fuglsang-Damgaard drew attention to the ability of confession to create a sense of communion, and he expressed the result in the following words : "Then he who suffers and sorrows is no longer alone. He is taken into the larger community which holds a united view about sin and grace. Indeed, exactly on that matter over which the individual may feel himself most lonely and abandoned, because he is rejected by other people, down in the depths of sin, he meets with the solidarity of love. And because it is God's love, the solidarity is absolute".[27]

The confessor's influence makes itself felt in all the phases of confession. He serves as recipient of the confessant's emotional discharge, which he makes easier through his personal involvement and judicious manner of proceeding. He is the authority before whom the distressed

---

[26] It is hardly astonishing that Carl Rogers has become a most important man in the eyes of American pastoral psychologists. He has even been made a "theologian" by Thomas C. Oden. A summary of Oden's views on Rogers is given by Dietrich Stollberg in *"Die Theologie Carl Rogers"* (in *Therapeutische Seelsorge*, 2nd ed. : Munich, 1970; p. 361 ff).

[27] H. Fuglsang-Damgaard, *"Privatskriftemaalet"* (Private Confession), in *Svensk teologisk kvartalskrift*, 1939; p. 45 f.

and perplexed sinner examines his personal situation and becomes clear about himself. Because of the confidence inspired in him and because he unrestrainedly reveals what he has within to the confessor, the confessor becomes the object of special feelings of communion on his part, and of an emotional attachment that may often be very strong; this is particularly so since the confessant expects to attain salvation and release through the confessor's help and intervention. In some cases, the confessant's need to surrender himself wholly to the confessor's authority appears therefore to be the primary element in his attitude. During confession the prior conditions mentioned, advantageous to the exercise of personal influence on the confessant, are strengthened by the confessor's manner of proceeding— by his personal interest, by his willingness to share the burden of sin, to help and guide, comfort and sustain the distressed sinner. This course renders the sinner very susceptible to suggestion during confession; he becomes ready to adopt without question the confessor's advice and directions—and the chief aim of these is in general to lead the sinner on to experience the foregiveness of sins as an actual fact, and moreover the counsel should be of practical guidance in his future way of life.

CHAPTER ELEVEN

HOW CAN GUILT-LADEN MEMORIES BE KEPT
FROM CONSCIOUSNESS?

We had reason, when dealing with the assimilative process in confession, to give our attention to the question of whether unconscious memories could be thought to enter consciousness during the act of confession or in connection with it. We found then that they might be thought to do so, and the cause of this emergence was stated to be the patient's interest in recollecting. and his concentration on guilt-laden memories deriving from that interest. When we now attempt to answer the question of how memories can be ejected from consciousness, how reproduction of them may often be prevented over long periods, the supposition at once presents itself that here again the explanation is self-interest. And psychoanalysis in particular claims that forgetting an affective memory may thus be explained. That view has been confirmed by psychologists who are not psychoanalysts, though usually they emphasize at the same time that it cannot be applied to forgetfulness in general but only to certain forms of forgetting.

When people apply Freud's theory on forgetting, they have recourse as a rule to his idea of repression, and here they are sometimes unclear about what repression really implies in Freudian theory. If the term is to be employed as an explanation for a certain form of forgetfulness, its meaning must necessarily undergo alteration. Of course for Freud the term signified a process that takes place wholly in the unconscious. According to him, the instinctual drive—libido—forcing its way up from the Unconscious (*das Es*) and trying to gain expression, is banned by the censor; this, also functioning unconsciously, thrusts back the instinctual desires unwanted by the superego. For Freud, then, not only the process of repression itself but also a certain part of what is repressed—drives and desires, including that central complex of neuroses, the Oedipus complex—belong to the sphere of the unconscious.

Criticism against Freud's theory of repression is often directed precisely against his assumption that repression comes under the *"Unbewusst"* system, the critics claiming that matters repressed to the unconscious must to some degree have been present in consciousness. But in spite of such opposition, they would like to retain the Freudian concept of *Verdrängung*, though with the reservation that the process may also be regarded as taking place with the aid of the conscious will and that it aims at repression of conscious knowledge.[1] The reason why people often apply the term appears to be connected with its particular usefulness in emphasizing the dynamic element of psychic life.[2]

Oskar Pfister, a member of the psychoanalytical school, advocated extending or altering the concept of "repression" in the way indicated; he deviated thereby from the master's intentions. He spoke about several degrees of repression. "Matters repressed—that is to say, what has been expelled from consciousness along with accretions below the level of consciousness—are, on the one hand, preconscious only if they have reached merely a slight degree of repression and, on the other hand, are unconscious in a stricter sense when a higher degree of repression is involved, an amount that can be overcome only by strong motives and especially by analysis".[3] And Pfister assumed that repression may vary a great deal in power and extent.[4] The process can be thought to take place consciously and include conscious knowledge. One easily perceives that from the Freudian point of view that phrase "unconscious in a narrower sense", with its assumption that there are various degrees of repression, must appear completely mistaken.

---

[1] Such an amplification of the range covered by repression commonly appears during discussions. Linus Bopp commented on the narrowness of the psychoanalytical view on the point. He said (*op. cit.*; p. 33) that psychoanalysis "considers as belonging to the unconscious what has never been conscious, indeed what can never become conscious. But in actual fact extremely much of what has sunk down into the unconscious was once conscious". Bopp advocated (page 37) an extension of the repression concept to include conscious knowledge of the kind. Tor Andrae, too, evidently had such an enlargement of the idea in mind (*Psykoanalys och religion*; p. 65). Note especially in what follows here the account of Maeder's view in the matter, p. 181.

[2] Even a specialist in the field extremely critical of Freud and psychoanalysis, Rudolf Allers, was willing to acknowledge the value of the repression theory where understanding of forgetfulness and inadvertent mistakes is concerned, also to explain the determining of trains of thought "through certain—moreover not always unconscious —repercussive experiences". (Rudolf Allers, *Über Psychoanalyse*; Berlin, 1922; p. 41.)

[3] Oskar Pfister, *Die psychanalytische Methode* (Leipzig, 1924); p. 60.

[4] Pfister said (*ibid.*; p. 143 f.) : *"Für mich ist Freuds Vorbewusstes das Schwachverdrängte, sein 'Unbewusstes' das Starkverdrängte, wobei ich die verschiedensten Intensitäten und Grade der Verdrängung anerkenne".*

But the remarkable thing is that, even if Freud did not then use the word "repression", in certain context he himself seems to have diverged from his fundamental concept and approached a standpoint similar to that taken by Pfister. He did so when dealing with "the psychopathology of everyday life" and the various kinds of inadvertent mistakes there, which include those of forgetfulness. In particular, the forgetting of names was subjected to analysis. Such slips were explained as the result of conflicts between contending tendencies. These were seen as compromise solutions between clashing interests, like dreams and the symptoms of neuroses. Freud said in effect that a disturbing tendency which interferes with orderly everyday life and causes a person to make slips may be thought to exist at various levels of consciousness or different stages of repression. They are: (1) when the person knows about the tendency and knows that it is present before the slip but wishes to keep it temporarily in abeyance; (2) when the person knows about the tendency in a general way but is not clear that it comes up before the slip; (3) when the person has no awareness at all of the troubling tendency and refuses energetically to hear any talk on the subject.[5] It is, then, this last stage which corresponds to Freudian repression in a genuine sense. In order that we may use the concept to explain a certain type of forgetfulness— the active kind which depends on an impulse of the will—we must, like Pfister and others, extend the idea to include the first two stages, where it is assumed that repression can take place consciously as well as unconsciously, and that conscious knowledge can be its object.[6]

---

[5] S. Freud, *op. cit.*; p. 54 f.

[6] In other contexts, too, Freud so portrayed the process of repression that, in actual fact, his reasoning results in the view of repression as being occasionally a conscious act of the will directed at fully conscious knowledge. This applies particularly to his earlier studies of the process. His hypothesis concerning "*Abwehr*"—previously dealt with here— may be recalled. He considered the action to be fully conscious and to cover conscious desires and impulses. (Cf. Pfister, *op. cit.*; p. 60. With manifest regret, Pfister there observes that Freud later abandoned this theory of repression.) Similar views on Freud's part can be gathered from his work *Über Psychoanalyse*. (Evidently with Freud's approval, this collection of lectures, delivered to an American university public in 1909, was published—Vienna, 1922—in a separate edition, and it was included in his *Gesammelte Schriften*, vol. IV—Vienna, 1924—from which it is cited here.) According to the main viewpoint here repression is an unconscious action, but judging from the examples Freud gave, he obviously thought that repression may take in conscious knowledge, and it must consequently be assumed that a conscious act of volition is involved in the process. (See the example, *op. cit.*; p. 367 f., and the rough but instructive comparison in what follows here.)

The explanation that Freud gave for such active forgetfulness has won general acceptance. He said that the operative power involved— the underlying drive which causes people to forget—is "the psychic flight from displeasure". They forget what they *want* to forget : they fail to remember a resolution that would infringe on their comfort and natural inclination, fail to recall a name which in one way or another they associate with displeasure. And the reproduction of memories here is prevented by a single basic tendency : aversion to remembering "something that was associated with disagreeable feelings and which on being reproduced would renew the displeasure".[7] But the affect-laden and suppressed memories do, nevertheless, gain expression of a kind through the person's inadvertent slips.

When, like Ernest Jones, people wish to apply the theory involved to all cases of forgetfulness, of course they carry things too far. Only the most elaborate experiments with association could lend seemingly clear support to such a generalization. One frequent reason why people forget is naturally the wear and tear to which memories are exposed by continuous gathering in of the facts which experience supplies. But it is hard to deny that Freud gave a highly likely explanation of active forgetfullness—that is to say, for the manner in which memories are repressed to the unconscious, this process obviously taking place under sway of the will or of self-interest.

It was evidently psychiatric observation that led Freud to his theory on forgetting. Cases appear in psychiatric practice where patients obviously suppress from current consciousness experiences that are unpleasant to them or inimical to their way of life. This occurs particularly with hysterics. The behaviour of a patient suffering from this form of mental illness may suggest that he deliberately ignores discomfiting events in his past or other disagreeable experience. The element of simulation which often seems characteristic of hysteria can be explained in this way. Indeed, cases occur of cured hysterics who accuse themselves of having previously pretended. It seems to them that they deliberately deceived their doctor. To give an instance : after the recovery of Anna O., Breuer's patient, she burst into self-recriminations which she explained by saying that even in her severest attacks of hysteria a calm and acute observer occupied a corner of her brain and quietly watched all her "crazy tricks".

The cause of hysterical symptoms, in part voluntary, indicates

---

[7] S. Freud, *Vorlesungen*, p. 67 f.

that a person may easily suppress memories or impulses which are incompatible with the behaviour that he has decided to follow. In psychiatry the phenomenon involved is commonly called "opportune forgetfulness". Bror Gadelius cited an excellent example of it: the case of a patient whom he called "the man without memory".[8] In this patient hysterical repression was found of all memories from before a certain date. Its cause was an instinctual impulse to escape from the very unpleasant demands placed on the man. Gadelius considered his forgetfulness to be founded on "repression of all conceptions or memories incompatible with his well-being or even inimical to his existence". The hysterical or psychogenic amnesia in question was, Gadelius believed, caused by a hypertrophy of the repression operative in normal mental life and affecting inopportune conceptions and memories. Gadelius called this normal psychic activity that controls our thoughts and actions the "elective" function.

Earlier here, when dealing with the reproduction of unconscious memories during confession, we examined the activity involved and then construed it as being dependent on a current need or interest. The fact that forgetting, brushing aside or repressing knowledge and preventing its reproduction may derive from self-interest—this we have now received good reason from psychiatry to assume. And it appears very probable that the interest is the psychic flight from displeasure.

That view is confirmed not only by psychiatry but also by the normal experience of people in general. John Elmgren, the Swedish psychologist who devoted special study to the functioning of memory, said: "The general law seems, however, to be that, while pleasant experience becomes consolidated in the memory, unpleasant and painful memories fade more quickly until they dissolve completely and are effaced".[9] Of course individual differences, deriving from individual temperament and character, might seem to go against this view. But they may be considered exceptions that prove the rule. Surely everyone can observe in the ordinary intercourse of human beings that, while they commonly dwell on happy recollections from the past, their memories of sombre and less agreeable events subside, become dulled and are forgotten. Of course there are occurrences which have affected the life of the personality too profoundly for them to be forgotten. Opposing tendencies appear to be involved here:

---

[8] B. Gadelius, *Det mänsliga själslivet* (Human Mental Life), vol. II; p. 230 ff.

[9] John Elmgren, *Minnet* (The Memory: Stockholm, 1935); p. 185.

one trend impels towards forgetfulness and the other towards reproduction of remembered facts. We shall in what follows have occasion to
take up discussion of this matter.

Experimental psychology lends a good measure of support to the
general law which is accepted here to cover active forgetfulness.
Though rather superficial experiences are concerned in the tests,
they supply evidence that runs along the same line as the Freudian
theory and thus serves to support it. For instance, Elmgren spoke
about memorizing words which have a pleasant or an unpleasant
feeling and tone. Experiments in the matter show that agreeable
or pleasure-giving words remain more easily in the memory than do
unpleasurable words.

A member of the *gestalt* psychological school, Bluma Zeigarnik,
carried out thoroughgoing experiments to ascertain whether completed
or uncompleted actions are better retained by consciousness.[10] Subjects
of the experiments, who varied in age, were set a number of tasks.
They were allowed to complete half of these, but the leader broke off
the second half at the point where subjects were most deeply at work.
Interrupted and finished tasks followed in no systematic order. It
then became apparent that the uncompleted tasks were more easily
retained by the memory than those completed. Unfinished work
leaves a certain tension in the psyche; this is because of the instinctual
impulse to finish it or the interest felt in getting it done. The tension
involved was used to explain why recollections of such work are more
easily retained by the memory and more readily produced. But (and
now we come to what is of special interest in our investigation) when
some subjects of the experiments responded to certain tasks with a
feeling of inadequacy or powerlessness, the memory tests revealed
that the tasks were more easily forgotten than in other instances.
According to Bluma Zeignarik, in such cases the subjects forgot
because they were disturbed by their insufficient ability. Forgetfulness was there occasioned by a sense of inferiority; the memory had
been "encapsulated" or repressed because it was unpleasant.

Two American psychologists, S. Rosenzweig and G. Mason, under-
took similar experiments with the principal aim of finding out whether
Freud's theory of forgetting holds true.[11] They first took up Bluma

---

[10] Bluma Zeigarnik, "*Über das Behalten von erledigten und unerledigten Handlungen*",
in *Psychologische Forschung*, vol. IX (Berlin, 1927); pp. 1-85. Cf. J. Elmgren, "*Gestalt
Psychology*", in *Göteborgs Högskolas årsskrift*, 1938; pp. 265-280.

[11] "An Experimental Study of Memory in Relation to the Theory of Repression",
in *The British Journal of Psychology*, 24 (1933-34); pp. 247-265.

Zeigarnik's findings about memories associated with feelings of inferiority or uneasiness. Experiments were carried out with children of different ages, tasks being assigned to them. The children could not accomplish some of these. Later, when they were required to enumerate the tasks that they had been given, it became clear that their response varied in accordance with their age. The more mature children who possessed greater assurance recalled best what they had done successfully; but younger and less mature children remembered unsuccessful activity as well as, if not better than, what had been successful. The difference evidently depended on psychic development. Children of greater self-assurance pay closer attention to their personal valuation, are more jealous of their prestige, and consequently they suppress memories that are unenhancing to their self-regard. Failed activities have acquired a distateful character because they inflicted on the child's self-esteem, and so they are repressed. This, the authors of the study pointed out, accords with Freud's theory on repression.[12]

Thus, the Freudian thesis that people forget what they wish to forget—forget what is unpleasant, discomfiting, incompatible with the personality's line of action—receives support from psychiatric observation of clinical cases, from the normal experience of people generally, and from the carefully executed tests of experimental psychology. An elementary instinct seems to be in operation here, what Freud called the psychic flight from displeasure.

Obviously, the principle he applied to forgetfulness provides a very likely explanation for the way guilt-laden memories may be suppressed and prevented from coming to consciousness. The extremely discomfiting character of guilt feelings doubtless needs no lengthy demonstration. Their unpleasantness was apparent from our discussion of remorse. The tendency to flee from displeasure works towards the suppression of disagreeable experiences with the result that they can be more or less completely forgotten. Of course the degree of forgetfulness varies with each individual person and with the sensitiveness of his conscience, but there appears to be a general, and natural, trend towards forgetting.

People have, however, unpleasurable experiences that they cannot forget. There are guilt-charged memories which have gained so profound

---

[12] *Ibid.*; p. 258. The concept of repression is accepted here without any very close definition. It is evidently employed in the "amplified" way. Other experimental studies have confirmed the results adduced here. See Shakow and Rapaport, *op. cit.*; p. 131.

a hold, which possess such radical consequence in the life of the personality, that they cannot be forgotten. The existence of these seems of
course to run directly counter to the principle on active forgetfulness
accepted here. Freud responded to the criticism simply by observing
what is justified in it; he did not consider that it cancelled out his
previous reasoning. It is important he said, that people should start
taking into account the fact "that mental life is a battlefield and
an arena for conflicting tendencies, or, to express it unmetaphorically,
that mental life is made up of contradictions and antitheses. Evidence
that a definite tendency exists there provides no grounds for excluding
that the opposite tendency is present. There is room for both. What
matters is simply how the contradictions are ranged in relation to
each other and what effects emanate from one or the other".[13]

The psychology of memory gives a place to this particular reproductive tendency which seems to be attached to certain memories
of a fundamentally affective kind : to a grief or an anxiety or a problem
that has long been at the centre of psychic activity. Such recollections
may be said to possess an inherent power that forces them up into
consciousness. They can appear there spontaneously. They then
come to mind without any demonstrable agency of an association.
In the phrase of G. E. Müller, this movement of certain recollections
is the "perseverance tendency".[14] We have, incidentally, earlier met
with a variation of it in the account given about Bluma Zeigarnik's
experiments. The reason why uncompleted solutions to problems
there were more easily remembered may well be interpreted with
such a persistent force in view.[15] But it is not only because of the
perseverance tendency, because strongly emotional recollections have
an innate power of reproduction, that they remain in the memory;
of course it is also because they are easily brought to mind by outward
stimuli. Associations are likely to be made with them. A person's
concepts revolve about such a recollection, and his thoughts all radiate
towards it as to a focal point. The affect binds life of the imagination
in the direction of the object to which it is itself attached.

We have thus to take into account, on the one hand, the way
unpleasant experiences tend to be forgotten, the flight from displeasure,

---

[13] S. Freud, *op. cit.*; p. 69 f.

[14] A. Messer, *op. cit.*; p. 265 f. Cf. p. 276.

[15] Cf. W. Stern's review of Bluma Zeigarnik's work in *Zeitschrift für angewandte
Psychologie*, 29 (Leipzig, 1928); p. 422 f.

and on the other hand we must accept a tendency to accept unpleasant memories, the perseverance tendency, and the activity of association. This double situation may well serve to illuminate the state in which the confessant finds himself. Particularly, it reveals how the need to confess may become irresistible. For one readily understands that if an unpleasurable memory—where religious confession is concerned, the recollection of a sin, of an event producing strong guilt feelings— exists, so to speak, in a magnetic field where the two opposite poles exert great force at the same time, then mental tension will finally become unbearable. We know from dynamic psychology that a large amount of psychic energy is required to maintain such tension. Far more may be needed than the person is able to supply, and mental disorders can appear if mental tension is not allowed to subside by clearing away the centre of trouble. The person may reach a state where confession compels itself forth. This seems to be the background of a spontaneous confession.

If we are to take a realistic view, however, we are forced to accept that people succeed very extensively in keeping unpleasurable memories from consciousness. And where suppression of guilt-charged recollections is concerned the process appears to include not only repression of individual events but also the entire drive that moves a person towards ethics and religion : which is to say, the tendency to take in real earnest the recollections that induce guilt. If with Freud there was primarily question of desire, of the libido, being suppressed, here the thing is suppression of the instinct to surrender oneself, of the drive towards an ethical ideal and a religious object.

This is not the place for a thorough examination of what lies behind the life of the conscience and what causes an instinctual movement towards the ideal. Let it be enough to observe that forces of the kind exist, and they are of extreme importance to the personality. Freud was not backward in perceiving this. In the often crude campaign against him and his school, it is commonly argued that he was an advocate and prophet of permissiveness; in other words, it is advanced that his theories and practice, taken as a whole, were based on the aim of liberating people from moral values. He is supposed to have held that the calamitous effect of such values may be seen in repression, inhibitions and the formation of complexes. Because of this situation, the inhibited person ought to be freed from those values, should be put in a state where he can live out his libido, so as to achieve health and harmony. As a number of psychoanalysts have derived such views from Freud's theories, it cannot very well be denied that something does lie in the contention involved. But one might contend with greater justification that Freud laid more emphasis than most analysts have done on the enormous part played by the conscience. His assumption of a censor in the mind and of repression certainly drew attention to the strength of moral forces.[16] And he demonstrated that the position occupied by those forces is not superficial; they go down to the deepest level of the mind and form part of the unconscious system which gives rise to repression. Freud remarked on the consequent wrongness of recommending to a neurotic whose trouble originates from repressed libido that he should give full expression to his lust. If the person does so, he will immediately acquire a new form of neurosis coming from the drive that previously was the active element in repression.[17]

Thus, it is seen that Freud did not narrowly accentuate repression of the sexual instinct as the cause of neurosis; he showed how repression of the moral force or the ego drive can produce calamitious psychic disorders. According to him, what is required for a normal psychic life seems to be a harmonious balance between the forces on either side. If the clinical cases with which psychoanalysis is usually concerned are interpreted as involving repression of the libido, that constitutes good evidence of the part moral authority plays in the personality and the power it exerts there. But, obviously, such authority may bear little weight in the determination of people's actions. And the moral side of the personality can be repressed.

When taking up the theory of repression, the Finnish psychologist Eino Kaila construed it in the widest sense and said of the idea: "Any need at all may in certain circumstances provoke repression; this is by no means because the forces exercising suppressive effect are always of a higher nature and belong to the 'superego' and not because the object of repression is of a lower kind, merely stimuli from the animal sphere. What happens may be exactly the contrary:

---

[16] With a disciple's admiration for his master, O. Pfister said on the subject (*op. cit.*; p. 60): "*Damit war in unvergleichlich eindrucksvoller Weise die ungeheure Macht des Sittlichen festgestellt, und keine frühere Psychologie durfte sich rühmen, eine ähnliche Würdigung des sittlichen Faktors im Menschen erzielt zu haben*".

[17] S. Freud, *op. cit.*; p. 458 f. Elsewhere, Freud said that, if one measures by ethical standards, "one as often sees people succumb to mental illness when they cast away an ideal as when they wish to live up to one". (Freud, "*Über neurotische Erkrankungstypen*", in *Gesammelte Schriften*, vol. V—Vienna, 1924—p. 404).

for example, "the voice of conscience" may meet with suppression and be caught by the forces which have a repressive effect, by animal desire, for instance".[18] Arvid Runestam, the Swedish theologian, pointed out in his book *Psychoanalysis and Christianity*[19] how life of the conscience can be subjected to systematic repression. He said that with modern man there is often question of ethical and religious life being repressed as a whole. Natural desire is given admittance and the moral force is suppressed in consequence. The moral element is often too weak to prevent instinctual impulses from appearing, but meanwhile it possesses sufficient strength to produce remorse over manifestation of the libido. All this may be thought to take place unconsciously, but what transpires in the depths of the mind has its effect and often results in neurosis.

Theodor Müncker was another who took up Freud's teachings on repression, but he found "excessive bias" in Freud's way of tracing all repressions to sexual drives. "Repression", he said, "is a common manner of dealing with the experiences where everything felt as unpleasant is concerned".[20] Thus, the dictates of conscience may be instinctively thrust aside. The driving force involved here comes from an attempt to preserve the person's self-esteem, shaken by a remorseful conscience. Müncker held repression to be basically self-dissimulation, "an ostrich-like policy towards unpleasant mental processes".[21] And he pointed out the danger of repressing qualms of conscience in such fashion. He said—which of course Freud also stressed—that remorse may manifest itself in mental disorders.

The Swiss psychiatrist A. Maeder gave many good examples of neuroses caused by repression of the conscience. The principles he proceeded from are those on which analytical (Jung's) psychology is based. His originality among analysts may be said to reside in the fact that his therapy turned to account the moral tendency evident in the formation of neuroses, and that he regarded the patient's moral transformation or change of heart as the royal road to recovery.

---

[18] Eino Kaila, *Personlighetens psykologi* (Psychology of the Personality; Stockholm, 1939); p. 288 f.

[19] (Rock Island, 1958.)

[20] T. Müncker, *op. cit.*; p. 193.

[21] *Ibid.* See also A. Uleyn, *Pastorale Psychologie en Schuldervaring* (Bruges, 1964), n particular p. 200 ff.

From Maeder's collection of cases let us cite two examples of such "conscience neuroses".[22]

For some years a woman of thirty has complained that she suffers sensations of uneasiness and is in a depressed state. She no longer takes much interest in anything; she feels empty and arid, is disoriented and generally disappointed in life. As to what causes her mental condition, she herself knows nothing. During the period when she is receiving psychiatric treatment her husband dies. She has not been capable of drawing close to him spiritually during his brief illness and giving him solace at the hour of his death. Nor can she summon up genuine grief afterwards. Her disagreeable sensations increase, and a number of physical symptoms appear; all of these indicate that she is suffering from some stomach trouble. She is convinced herself that she has tapeworm. Terrifying nightmares harass her at night, and insomnia that no sleeping medicine can cure comes upon her. A physical examination reveals that there is great restraint, inhibition verging on paralysis, in the functioning of her stomach and intestines. It cannot be established that she has tapeworm. What a psychological analysis reveals is as follows. Affects which did not gain their natural outlet have been released by her husband's death. Of course her ability to give expression to her feelings has been poor. Instead of these being manifested, a typical hysterical conversion has, according to Maeder, taken place. Her mental agitation has found an outlet by affecting her digestive apparatus and paralyzing it. As for her anguished dreams, in which her husband appears as pursuer, they express a critical feeling towards herself and a sense of inferiority. Both have been brought on by her husband's death. Her husband led an upright life and was morally strict. But her life has been exactly the contrary. From early youth, she has "rushed into a series of adventures and gradually emerged a mere shadow of herself". She broods over the self-reproaches incarnated by the dream figure of her husband. As result, she has become sleepless. She interprets the physical difficulties caused by conversion of her affects as coming from tapeworm. In fact, the tapeworm is purely a symbol of her distressing moral situation and her suppressed conscience. She has come from an austerely Christian home and acquired an earnest and ethical outlook on life. But in adult years she has become emancipated and followed a "free way of life". She regards this as being in accord with her particular temperament. "With the passing of time, she has constructed her own

---

[22] A. Maeder, *Die Richtung im Seelenleben* (Zurich, 1928).

safety system : an artificial rationalization by which she has justified her situation to herself and switched off promptings of the inward voice. She has succeeded only too well. We have already seen at whose expense, for we know that she gradually forfeited her joy in living, her spontaneity and indeed even the sense of leading her personal life. By repressing admonitions, protests and reproaches from within, she has, as it were, lost her spiritual life and become a stranger to herself. What has been repressed now returns in a violent reaction; it overwhelms her in the peculiar form of her half physical and half psychic illness". Maeder now conveys this interpretation of her illness to her; she apparently accepts it, and an improvement in her general state immediately results. Subsequent treatment brings her a deeper conviction that her illness has been rightly construed; she evidently arrives at a new way of behaviour and attains mental health.

Another of Maeder's cases is also enlightening. Here the patient wakes up in the middle of a night filled with the affect-charged idea that it is dangerous for him to drink. He grows frightened and decides that he will give up drinking spirits. Some days later, he becomes aware that he has been suffering from an almost unconscious anxiety : he may have stomach cancer. But a medical examination does not support his fear. What later comes to light is that he secretly lives in an extra-marital relationship, and this sometimes disturbs him. He does not admit that it does, and he invents excuses for the situation. By means of these, he has succeeded in repressing his moral conflict, but this manifests itself indirectly as worry about cancer. The anxiety expresses "in veiled form the danger of the situation. A destructive psychic process is taking place within him, and he first becomes aware of it in this roundabout manner". Maeder concludes his case histories with a variation of the classical phrase about what happens when Nature is ignored. "If you chase away the reproaches of conscience, they only come back all the stronger !"

The most striking thing about Maeder's explanations of his cases, when they are compared with those customarily offered by the Freudian school, is his interpretation of symbols. Obviously, to a faithful Freudian the tapeworm in the case of the woman could only be a sexual symbol, a sign of repressed sexual libido; and in the other case a similar construction would doubtless be placed on cancer. The fact that Maeder's explanations demonstrate the narrowness of the way symbols are interpreted by orthodox psychoanalysis is one reason why they inspire interest. His approach naturally cohered with his general outlook on the mental illnesses involved. He gained a clear picture of his patients' psychic state from their accounts of factors in their lives and of their dreams, and he assumed that their troubles were caused by repression of conscience. His interpretation of the predominant symbols came as a later consequence of the over-all view he took. And this comprehensive approach seems the only sound basis on which to interpret symbols. If undertaken realistically and without preconceived ideas, it will evidently do justice to cases where the force that initiates the formation of neuroses is repression of the moral tendency. Thus, it supplies a corrective to the biassed psycho-analytical interpretation of symbols.

In the case of the man, another element that deserves attention is the process of repression. This clearly begins quite consciously, for he is disturbed now and then by his own way of behaving. He works to suppress the reproaches of his conscience, and he believes that he has entirely succeeded when the moral tendency finds expression in the form of compulsive ideas which force him to consult the doctor. Concerning the repression of conscience, Maeder did in fact speak about various degrees of unconsciousness.

A similar conception of how the conscience is repressed has been put forward by O. H. Mowrer, the eminent American psychologist.[23] His opinion on the matter has drawn much attention because of his radical outlook. He would evidently like to find the causes of all functional neuroses, of psychic disorders as a whole, in a sense of guilt. As predecessors in taking such a view, he mentions particularly Runestam, Boisen and Stekel.

Mowrer considers that a patient can regain mental health only by taking his guilt in real earnest and expressing it in such a way that it is acknowledged and avowed. Special emphasis is laid on confession : "It appears that the central fact in personal disorder is real *guilt* and that it can be radically resolved only by confession".[24]

According to Mowrer, confession is not enough, however. There must be a "restitution" as well : amends must be made in the form of penance. When reading Mowrer here, one gets the impression of a criminal having to redress his crime; the patient must suffer if his mental balance is to be restored. The penance involved should be directed in some way towards restoring communion and at re-establish-

---

[23] O. H. Mowrer, *The Crisis in Psychiatry and Religion* (New Jersey, 1961).
[24] *Ibid.*; p. 217.

ing severed personal relationships. That lies in the internal logic
of events. As the sin has involved rupture with the community and
isolation of the individual, restitution should aim at restoral of the
ties that unite people together.

The examples which Mowrer describes to support his views are of
much interest, and, though more complicated, they may be compared
with the cases from Maeder's practice cited here. As with Maeder,
the repression of guilt feelings and the making of confession are of
central importance to Mowrer.

In the discussion devoted to Mowrer's sweeping opinions,[25] the
psychiatrist Sidney M. Jourard made a statement which has since
been quoted with some approval by Mowrer himself. Jourard said :
"Clinical experience suggests that neither Freud nor Mowrer is wholly
correct or wholly incorrect. Rather it can be found that some neurotic
patients do indeed have a conscience that is too strict; in order to
remain guilt-free they must refrain from all pleasurable activities
including those which society condones. Other patients may be found
with the make-up which Mowrer has regarded as nuclear to all neurosis
—they repress conscience so they can break social taboos without
conscious guilt".

Attempting to resolve the antagonism in what we regard as a
sensible manner, Jourard concluded by saying : "Consciences *are
not all alike* among all members of a given society. Some consciences
are stricter than the society requires, some are more lenient, some
are quite deviant from the social value system, and many are highly
conflicted".[26]

As regards repression of the conscience, we have seen that it can be
unconscious or can be thought to involve different degrees of consciousness. And it seems significant from the viewpoint of religious confession
to speak about various degrees of repression. We may observe that
with religiously active people guilt-charged memories are only slightly
repressed. In pious Catholics, for example, such memories are latent
and frequently emerge into consciousness because the people are
well-schooled by penance and by the practice of confession for the
penitential remorse enjoined by the Church. If we examine cases of

---

[25] Concerning Mowrer's exaggerated criticism of psychiatry and the churches, see
the review in *Journal for the Scientific Study of Religion*, 1961, p. 125, and an article in
Insight, 1967.

[26] Quoted from Mowrer, *op. cit.*; pp. 26-27.

this kind where repression of the conscience scarcely exists or is very weak, we can imagine a gradual increase in the strength of repression leading towards a stage where the moral function is unconsciously repressed and the person is unaware that his action incurs any guilt or any offence against an ethical rule.

Actually, a person living a completely "blameless" life, without any awareness of guilt at all, would seem to be a fairly rare phenomenon. Earlier, we witnessed instances of confessants who appear to have succeeded wholly in repressing their consciences, their moral strength, before making confession. When God then becomes a reality for them they observe that they are sinners; self-objectification takes place, and they look on themselves and their lives from a new point of view; this shows individual memories to be particularly laden with guilt, and they are confessed. As is apparent from what has been said here about the interplay of forces that manifests itself in repression, the confessor is moved by a sound instinct when he regards the different sins confessed as expressions of the drives which repress the moral force. The confessor's observation of what these are, brought forward and readily accepted by the confessant himself, means that the balance required for normal life between forces and needs of the personality can be re-established. The process which then takes place is fortified by the confessor's advice and guidance, and the confessant experiences it as a transformation of his personality, as a conversion.

In the chapter that follows we shall have occasion to dwell somewhat more thoroughly on the relation between confession and conversion.

PART FOUR

CHAPTER TWELVE

WHAT IS CHARACTERISTIC OF CHRISTIAN CONFESSION

The moral tendency of human beings finds expression in Christian confession. What distinguishes such confession from the secular kind is of course that offenses against ethical rules are here confessed as sins, as crimes against the will of God; also, the Christian confessant is seeking God's foregiveness by his confession, and he is prepared to be guided henceforth by God's will in order to live a better life. Thus, his confession denotes a change of heart, a *metánoia* or conversion.

We might define conversion as a psychological act in the way J. B. Pratt did. He said: "The only essential part of it is just this new birth by which a man ceases to be a mere psychological thing or a divided self and becomes a unified being with a definite direction under the guidance of a group of consistent and harmonious purposes or ideals".[1] This definition seems to cover rather well what transpires in a sincere confession or in the process which reaches culmination or receives corroboration during confession. Naturally, while observing this we must take into consideration that the definition is of a framing character and intended to comprise all forms of conversion; it therefore includes those of a non-Christian variety and indeed even from Christianity to a positivist conception of life (as in the example Pratt cited of the Italian philosopher Roberto Ardigo[2]). Naturally, too, the process and what it imports vary in accordance with the faith concerned. It is therefore of weight in our context here to establish the significance and consequences of conversion in the Christian sphere. What then seems to be essential is that the confessant places himself under the Divine Will and makes the values adherent there those highest in his life, all other norms and aims being subjected to them. It is of special importance to emphasize that conversion should be regarded as a conscious action, an act of the personal will bringing a resolution in favour of of the Divine Will and of the highest ideals.[3] During this conscious act the person feels himself a free being;

---

[1] J. B. Pratt, *op. cit.*; p. 123.

[2] Pratt, *op. cit.*; p. 126 f.

[3] In his work *Religious Conversion* (London, 1927), Sante de Sanctis laid particular

he feels also that he gains the ability and the strength to govern his conflicting instinctual drives and to assign them their places in the hierarchy of forces and values which ought all to serve the Divine Will.

What Pratt questioned was whether the sense of guilt and of remorse for sins truly plays such a dominant part in the process of conversion as people have generally sought to maintain. He for his own part took the view that it does not. Since the matter is of special interest in an investigation of the connection which the avowal of sins in confession bears to conversion, we may give it some attention here.

Pratt carried on a controversy against Starbuck's and James's view on conversion. He thought that their studies were based on cases where conversion had been brought about by Anglo-Saxon revivalist preaching of a kind that derived from Luther and Calvin. The aim of such preaching was to induce a sense of guilt, to convince the sinner that he was in a hopeless situation and incapable of extricating himself by his own efforts. In uttermost darkness, he could do nothing but leave all to the Grace of God. Only when he had come to such understanding of his plight and ceased to struggle forward alone could he hope for God's intervention, for salvation through Grace. Conversions like those of John Bunyan and David Brainerd—which Pratt regarded as typical—had come about through revivalist preaching of the sort mentioned. Before the "emergence of Grace", the two suffered long periods of the most agonizing uncertainty about their redemption, and they systematically cultivated a sense of guilt. Consequently, they were reduced at intervals to a depressive state in which they believed that they were condemned by God. They dwelt in unblessed expectation that God's Grace might descend on them, that they would be free from their burden of guilt. At last they experienced liberation. Their conversion was complete.

When such psychologists as Starbuck and James took to studying the psychology of conversion, they encountered stories of conversions like those of Bunyan and Brainerd. They then, from cases of that kind, proceeded to work out their theories about the course and stages of conversion. Such cases—the result of a definite type of religion, of a special theological outlook and type of preaching—were thus

---

stress on the operation of unconscious factors, or "the complex", in explaining the process of conversion, but he emphasized that the person must consciously and "of his own will" accept the change which has taken place in his unconscious if a true conversion is to be attained. (Page 253.)

turned into typical examples of conversion as a whole. Afterwards, theologians and preachers paid tribute to the psychologists for the sound picture provided of the psychology involved. A fine circle! exclaimed Pratt in effect. He held that sin and a sense of guilt are by no means usual phenomena in conversion. The commonest motive there is the search for a supreme value, or it is the striving to escape from a miserable state, consequent on vice and misdemeanour, and to enter a purer, brighter and calmer life. The theory that people must give up or restrain their efforts here, a matter of such importance in the theology and psychology described, was regarded by Pratt as one of the most pernicious ideas put forward. What he placed among the most important fulcrums of conversion was rather a struggle towards the possibility of a new life.

Undeniably, it occasions some surprise that a psychologist of religion should ascribe as little importance as Pratt did to the part played in the process of conversion by remorse over sins. His view on the subject seems to have been dictated more by a marked aversion to Anglo-Saxon revivalist preaching and the religiosity in revivalist circles than by note of evident facts to be considered. He showed a tendency to tone down the importance of eminent conversions—those of Saint Augustine and Luther, for instance—where the essential factor was repentance; he drew attention instead to examples where the intellectual element—the search for truth and for a meaning in life—was dominant. Significantly, of the four cases he put forward initially to substantiate his view, the first was the conversion of a scientist from Christianity to positivism, two were drawn from the sphere of Indian religion, and only the fourth came from Christianity. Beyond these cases, he confirmed his stand mainly by pointing out that repentance does not play any vital part in the accounts of conversion given by the New Testament, and he said the same about examples he had investigated in the Salvation Army. As for the New Testament, his opinion may easily be disproved; reference to the Gospel according to St. Luke will probably suffice in the matter.[4] And it is surely clear enough that contrition often plays a decisive part in the change of heart undergone by adepts of the Salvation Army; that applies as well to other revivalist organizations which work methodically to arouse a feeling of remorse and a desire for penance. Consequently,

---

[4] See, for instance, the story of the sinful woman in Simon's house (*Luke* 7:36 ff.) and the parable concerning the Prodigal Son (*Luke* 15:11 ff.).

such a failure as Pratt's either to accept or to take into consideration the importance of guilt feelings in genuine conversion implies in our opinion misjudgement of known facts.

Pratt was surely right that the theology and preaching which prevail determine the type of conversion that will take place. It follows, however, that the conversion not only of a person who has been brought up in an Anglo-Saxon revivalist environment but of one simply with a Christian background will be coloured by an awareness of guilt, and this will often be the weightiest reason for his conversion. For where the Christian faith is concerned we never seem able to avoid according guilt feelings a central position among incentives to conversion. True, they are not by any means the only grounds for conversion. But Starbuck—though so attacked by Pratt—did not mean to say that they were. Of the people who replied to his inquiry about the reasons for their conversions, fifteen per cent of the women and eighteen per cent of the men gave remorse and a sense of guilt as being decisive.[5]

Another of Pratt's reproaches against Starbuck and James was directed at their assumption that conversion implies "a struggle to escape from sin rather than a striving towards righteousness", also at their acceptance that the final and decisive stage in the process of conversion is the person's relinquishment of his efforts, and indeed of himself, when he feels himself seized by the divine power. In Pratt's eyes what occurred ran exactly counter to this. He regarded conversion as basically an endeavour to attain righteousness and to enter a new, pure life. The factor of volition was paramount, and he considered the view that self-surrender and passivity came at the last phase to be pernicious because it gave rise to cases, such as Bunyan's and Brainerd's, of wretched brooding and continual lamentation over a sinful state.

In answer to this it can simply be stated that Starbuck and James spoke about the struggle to escape from sin and thus provided ample scope for the element of will in the conversion process. Of course they did not extract from thin air their theory about self-surrender at the last phase: it reflected definite experiences in typical cases. As for whether conversion is characterized by the struggle to escape

---

[5] E. D. Starbuck, *The Psychology of Religion*, 4th ed. (London, 1914); p. 52. Cf. Fritz Giese, "*Kinderpsychologie*", in *Handbuch der vergleichenden Psychologie*, ed. by G. Kafka : vol. I (Munich, 1922); p. 368.

from sin or to attain righteousness,[6] it seems possible to settle the matter merely by supposing that both factors are in operation where Christian confession is concerned. The process when feelings of guilt appear is this : at the same time as the sinner perceives his sinfulness and confesses it he attempts to fight against it, and he is aided in his resistance by reaching out after the power which he believes can liberate him and enable him to live a better and purer life. As we previously observed, imbued within contrition there is a striving away from sin; if profound, this struggle depends of its nature on the sinner's comprehension, however obscure, that he can be free from sin. Thus the remorse is inspired inherently by a longing to get away, a drive to escape, from sinfulness and to arrive at a purer state.[7]

In his discussion of confession Pratt criticized the psychologists of religion for exaggerating the frequency of sudden conversion, and on this it seems that we must agree with him. Because "sudden conversion" is an enigma, it has attracted much attention among psychologists, and too great stress has been laid on it in consequence. Pratt pointed out that a gradual progress towards conversion occurs far more often; and in fact this constitutes the normal course. An abrupt and strongly affective conversion proves genuine only in certain extraordinary cases involving people of nervous disposition. Pratt said that nine times out of ten the "sudden" type of conversion is produced because tradition and preaching have insisted on it. His view appears to be justified. It should be remarked here that ever since William James advanced his theory of "unconscious incubation" there has been a tendency to exaggerate the importance of the unconscious element in conversion. People seem too inclined to regard conversion as a phenomenon that has emerged precipitately, without any advance warning, and has at a single stroke brought about a transformation of the personality. An "unconscious incubation" is said to have taken place. Earlier, tendencies towards a change in the person's values and way of life have been present in his unconscious, and these may

---

[6] Starbuck, incidentally, in the account he gave of the reasons for conversion, paid due regard to the struggle for righteousness. He even estimated this incentive to be somewhat more usual than contrition and guilt feelings; fifteen per cent of the men and twenty per cent of the women had reported such grounds for their conversions. (Starbuck, *op. cit.*; p. 52.)

[7] Cf. G. W. Allport's *The Individual and his Religion* (New York, 1968 : p. 149) concerning faith as an endeavour towards, for one thing, personal perfection.

have attempted now and then to penetrate into consciousness but been suppressed. They have meanwhile drawn more strength and concepts; they have grown into powerful complexes which have matured and finally, on a suitable occasion, pressed forward into consciousness, where they have taken over completely, bringing an abrupt reassessment of values and a change in the personality.

It would of course be difficult to supply another explanation than this for some cases which come to mind. But in general an endeavour or a tendency that truly impels towards a transformation of life does not allow itself to be wholly repressed. Consciousness will certainly be reminded of its existence from time to time, and new justifications to strengthen it may then appear. We can thus think of the process as continuing gradually towards its culmination, to a new immediacy and power; it goes on until, because of experiences that life brings to the person or influence that people in his environment exert, the whole context of values represented becomes so powerful and vivid in his consciousness that the tendency takes complete possession and transforms his personality. It would seem that most cases of "sudden conversion" are preceded by a more or less conscious procedure of this kind. What we observed earlier concerning repression of the moral tendency is of course in line with such a view.

Thus, our discussion of conversion has shown, among other things, that we must consider remorse for sins and struggle against sinfulness to be central and genuine reasons for Christian conversion. Christian confession should be placed against this background. Progress towards conversion reaches its climax in confession : the person arrives there at the final and crucial phase where his sin and its context become clear in his consciousness and are repented, where he makes a deliberate decision that in future his life will be under the will of God.

But the question arises : Are all the forms of confession that we have seen instanced in this study truly religious and Christian in character ? Is such a character not attributable only to forms which stress an institutional aspect—those met with in the Catholic Church and practised in Protestantism by certain churchmen and priest-like spiritual leaders ? The question has an important bearing on our investigation into the relation between confession and conversion. For, if a certain kind of confession which has been dealt with in the foregoing does not actually possess the nature of a religious act, then of course we cannot regard it as belonging to the process of conversion. It was evidently such a view of the matter that led H. I. Schou to equate private confession with profane confession. By "private confession" Schou meant "a purely personal avowal made by one person to another without religious aim"; he thus distinguished it from ecclesiastical confession, which prepares for absolution and Holy Communion.[8] Schou believed that only the latter kind has a religious objective. It is plain that, so regarded, private confession becomes primarily confession made to a layman, and such confession may appear at times to be simply an avowal from one person to another. But if we examine the situation there more closely we find that the religious aim may still be present, provided that a sin, deeply felt and profoundly repented, is earnestly confessed. The very fact that the sinner feels his error or his shortcoming to be a sin surely indicates that a religious reality is in some way animate for him, and the choice of a religiously experienced person as his confessor shows that he considers God to be present or participant in the act of confession, or it shows that he believes he will feel the presence of God as a result of confession when absolution comes to him as an actual fact. But among religiously inexperienced people God may be only dimly conceived. The God towards whom they wish to turn for liberation may not be known to them. Or they may feel that they have been rejected by God, and by other people, because their sins are so severe. They need guidance and help in order to arrive at a real confession. Perhaps they need to hear from a person who is more experienced in religious matters that God truly *can* liberate them. Earlier here we saw many cases of this kind. We might recollect especially the Laestadians in Lainio and the first confession received by Blumhardt. But such confessants generally do feel, even if obscurely at times, the presence of God, and they sense that this gives their confessions a solemn seriousness and far-reaching significance. Ultimately, what they wish to reach in their confession is not the confessor but a higher and stronger Power behind him : they want to experience the presence of that Power; they want that Power to help them escape from the sinful state in which they find themselves and which they can no longer bear. The confessor is able to serve as intermediary between them and God by providing new insights into the nature of God or by leading them to certainty about the remission of sins.

On the other hand, the part played by the confessor may be passive. The confessant may experience the reality of absolution so strongly

---

[8] H. I. Schou, *op. cit.* in *Kirke og kultur*, 1933; p. 577.

during confession that he does not need any mediation by the person to whom he confesses. We might illustrate this by an example from the Oxford Group movement. Though the case in question has already been cited in our account of self-objectification during confession, it has its interest here as well. The confessant relates : "I shared everything that lay on my mind with a friend; I revealed my weakest side to him, and he did the same to me. And while I was telling him what oppressed me, I suddenly realized what a worthless creature I actually was, how I valued myself too highly, loved myself. I talked and talked until there really was nothing more to tell and—I was free. At the instant when I felt what a burden of sin weighed on me, God took me to Him. I passed everything on to Him—and from that moment I felt that I was the happiest person on earth".[9]

It is here as if the confessor's part were confined to prompting forth a total confession. After he has done this, the confession continues as a long monologue which is gradually directed more to God than to the listening friend. That such is the case appears from the words : "... I was free. At the instant when I felt what a burden of sin weighed on me, God took me to Him..." It follows that our example shows a confession "from one person to another" where in the course of the confession the religious reality grows very important to the confessant : indeed, God Himself finally becomes the real confessor. Luther, who advocated both confession to a member of the clergy and to a Christian layman, was anxious to stress that the confessant always has to do with God.[10]

What gives religious confession its particular character and distinguishes it from other forms of confession is, then, that the confessant feels the presence of God. Provided that the confession is made in real earnest, this applies both to the church type of confession, with its institutional element, and to confession received by a layman. Ultimately, confession derives its value for the confessant from its religious dignity and religious atmosphere. Because of this, its connection with religious conversion seems in essence to be clear. The connection is particularly evident when we look at those revivalist movements in which confession has become a practice. We observed how confession has been used as an act of initiation by the Laestadian movement, by the Oxford Group one and others, such as that led by

---

[9] *Ermatinger Tagebuch* (previously quoted here in Chapter IX).
[10] Regarding Luther's views on confession, see what was said here in Chapter I, p. 4.

Blumhardt, of a more local kind. There confession emerged as an element in conversion, as its summit and conclusion. The act of confession became an expression—the confirmation—of the conversion process.

As regards the practice of confession in revivalist movements, we can easily discern a connection with conversion because of the change of heart implied and the fundamental break with previous norms and way of life, the "transformation of all values"; but in the Catholic Church, where confession has more the character of a spiritual exercise, its connection with conversion is perhaps more difficult to accept. Apart from cases of basic conversion which may arise, what matters in Catholic confession is that it allows expression to the continually renewed need for penance and improvement on the part of already Christian people. But with this form of confession, too, we may justifiably speak about conversion inasmuch as a change of heart takes place when, after an examination of conscience and earnest repentance, serious sins are confessed. Here again confession means that the sinner is brought to an understanding of his own nature and of the tendencies in it which have caused his sin or sins. According to the procedure of Catholic confession, penitents are called upon to experience profound remorse—*contritio*, a "broken-heartedness" which in fact comprises a change of heart—and in consequence of this they must consciously resolve to sin no further. Thus, in Catholic theology such a change of heart or conversion is adduced as a result of confession.[11] The person's guilt is effaced, and he can make a new start. Cleansed of sin, unified in strength, he can direct himself at following dictates of the Divine Will and accomplishing the aims it imposes on him. As we have accepted the view that conversion is a change of heart which brings integration of conflicting psychological tendencies and produces organization of the character, we are surely entitled to regard the Catholic form of confession, too, as an important element in conversion.

---

[11] See L. Bopp (*op. cit.*; p. 79) who stated that through penance "the person arrives at unity and completion. He is saved from his self-division, his schizothymia. He has found health in the furthest depth of his soul, and with his full strength he can turn to his new goal". Cf. G. Wunderle on conversion as the aim of penitence and confession (*op. cit.*; p. 5) : "The resolution is to be regarded as a special act concluding the whole spiritual process, and with it *conversio*, the turn to faith of the inward being, is wholly completed".

It will be seen that our discussion of the connection between confession and conversion has further underlined the function of confession
as a unifying factor—a function previously illustrated in the chapter
here on assimilation. We there observed that, to a considerable extent,
the feeling of relief after confession may be explained by the fact
that a confession involving conversion and synthesis of the personality
marks the end of conflicts with the conscience and of strife among
various tendencies in the personality. We brought out there how
affective discharge—abreaction—is in the main what causes a sense
of release. Doubtless this holds true particularly in cases where remorseful affects are very intense, but it generally applies when feelings
of remorse have appeared. The discharge of such affects would seem
to provide an explanation that fits the direct and instantaneous
relief experienced after confession, especially if a great mobilization
of affects has occurred before and during the act; and the synthesizing
activity which meanwhile results from confession causes the relief to
subsist, turning into calmness and peace of mind that continue for a
rather long time. The synthesis which takes place in confession thus
accounts for a good deal of the beneficial effect that confession exerts.
It accounts equally for the great importance attributed in some quarters to confession as part of general mental hygiene. The significance
of the synthesizing function would be greatly accentuated if it were
possible to demonstrate that this meets, and fulfils, a basic psychic
need for unity. A deeper background would then be given to the need
for confession and absolution, the longing for an instructing authority,
and on the other hand to the so widely-attested feeling of relief after
confession.

In general psychology much discussion has been devoted to the
supposition that a synthesizing tendency exists in the psyche and
explains the cohesion of the ego or the continuity of the personality.
William Wundt advanced a theory of "apperception" :[12] this he
defined as activity, both instinctive and voluntary, that decides what
will be placed in the limelight of consciousness; it functions as a
central creative power of the psyche and has a regulating effect on
the development of ideas and impressions, drawing them together,
dividing them up, leading or hampering the process.[13] Harald Höffding

---

[12] For the history of this concept, the various opinions about it and its consequence
in modern psychology and pedagogy, see the article "*Apperzeption*" in *Pädagogisches
Lexikon*.

[13] See A Messer, *op. cit.*; p. 14. Messer devoted special studies to the concept.

gave a number of reasons for assuming the existence of such a synthesizing force in mental life. Without it, there could be no cohesion of
knowledge and feelings; there could not even be any real volition.[14] He
took Kant's word for it that the synthesis proceeds from "a blind,
though indispensible, mental operation without which we should have
no knowledge at all, but of which we only rarely become aware".[15]

The French psychologist Charles Blondel submitted the theories on
psychic synthesis to a critical examination, and he found that they
are generally weighed down by metaphysical suppositions.[16] He made
objection to certain statements coming precisely from Höffding, for
instance to the remark : "Spiritual existence has synthesis as its
fundamental form". And he cited similar declarations by the psychologist G. Dwelshauver, who had a predilection for calling synthesis an
"action of the spirit". Passing an over-all judgement on theories about
a psychic tendency creating unity, Blondel added that, if one disre-
gards the metaphysical content with which the theories are charged,
they do not really say very much. Simply they assert that a synthesis
occurs, they are unable to explain *how* it takes place. "We still do not
know exactly what the mechanism is in our sensations or memories,
and what we want to know are the general laws by which these are
joined together".

Although Blondel warned against too confident and unreflective
use of the theory he criticized, he did not wish to abandon it himself.
He agreed with the supposition that a synthesis really does take
place, but he desired to limit its scope to that of a rational activity.

In attempts at solving the difficulties presented by the synthetical-
tendency theory, the usual course followed in modern psychology,
in order to gain a correct idea of a psychological phenomenon, has
been to regard it from the standpoint of the goal involved. It is said
that the problem of cohesion in mental life—the ego problem—can
only be solved by asking, not "Who am I ?", but "Where do we come
upon our egos ?" A psyche in operation finds unity precisely through
the operation in which it is engaged, an operation which implies a
purpose and a direction towards a goal and a purpose. Thus it is the
striving towards a goal that creates unity of the psyche. This means

---

[14] Harald Höffding, *Psykologi i Omrids* (General Survey of Psychology; 4th ed.
Copenhagen, 1898) : p. 55 ff.

[15] *Ibid.*; p. 58.

[16] Charles Blondel, *L'Activité automatique et l'activité synthétique*, in *Nouveau Traité
de psychologie*, vol. IV (Paris, 1934); pp. 341-385.

that the concept of the ego, or of the personality, becomes purely functional.

The question is whether the problem of the synthetical tendency can be approached in this way alone. All the same, acceptance of a theory that the psychic equipment possesses an ability, or a tendency, to create unity seems inescapable. Here psychiatry might, it seems to us, help resolve the matter. For psychiatry teaches us that the mentally-divided person lacks an essential function : because of this lack, even the simplest objective cannot at times summon his forces to perform a proper action. The thing wanting is precisely an elementary ability to pull oneself together, to order and unite mental powers and direct them at a definite aim. In the long run, a capacity of the psychic equipment to create unity seems to be a requirement for purposeful action. That a disposition to establish unity makes itself felt as a primary psychic power is of course indicated by the fact that many patients who suffer from neuroses manifest great dissatisfaction with their dissociated mental condition and show a marked desire to recover from it. Unity of the mind is required for its health.[17] Pierre Janet, the psychiatrist whose observations and investigations have—along with Freud's—contributed most to normal psychology, remarked generally on the significance and operation of the tendency in question : "The tendency towards synthesis and personality is what commonly characterizes psychic phenomena".[18]

In certain quarters of psychiatry the synthetical activity has been strongly highlighted as one of the basic forces in mental life. Indeed, the whole process of mental healing has been hinged upon it. This trend derives from the psychoanalytical school. It has been represented particularly by Alois Maeder[19]—who of course pursued a line close to Jung's—and the Swedish psychiatrist Poul Bjerre,[20] who did not

---

[17] The Swedish psychologist John Landquist, said in his *Själens enhet* (Unity of the Mind : Stockholm, 1935; page 109) : "The fact that psychiatry places much more emphasis on cohesion and wholeness of the mind than do the ordinary handbooks of normal psychology is worth reflection". And again (page 110) : "Psychiatry teaches us in a penetrating way how firmly the mind coheres and how well connected its structure is in a normal person, what havoc and suffering are brought by a disturbance of this cohesion, and how necessary such connectedness is to a person's state".

[18] Quoted by Blondel, *op. cit.*; p. 357.

[19] A. Maeder, *op. cit.* See especially Chapter II on "The Conscience and Direction". Cf. Maeder's work *Wege zur seelischen Heilung* (1945).

[20] For the essentials of Poul Bjerre's concept, see *Själsläkekonst och själavård* (The Art of Mental Healing and Cure of Souls : Stockholm, 1935); pp. 151-204.

acknowledge that he owed anything to either Jung or Maeder. These two psychiatrists laid the main weight in their treatment on psycho-synthesis, rather than on analysis. True, in the view they followed analysis is necessary in order to uncover the causes of nervous distur-bances or of the conflicts which the patient has come to the doctor to have resolved. But synthesis follows after analysis, and here all the doctor can do is serve as guide and supervisor for the psychic activity taking place in the patient's unconscious mind. Maeder drew attention to a prospective tendency in the patient's dreams :[21] to how, through the symbolical language of dreams, the unconscious provides ways for the resolution of conflicts and for re-establishment of unity and cohesion in the personality.

The basic idea was the same with Bjerre : particularly in his book on the natural system of dreams,[22] he supplied ingenious interpre-tations of his patients' dreams. He wished to show how these changed in the course of treatment, thus revealing development towards complete synthesis of the patient's personality : towards recovery. Throughout this process, the unconscious psycho-synthetic tendency provides the motive power. The assumption that nature possesses a healing power of its own is, Bjerre claimed, as self-evident where the mind is concerned as with the body. If it were not for such a force the practice of medicine would be impossible. And in restoring health to a sick mind, a natural power of the sort is again at work as the psychiatrist's ally. The tendency operates during sleep and manifests itself in dreams—likened by Bjerre to the creations of an artist. Just as the artist's works give him symbolical expression for his artistic aspirations, his intuitions and feelings—his entire personality—dreams come to symbolize the solution of the problem in the patient's life. The objective is to interpret these symbols and get the patient to perceive the truth which is either contained in his mind already or at which he arrives through the workings of his innate psycho-synthetical tendency.

Though a critical attitude may be taken towards this line of reason-ing and its consequences, we seem unable to deny that it comprises a

---

[21] Cf. C. G. Jung's *Das Unbewusste im normalen u. kranken Seelenleben*. Dreams indicate the way to remove conflicts by revealing the collective unconscious and the archetypes, with their mysterious powers aroused by the conflicts in the depths of the mind. The dreams "move along an advancing line and ally themselves with the instructor".

[22] Poul Bjerre, *Die Träume als Heilungsweg der Seele* (Zurich and Leipzig, 1936).

fruitful point of view and contains a truthful element.[23] It is some-what difficult to contest the assumption that a special healing power exists in the mind and that a psycho-synthetical tendency is the basic cause of this regenerative power.

The survey by Ford and Urban, previously cited here, discussed the question involved : Are there really such forces in the psyche as "innate organizing principles" ?

A number of specialists, Adler, Rank and Rogers among them, are mentioned as representing the view that there are. What made these psychiatrists take it ? "They may have identified a fundamental, innate attribute", says the survey. Its author holds that more research should be carried out in the field, and he adds : "There is no doubt that adult behavior is highly organized and systemized. Certainly many psychotherapists have reported that the feeling of losing behavioral control or falling apart is often terrifying for the patients".[24]

Heinz Hartmann and his epoch-making view on personality might also be mentioned here. Hartmann speaks about "ego-apparatuses" as being required for the life of the personality. And, according to him there is an organizing principle over these apparatuses : what he called "the synthetic function".[25]

It may thus be assumed with good support that the striving towards assembly of the various psychic tendencies and experiences, their organization and unity, constitutes a force inherent in the mind, a force that asserts itself in normal psychic life and, when psychic dissociation causes disorders, works to re-establish and unify the split personality. This supposition sheds new light on our view of confession as a factor that creates unity. It illuminates this view more profoundly and helps substantially to explain both the need for confession and the sense of relief that, according to so-frequent testimony, confession brings.[26]

---

[23] The criticism against psychoanalysis because of its suggestive influence, an influence that produces the symbols—or the interpretation of symbols—which the doctor wants, appears to be applicable in Bjerre's case.

[24] Ford and Urban, op. cit.; p. 612.

[25] Concerning Hartmann, see Wordsworth and Sheehan, *Contemporary Schools of Psychotherapy* (New York, 1964). Cf. Erik Homburger Erikson on "ego synthesis" as "an ordering process", *Insight and Responsibility* (New York, 1964).

[26] A. Boisen took the sense of guilt and the subsequent emotional disturbance as a sign of health, a force leading to psychological unification. In a letter of 1943 to H. E. Fosdick, Boisen wrote : "The emotional disturbance which follows [the sense of guilt] is

But of course synthesis of divided mental life is accomplished in secular psychotherapy, too. When such therapy is compared with confession, the question arises whether confession possesses any peculiar ability to create unity precisely because of its religious character. We shall cite in what follows some statements from psychiatric quarters which seem to confirm that it does.

Authoritative psychiatrists readily admit that confession generally exerts a most beneficial effect. We witnessed Pierre Janet's appreciation of it when we described his view on the need for psychic guidance. Janet felt able to conclude with certainty that many psychically-weak individuals escape disorders because they are under the moral discipline of the Church : because they go to their confessors at regular intervals and then receive solace in their troubles, new instructions for the conduct of their lives and new courage to lead them. Janet expressly emphasized that he valued confession as an institution. "Regular confession seems to have been invented by an alienist of genius who wished to treat those obsessed", he said.[27]

Here the merit of religious confession is evidently regarded as residing mainly in the comfort and renewed courage it affords to people suffering states of anxiety and depression, in the fact that it provides an ability to hold conflicting forces together in the mind, thus preventing them from causing an obvious split in the personality and symptoms of mental illness.

Jung gave rather illuminating, if indirect, evidence of what institutionalized confession means for mental health when he stated that among the many hundreds of patients, from all the civilized countries, whom he had treated over the years, the great majority were Protestants and only five or six were Catholics.[28] He submitted a questionnaire to Swiss, German and French Protestants, also to a number of Catholics, in order to discover whether when in a state of conflicts or mental distress they preferred to go to a churchman or to a psychiatrist, and what decided their choice. The response he received was as follows. Fifty-seven per cent. of the Protestants and only twenty-five per cent. of the Catholics chose to go to a doctor. While a mere eight per cent. of the Protestants said that they were willing to go to a clergyman,

---

then analogous to fever or inflammation in the body. It is not an evil but a manifestation of nature's power to heal". (Quoted from O. H. Mowrer's *The Crisis in Modern Psychiatry and Religion*: p. 66.)

[27] P. Janet, *Les Obsessions et la psychasthénie*; p. 707.

[28] C. G. Jung, *Psychotherapie und Seelsorge* (Zurich, 1932); p. 12.

as many as fifty-eight per cent. of the Catholics wanted to go to a priest. The rest of those questioned could not make up their minds one way or the other : thirty-five per cent. of the Protestants and only seventeen per cent. of the Catholics were undecided. Jung's report on the results of this questionnaire is too brief for us to draw any absolutely sure conclusions. One would like to know, among other things, whether the Protestants questioned really were active Christians. It is an obvious consequence of secularization that many people have come to take their spiritual troubles—what should not actually be regarded as psychic disturbances—to a psychiatrist rather to a churchman. Nevertheless, the results produced by Jung's inquiry were sufficiently clear for us to regard them—along with the evidence he supplied about the religious background of his patients —as confirming that confession, particularly in its institutionalized Catholic form, is an important factor in mental hygiene.

The statements from psychiatrists cited here apply to the general significance of confession where such hygiene is concerned. Bror Gadelius was among those who have drawn attention to the specific effect and therapeutic consequences of the religious factor. A trifle unwillingly, he stated his appreciation of the value which this factor possesses for psychotherapy. In a discussion with Fjellbu as to whether the Christian "cure of souls" may be considered superior to secular mental care, he said : "I readily admit that in suitable cases the religiously Christian 'cure of souls' *can* be superior to psychotherapy without religious engagement from a doctor".[29] And he went on to consider it a virtue in a psychotherapist's equipment "if, unaffected by scientific training, he has been able to retain his original childhood faith".

More spontaneously and unreservedly, the English psychiatrist A. Hadfield expressed an opinion along the same lines : "Speaking as a student of psychotherapy, who as such has no concern with theology, I am convinced that the Christian religion is one of the most valuable and potent influences that we possess for producing that harmony and peace of mind and that confidence of soul which is needed to bring health and power to a large proportion of nervous patients. In some cases I have attempted to cure patients with suggestions of quietness and confidence but without success until I have linked those suggestions on to that faith in the power of God which is

---

[29] B. Gadelius, *Tro och helbrägagörelse* (Belief and Faith-healing); p. 30.

the substance of the Christian's confidence and hope. Then the patient
has become strong".[30] This statement recalls the attempts made to
utilize the therapeutic power of religion systematically in a particular
method of healing : for example, the efforts of the American "Emma-
nuel" movement.[31] Whatever opinion may be held of these, they do
supply good evidence that a special healing power resides in religious
experiences.

Jung gave universal application to the judgement which he passed
on the importance of religion to mental health. He declared that
among all patients of his more than thirty-five years old, none could
be found "whose problem was not finally that of religious attitude".
He went on : "In fact, every one of them suffers ultimately from
what living religions have at all periods given to their faithful, and no
patient has really recovered his health without having regained
his religious attitude : which of course has nothing to do with confession
or membership in a church".[32]

It is perhaps not wholly clear what Jung meant by "religious
attitude". Where neurotic patients were concerned, he seems generally
to have had in mind the achieving of insight into the symbols created
by the collective unconscious and into the archetypes, of reverence
for such sources of strength hidden in the depths of the mind. According
to Jung, patients may often be impressed by the solutions to their
personal problems which those profound supra-individual powers
reveal and make possible; by yielding to the solutions, they attain
unification of their psychic life, divided by neurosis. When we study
Jung's account of the course which the healing process takes, we
understand that in Jungian therapy the doctor plays no less a part as
intermediary between the patient's unconscious and conscious lives
than he does in Freudian psychoanalysis; we realize also that, as
Jung himself stressed, a principal element in treatment is the influence
which the doctor exerts on the patient with a purely instructive aim
in mind. For Jung, the collective unconscious and archetypes evidently
constituted the religious object. The gods of historical religions were

---

[30] Quoted by W. B. Selbie in *The Psychology of Religion* (Oxford, 1924); p. 24.

[31] See Tor Andrae's *Psykoanalys och religion* (Psychoanalysis and Religion); p. 24 ff.

[32] Jung, *op. cit.*; p. 12. Cf. (p. 14) : "It seems to me that neuroses have considerably
increased in correlation with the decline in religious life". Cf., too, a similar statement
from the psychiatrist P. J. Möbius : "If we consider how absence of religion increases our
helplessness against the storms of life, its relation to nervosity cannot be in doubt".
(Quoted by Selbie, *op. cit.*; p. 25).

simply projections of the archetypes. But the matter of most interest to us here is the decisive importance for mental health which Jung attributed to the religious attitude and the fact that he regarded the living religions as the great psychotherapeutic systems of mankind : systems largely abandoned in modern times, not without detriment to mental health.

As we attempt now to discover on what the therapeutic effect of the religious factor is based, we might follow the frequent course in discussions about the psychology of religion and mention religious needs which could conceivably be satisfied by the religious experience. It is then tempting to adduce—as did Selbie, for instance—the existence of a special psychic receptivity to religious experience and of a need that demands satisfaction. With reference to the statement by Hadfield quoted earlier here, about his success with suggestions founded on religion, Selbie said : "Such a result would hardly be possible, nor could such methods be defended, apart from the existence of a religious nature in Man prepared to respond to suggestions of the kind indicated. The psychology of religion at once justifies such an interpretation of human nature and serves to indicate the right conditions and methods of such an appeal".[33]

What Selbie means here by a "religious nature" is evidently the same thing as a predisposition or attitude for religious experience. And we may agree with Tor Andrae that such an aptitude consists of "the ability to carry out a psychic function, inasmuch as this ability is based on an innate character possessed by the subject".[34] The predisposition would then appear to be an inherent ability to know religious experience. But even if we accept the hypothesis of a special religious aptitude, the specific effect of religious experience remains to be explained. This is so because the assumption that a special aptitude for religion exists in Man does not suffice; the question must be asked : What central needs in the person gain satisfaction from the response that comes through the religious function, which is based on natural tendency ? Though in the past Selbie and others have merely referred to a "religious nature" without further analysis, it is only by asking this question that we can arrive at a genuine and differentiated explanation of the effect that religious experience produces.

---

[33] W. B. Selbie, op. cit.; p. 24 f.

[34] Tor Andrae, "Die Frage der religiösen Anlage", in Uppsala universitets årskrift, 1932; p. 72.

The reasoning that Man does possess a "religious nature" finds an analogy in Viktor Frankl's "working hypothesis" that human nature looks beyond itself, beyond mere physical and mental existence. While in a Nazi concentration camp during the Second World War, Frankl had many opportunities to witness the importance which belief in some kind of future holds for people : what it means for the very continuation of life, for the ability to endure.

In Frankl's view, the absence of anything to believe in, the failure to find any meaning in life, is the misfortune of many people in our time. They suffer from what he calls an "existential vacuum", or from "existential frustration". He believes that the need to find meaning and coherence in life is of such fundamental importance for mental health that, from lack of faith, many people fall prey to mental illness. He terms the form of mental disturbance here *"noogen neuroses"*. And after thorough research he considered he could establish that twenty per cent. of neuroses may be placed in this category.

Frankl emphasizes strongly the close link between human nature and the function he describes; he did so when criticizing older psycho-analysis for confining itself to "depth psychology". There should also be a "height psychology" (*"Tiefenpsychologie-Höhenpsychologie"*), a psychology that takes into account not only the will to pleasure but also the "will to meaning". This, too, may be found deep in the unconscious, but it is often repressed. When quelled it does not always involve the existence of a religious faith, though it may do so. According to Frankl, in fortunate cases a long restrained and repressed tendency to believe— *"die Quellen einer ursprünglichen unbewussten verdrängten Glaubigkeit"*—may be discovered in the course of treatment.

The success gained by "logotherapy", Frankl's form of therapy, shows of course that his views have proved fruitful. Like other great German-language analysts, he has established his school in psychiatry, and his ideas have naturally been important in the religious cure of souls.

It can surely be said that these confirm the opinions of Jung—one of his masters—on the importance which religions possesses for mental health, and in particular Jung's view that the central problem of mankind finds its solution in religions. However, we do not hear about the archetypes from Frankl. He is practical and simple, but firm, in his conviction that the need for meaning and coherence must be allowed expression if people are to achieve happiness. The leading criterion of mental health is, he says, *"Sinn-Orientiertheit"*—

orientation of meaning—and he cites thorough tests carried out on the subject. He also adduces physiological examinations which show that need for meaningfulness in the functions reaches down into "the biological fundament of the human spirit".[35]

Frankl's view of the primordial need to find meaning is supported by the research of others. Mention can be made here of the work described by J. Milton Yinger in his paper "A Structural Examination of Religion".[36] In the course of this work, a great number of college students were asked about what was truly of profound concern to them; the resultant "expressions of ultimate concern" contained answers to such principal questions as : What is the meaning of life ? What is its aim ? How are people to attain a proper relation to God ? And so on.

We may compare with Yinger's survey a similar one carried out by Morton King and called "Measuring the Religious Variable : Nine Proposed Dimensions".[37] Here a general religious factor was adduced from answers received to a number of existential questions.

What several other recent examinations of religious conversion have indicated can be of special interest in our context here. Summarizing these, J. E. Dittes says : "More recent observations have emphasized especially the constructive, integrative or 'problem-solving' functions of conversion".[38] In other words, a strong need manifests itself to neutralize the conflicting tendencies or instinctual drives which threaten to destroy the coherence of the personality : a need for unity, peace and harmony.

As we stressed previously, it is primarily this need which appears in an earnest Christian confession. And we saw earlier that the tendency towards unity may be regarded as founded on human nature. Conse-

---

[35] For the most part, the account given above follows an article by Frankl in *Psychotherapie und Seelsorge : Ein Tagungsbericht von der Elmauer Tagung für "Artzt und Seelsorger"* (Stuttgart, 1965). Among Frankl's many works, mention may be made to *Man's Search for Meaning : An Introduction to Logotherapy*, prefaced by Gordon W. Allport (Boston, 1962). Concerning the theological application of Frankl's views, see for instance D. F. Tweedie's *An Introduction to Christian Logotherapy* (Grand Rapids, 1963) and R. C. Leslie's *Jesus and Logotherapy* (New York, 1965). A survey and valuation of Frankl's achievement is given by Dieter Vyss in *Die tiefenpsychologischen Schulen* (Göttingen, 1966); p. 408 ff.

[36] *Journal for the Scientific Study of Religion*, 1969; p. 88 ff.

[37] *Ibid*, 1967; p. 173 ff.

[38] Lindsey and Aronson, *Handbook of Social Psychology*, vol. V (Reading, Mass. 1968); p. 648.

quently, it is quite comprehensible that the tendency should insist with a certain elemental power on receiving expression and realization. The effect of the religious factor in confession will, then, reside ultimately in the satisfaction of this need. We saw instances in the foregoing of the enthusiasm felt by newly-converted confessants after confession; we also witnessed examples of the appreciation which certain psychiatrists have shown for confession and of their view that in some cases religious experience has an excellent therapeutic capacity. We may thus assume that the religious experience in confession makes it possible for mental unity to be achieved in a *specially complete way.*

Obviously, the unity of a person's ambitions and aims is governed by his values and by the ends he has in view. If his goal is high enough to require the assembly of all the powers and aspirations in his personality, and if at the same time it is of such kind as to inspire all his devotion, then the most favourable conditions for true unification of his personality are evidently fulfilled. The Christian religion provides such a goal. For a Christian, God is in fact the highest moral authority. This most elevated value—the moral norm or ideal in life—gains importance for the person to the same extent that he feels himself seized by, and attaches himself to, his God. It appears to us that the specific effect which comes with confession lies in the inclination of this experience to absorb the person and all his deepest powers, thereby rooting the ethical norm deep within him.

Of course it is the ability of religion to grip a person completely and transform him which produces such statements as that from Selbie about the appurtenance of religion to human nature. A natural instinct for devotion would seem to find expression in religious experience, a devotion that takes hold of the entire person.[39] Pratt studied this devotion from many sides, and he said: "A man's religion is not merely a matter of his clear-cut conscious processes: it is bound up with his whole psycho-physical organism. Truly, he who loves God loves Him with all his heart and soul and mind and strength. He loves God not only with his soul and mind, but with his body too.

---

[39] Cf. E. Berggrav's *Religionens terskel* (The Threshold of Religion); p. 77 : "The instinct for devotion is also a natural force" (along with the instinct for self-assertion). See, too, Max Scheler's *Der Formalismus in der Ethik und die materiale Wertethik* (Halle-an der Saale, 1921); pp. 287-292. Here feelings of sympathy and the instinct for devotion are presented as the original elements in relation to the instinct for self-assertion.

Our religion goes deeper down into our lives than most things, and is knit up with all that we are".[40]

The psychological structure of religious experience was analyzed with particular thoroughness by the psychologist of religion Karl Girgensohn.[41] Though his experimental method was open to criticism, considerable value should in fact be accorded to it because of the sensible way he applied it.[42] Furthermore, he supplemented the purely experimental aspect by conversations with his subjects about certain basic religious concepts : for example, the foundations on which certainty of belief and trust rest. Into the bargain, he verified his results by correlating them with a number of well-known documents in religious literature.

Those results appear to confirm strikingly the main view we have established on what the specific effect of the religious experience is in confession—a viewpoint rendered natural by our knowledge about the shattering consequences of guilt feelings and the healing action of conversion. Like Pratt, Girgensohn spoke of the ability which religion possesses to engage deep forces of mental life, and he regarded the unifying effect this creates as the most important factor in religious experience. He found it evident "that religion is a highly involved synthetical performance of the mind which makes demands on all its fundamental powers and creates unity from a multitude of experiences and relations".[43] The very process of achieving that

---

[40] J. B. Pratt, op. cit.; p. 60. Cf. the following statement by the psychologist and exegete Carl Schneider, who to all appearances occupied himself considerably with analysis of mental disorders. On the subject of various psychotherapeutic methods, he said that if the therapist is treating people who are receptive to religious influence the best manner of proceeding is to attempt utilization of the possibility this offers. "Denn die religiösen Erlebnisse des Menschen sind die ganzheitlichsten überhaupt die immer wieder seine Gesamtstruktur mit all ihren dispositionellen Gegebenheiten ganz in Anspruch nehmen". (Carl Schneider, "Wie hat sich der Seelenführer zu verhalten ?" in Zeitschrift für Religionspsychologie (Gütersloh, 1929); pp. 355-363. The quotation is from p. 373.)

[41] Karl Girgensohn, Der seelische Aufbau des religiösen Erlebens (Leipzig, 1921).

[42] Cf. Friedrich Andres, "Das religiöse Leben und seine psychologische Erforschung", in Zeitschrift für Aszese und Mystik, vols. I-II (Würzburg, 1944); pp. 39-52. Andres, a Catholic and a professor at Bonn, here gives an account of criticism against the experimental method in the psychology of religion; he refutes this criticism and alleges that many Catholic specialists in the field have stated their appreciation of the method. Cf. Otto Ritschl's review of Girgensohn's work in Theologische Literaturzeitung (Leipzig, 1921); p. 331 ff. : special attention is paid to Girgensohn's delicacy of feeling and tact in his conversations with the subjects of his investigation.

[43] Girgensohn, op. cit.; p. 436.

dominant unity contains "the essential element in the religious structure".

It is interesting to observe how Girgensohn supposed this unity to be produced. Briefly, here are his basic ideas.[44] The cardinal thing in religious experience is the reflective element. The person must have gained some experience, acquired some knowledge—"intuition"— about what lies beyond the everyday : this ranges "all the confused fragments making towards a conception of the world into an enclosed whole" ;[45] it gives a resting-place and a rallying point to "the flight of phenomena". The ego must then establish a relation to this focus. Action takes place through the "ego functions".[46] These come in three groups. (1) Reflection on the divine are transformed from objective to subjective; that is, they are ranged with the person's own thoughts, are given expression as the person's own convictions. (2) The ego must now take an attitude to the divine reality, subject of its conviction. This action, if positive, finds particular manifestation in devotion, trust and love. (3) A consequence of the ego's devotion to the religious object is that the ego undergoes an "extensive and intensive" development.

The stages of religious experience which have occurred here are only distinguished from one another when submitted to psychological analysis. They are not felt to be separate when experienced; then two main elements are always present at the same time : the knowledge factor and that which comes as the ego takes a stand towards the reality it comprehends through reflection and ranges within itself.[47]

When studying Girgensohn's line of thought, one might pay particular attention to the second of those "ego functions" : devotion to, or trust in, the godhead, which appears to be at the very heart of the

---

[44] A summary of Girgensohn's results is given in the paper (cited above) by Friedrich Andres.

[45] Girgensohn, *loc. cit.* For a more thorough elucidation of this line of thought, see the chapter "*Die Intuitionen des religiösen Erlebens*", pp. 436-457.

[46] Described by Girgensohn in the chapter "*Die Ichfunktionen des religiösen Erlebens*", pp. 457-510.

[47] More recent American examinations which analyze factors in the structure of religious experience can be compared with Girgensohn's results here. Usually, a multi-dimensional view is taken. Dittes gives a table with five variables : the ideological ritualistic, experiental, intellectual and consequental dimensions. (Lindsey and Aronson, *op. cit.*; p. 648 f.) Cf. *Social Forces*, 1966; vol. XLV, pp. 246-254.

religious experience. Basing his view on statements received from the subjects in his investigation, Girgensohn said that two elements enter into the confidence engendered : on the one hand, the person opens himself to the object in which he trusts; on the other, he commits himself to it, assured that it can and will act rightly.[48] Trust takes the same form whether it is placed in another person or in a personally conceived religious object : it always contains the two elements mentioned. But of course there is a difference which lies in the intensity and whole-heartedness of the trust. Where God is involved "the opening of the ego is more heedless and sweeping than would be thinkable even in relation to the person who inspires most confidence, and the devotion with which one commits oneself is also more unreserved and intense, analogous to the great power and constancy of the Divine Will".[49]

Girgensohn's investigation thus emphasizes further our view that devotion, the act of trustful self-surrender, is the central element in religious experience. It also agrees with our view that the chief result of religious experience may be regarded as creation of unity in mental life. Earlier, when discussing confession and conversion, we pointed out that mental unity is created during conversion and emerges as a result of it. Consequently, Girgensohn's study confirms our opinion on the point. It also gives excellent support to our assumption that the specific effect of the religious factor in confession consists of an ability to unify the split personality in a particularly complete way. The religious object takes profound hold of the person and is capable of inducing his unreserved trust.

We have witnessed statements from Girgensohn and other psychologists energetically drawing attention to this quality of religious experience, considered in a general manner. It is worth stressing that the quality is even stronger when the experience is Christian. Naturally, the special character of a religious experience is determined by the concept a person has of God and His nature. We have of course just observed how Girgensohn called attention to the element of knowledge as an absolutely necessary condition for religious experience, if we are to qualify the experience involved as religious at all. It follows that with Christian religious experience the trust takes on a special colour and intensity; this is so because God is conceived of there as

---

[48] Girgensohn, in the chapter cited above; p. 465.
[49] *Ibid.*; p. 466.

the self-sacrificing love which calls for a response in kind from the person. This movement is the act of devotion, and all the person's powers are engaged and united behind it. Thus, in a Christian confession, earnestly felt and carried out, the best conditions are present for a particularly complete creation of unity among conflicting tendencies in the personality; for God absorbs the person's deepest forces and mobilizes them in the act of devotion. This ability of religious experience to bring about a complete synthesis of the personality appears very largely to explain why, according to objective testimony, Christian confession can produce results often surpassing those which secular confession can achieve; to explain also why from the standpoint of psychic health special value is attributed to confession.

We have in the foregoing sought to establish the peculiar character of Christian confession by observing it in relation to changes of heart or conversions that produce unity of volition and disposition in the personality. We have seen that there are good grounds for supposing this unifying effect to meet an innate psychic need for unity; finally, we have drawn attention to the fact that religious experience in its Christian form is, because of the profound act of devotion which it produces, particularly suited to create a complete synthesis of the personality.

BIBLIOGRAPHY

Allers, Rudolf, *Über Psychoanalyse. Abhandlungen aus der Neurologie, Psychiatrie, Psychologie u. ihren Grenzgebieten*, XVI. Berlin, 1922.

Allport, Gordon W., *The Individual and his Religion*, 8th ed. New York, 1968.

Andrae, Tor, *Mystikens psykologi*, Uppsala, 1926.

——, *Psykoanalys och religion*. Stockholm, 1927.

——, *"Die Frage der religiösen Anlage"*, in *Uppsala Universitets Årsskrift*, 1932.

Andres, Friedrich, *"Das religiöse Leben und seine psychologische Erforschung"*, in *Zeitschrift für Aszese und Mystik*, vol. I-II. Würzburg, 1944.

Begbie, Harold, *Life Changers*. London, 1923.

Berggrav, Eyvind, *Religionens terskel*. Oslo, 1924.

——, *Fångens själsliv*. Uppsala, 1929.

Birnbaum, Karl, *Die psychischen Heilmethoden*. Leipzig, 1927.

Bjerre, Poul, *Die Träume als Heilungsweg der Seele*. Zurich and Leipzig, 1936.

——, *Själsläkekonst och själavård*. Stockholm, 1935.

Blondel, Charles, *L'activité automatique et l'activité synthétique*, in *Nouveau traité de psychologie*, IV, ed. G. Dumas. Paris, 1934.

Bopp, Linus, *Moderne Psychanalyse, katholische Beichte und Pädagogik*. Kempten, 1923.

Bremond, Henri, *Histoire littéraire du sentiment religieux en France*, I-XI. Paris,1921-33 (Index 1936).

Breuer, Josef, and Freud, Sigmund, *Studien über Hysterie*. Leipzig and Vienna, 1895.

Brilioth, Yngve, *The Anglican Revival*. London, 1925.

Brown, William, *Psychology and Psychotherapy*. London, 1922.

Brunner, Emil, *"Mitt möte med Oxfordbevegelsen"*, in *Kirke og Kultur*, 1933.

Bumke, Oswald, *Die Psychoanalyse*. Berlin, 1931.

Buntzel, W., *Die Psychoanalyse und ihre seelsorgerliche Verwertung*, Göttingen, 1926.

Burr, Anna Robeson, *Religious Confessions and Confessants*, Boston, 1914.

Calvet, J., *Le renouveau catholique dans la littérature contemporaine*. Paris, 1931.

Clark, H.W., *The Psychology of Religion*. New York, 1958.

Condrau, Gion, *Angst und Schuld als Grundprobleme der Psychotherapie*. Bern, 1962.

Deinzer, J., *Wilhelm Löhes Leben*, I-III. Nuremberg and Gütersloh, 1874-92.

Delacroix, H., *Les Souvenirs. Nouveau traité de psychologie*, V. Paris, 1936.

Denzinger, H., and Bannwart, C., *Enchiridion symbolorum*, Freiburg-in-Breisgau, 1928.

Dittes, James, "Psychology of Religion", in *Handbook of Social Psychology*, ed. Lindsey and Aronson. Reading, Mass., 1968.

Dittrich, Ottmar, *Die Probleme der Sprachpsychologie*. Leipzig, 1913.

Dumas, Georges, *Les émotions. Nouveau traité de psychologie*, II. Paris, 1932.

Edquist, Carl, *Ropande röster i ödemarken*. Stockholm, 1916.

Edquist, Märta, *Lars Levi Laestadius*. Stockholm, 1922.

Elmgren, John, *Minnet*. Stockholm, 1935.

——, "Gestalt Psychology", in *Göteborgs Högskolas Årsskrift*, 1938.

——, *"Emotioner och sentiment"*, in *Psykologisk-pedagogisk uppslagsbok*. Stockholm, 1943.

Erikson, E. H., *Insight and Responsibility*. New York, 1964.

Ermatinger Tagebuch. Gotha, 1942.

Faber, Geoffrey, *Oxford Apostles.* London, 1933.

Ferenczi, S., *Bausteine zur Psychoanalyse,* I. Vienna, 1927.

Fjellbu, Arne, *Själavård.* Uppsala, 1934.

Fleege, G. A., *Den laestadianska rörelsen i Kyrkslätts församling.* Borga, 1910.

Ford, D. H., and Urban, H. B., *Systems of Psychotherapy.* New York, 1963.

Foucauld, Charles de, *Écrits spirituels.* Paris, 1930.

Frankl, V. E., *"Psychotherapie und religiöse Erfahrung",* in *Psychotherapie und Seelsorge : Ein Tagungsbericht von der Elmauer Tagung für "Artzt und Seelsorger".* Stuttgart, 1965.

——, *Man's Search for Meaning : An Introduction to Logotherapy.* Boston, 1962.

Freud, Sigmund, *Zur Psychopathologie des Alltagslebens.* Vienna, 1901.

——, *Handwörterbuch für Sexualwissenschaft.* Vienna, 1923.

——, *Gesammelte Schriften,* IV-V. Leipzig, Zurich, Vienna, 1924.

——, *Vorlesungen zur Einführung in die Psychoanalyse. Taschenausgabe.* Vienna, 1926.

Fuglesang-Damgaard, Hans, *"Privatskriftemaalets väsen og nödvändighed",* in *Kirke og Kultur,* 1933.

——, *Det enskilda skriftermalets förnyelse.* Stockholm, 1935.

——, *"Privatskriftemaalet",* in *Svensk teologisk kvartalsskrift,* 1939.

Gadelius, Bror, *Det mänskliga själslivet,* I-III. Stockholm, 1921-22.

——, *Tro och helbrägdagörelse.* Stockholm, 1934.

Giese, Fritz, "Kinderpsychologie", in *Handbuch der vergleichenden Psychologie,* I; ed. G. Kafka. Munich, 1922.

Girgensohn, Karl, *Der seelische Aufbau des religiösen Erlebens.* Leipzig, 1921.

Goyau, Georges, *Orientations catholiques.* Paris, 1925.

Gutzmann, Herrmann, *Psychologie der Sprache. Handbuch der vergleichende Psychologie,* II. Munich, 1922.

Hasselberg, Carl, *Under polstjärnan.* Uppsala, 1935.

Heiler, Friedrich, *Der Katholizismus.* Munich, 1923.

Huch, Ricarda, *Die Romantik,* II. Leipzig, 1920.

Huysmans, Joris-Karl, *En route.* Paris (no date).

Höffding, Harald, *Psykologi i Omrids;* 4th ed. Copenhagen, 1898.

Jahn, Ernst, *Wesen und Grenzen der Psychoanalyse. Artzt und Seelsorger,* IX. Schwerin-in-Mecklenburg, 1927.

James, William, *The Varieties of Religious Experience.* 1902.

Janet, Pierre, *Les obsessions et la psychasthénie.* Paris, 1903.

——, *Les médications psychologiques,* I-III. Paris, 1919-23.

——, *La tension psychologique et ses oscillations. Nouveau traité de psychologie,* IV. Paris, 1934.

Jastrow, Joseph, *The House that Freud Built.* London, 1933.

Joret, F.-D., *Aux sources de l'eau vive.* Lille, Paris, Bruges, 1928.

Jung, C. G., "The Question of the Therapeutic Value of Abreaction", in *The British Journal of Psychology,* Medical Section, 1921.

——, *Das Unbewusste im normalen und kranken Seelenleben.* Zurich, 1926.

——, *Psychotherapie und Seelsorge.* Zurich, 1932.

——, *Psychologische Typen.* Zurich and Leipzig, 1942.

Jörgensen, Johannes, *Mit Livs Legende,* IV. Copenhagen, 1918.

——, *Charles de Foucauld.* Copenhagen, 1934.

Kaila, Eino, *Personlighetens psykologi*. Stockholm, 1939.

King, M., "Measuring the Religious Variable", in *Journal for the Scientific Study of Religion*, 1967.

Kitchen, V.C., *I Was a Heathen*. London, 1934.

Kretschmer, Ernst, *Körperbau und Charakter*; 6th ed. Leipzig, 1925.

——, *Medizinische Psychologie*; 3rd ed. Leipzig, 1939.

Krogh-Tonning, Knud, *En Konvertits Erindringer*. Copenhagen, 1906.

Kronfeld, Arthur, *Psychotherapie*. Berlin, 1925.

Lagergren, Claes, *Mitt livs minnen*, IV. Stockholm, 1925.

Landquist, John, *Själens enhet*. Stockholm, 1935.

Laun, J.F., Unter Gottes Führung. Gotha, 1931.

Lea, H.C., *A History of Auricular Confession and Indulgences*, I-III. London, 1896.

Leute, Joseph, *Der katholische Priester*. Göttingen, 1914.

Liddon, H.P., *Life of Edward Bouverie Pusey*, I-IV. London, 1894-97.

Liebman, Joshua L., *Peace of Mind*. New York, 1946.

Lock, Walter, *John Keble*. London, 1895.

Luther, Martin, *Sämmtliche Werke*, XI. Erlangen, 1827.

——, *Werke*, XXI and XLIX. Weimar, 1923 and 1928.

Maeder, A., *Die Richtung im Seelenleben*. Zürich, 1928.

——, *Wege zur seelischen Heilung*. Zurich, 1944.

McDoughall, William, *An Introduction to Social Psychology*. London, 1908.

——, "The Revival of Emotional Memories and its Therapeutic Value", in *The British Journal of Psychology*, Medical Section, 1920.

——, *An Outline of Medical Psychology*. London, 1926.

McDougall, W., Energies of Man, 3rd ed. London, 1935.

——, *Psychoanalysis and Social Psychology*, London, 1936.

Messer, A., *Psychologie*. Leipzig, 1934.

Millon, T., *Theories of Psychopathology*. Philadelphia, 1967.

Moers, Martha, "*Zur Psychopathologie des Reueerlebnisses*", in *Zeitschrift für pädagogische Psychologie*, 1926.

Mowrer, O. H., *The Crisis in Psychiatry and Religion*. New Jersey, 1961.

Murray, E.J., *Motivation and Emotion*. New Jersey, 1964.

Muthmann, A., "*Psychiatrisch-theologische Grenzfragen*", in *Zeitschrift für Religions-psychologie*, I. Halle-an-der-Speer, 1908.

Müncker, T., *Die psychologischen Grundlagen der katholischen Sittenlehre, Handbuch der katholischen Sittenlehre*, II; ed. F. Tillmann. Düsseldorf, 1934.

Nachmansohn, Max, *Die Hauptströmungen der Psychotherapie der Gegenwart*. Zurich, 1933.

Ortolan, T., "Confession", in *Dictionnaire de théologie catholique*.

Pettazzoni, Rafaele, *La confessione dei peccati*, I-III. Bologna, 1929-36.

Pfister, Oskar, *Die psychanalytische Methode*. Leipzig, 1924.

Pratt, J.B., *The Religious Consciousness*, New York, 1921.

Purcell, E.S., *Life of Cardinal Manning*, I-II. London, 1896.

Rapaport, D.A., *Structure of Psychoanalytic Theory*. New York, 1960.

Rathke, N.N., "*Die lutherische Auffassung von der Privatberichte und ihre Bedeutung für das kirchliche Leben der Gegenwart*", in *Monatschrift für Pastoraltheologie*, 1917.

Rogers, Carl, *The Therapeutic Relation and its Impact*, 1969.

Rosegger, Peter, *Waldheimat. Ausgewählte Werke*. Vienna (no date).

Rosenzweig, S., and Mason, G., "An Experimental Study of Memory in Relation to the Theory of Repression", in *The British Journal of Psychology*, XXIV, 1933-34.

Runestam, Arvid, *Psychoanalysis and Christianity*. Rock Island, 1958.

Russell, A.J., *For Sinners Only*. London, 1934.

Sanctis, Sante de, *Religious Conversion*. London, 1927.

Scheler, Max, *Der Formalismus in der Ethik und die materiale Wertethik*. Halle-an-der-Speer, 1921.

Schmalhausen, S.D., *Our Changing Human Nature*. New York, 1929.

Schneider, Carl, "*Wie hat sich der Seelenführer zu verhalten?*", in *Zeitschrift für Religionspsychologie*. Gütersloh, 1929.

Schöllig, Otto, *Die Verwaltung der heiligen Sakramente*. Freiburg-in-Br., 1936.

Schou, H.I., "*Skriftemaalets betydning humant og kristligt set*", in *Kirke og Kultur*, 1933.

Selbie, W.B., *The Psychology of Religion*. Oxford, 1924.

Shakow, D., and Rapaport, D., *The Influence of Freud on American Psychology*. New York, 1964.

Shand, A.F., *The Foundations of Character*, 2nd ed. London, 1926.

Snoeck, Andreas, *Beichte und Psychoanalyse*. Frankfurt-am-Main, 1960.

Starbuck, E.D., *The Psychology of Religion*. Oxford, 1914.

Stollberg, Dietrich, *Therapeutische Seelsorge*. Munich, 1970.

Strauss, Erwin, *Wesen und Vorgang der Suggestion. Abhandlungen aus der Neurologie, Psychologie und ihren Grenzgebieten*, XXVIII. Berlin, 1925.

Thureau-Dangin, P., *La renaissance catholique en Angleterre*, I-III. Paris, 1903.

Uleyn, Arnold, *Pastorale Psychologie en Schuldervaring*. Brugge and Utrecht, 1964.

Vincent, Francis, *Saint François de Sales, Directeur d'âmes*. Paris, 1923.

Viollet, Jean, *La confession*. Paris, 1929.

Vyss, Dieter, *Die Tiefenpsychologischen Schulen von der Anfängen bis zur Gegenwart*. Göttingen, 1966.

Watkins, O.D., *A History of Penance*, I-II. London, 1920.

Wehrung, G., "*Wilhelm Löhe und seine Lehre von der Kirche*", in *Theologische Literaturzeitung*, 1941.

Woodworth, R.S., and Shehan, M., *Contemporary Schools of Psychology*. New York, 1964.

Wunderle, G., *Zur Psychologie der Reue*. Tübingen, 1921.

Yinger, J.M., "A Structural Examination of Religion", in *Journal for the Scientific Study of Religion*, 1969.

Zavalloni, P.R., *Psicologia pastorale*. Rome, 1965.

Zeigarnik, *Bluma, Über das Behalten von erledigten und unerledigten Handlungen. Psychologische Forschung*, IX. Berlin, 1927.

Zillboorg, Gregory, *Psychoanalysis and Religion*. London, 1967.

Zündel, Friedrich, *Johann Cristoph Blumhardt*. Giessen, 1926.

INDEX OF NAMES

218 INDEX OF NAMES